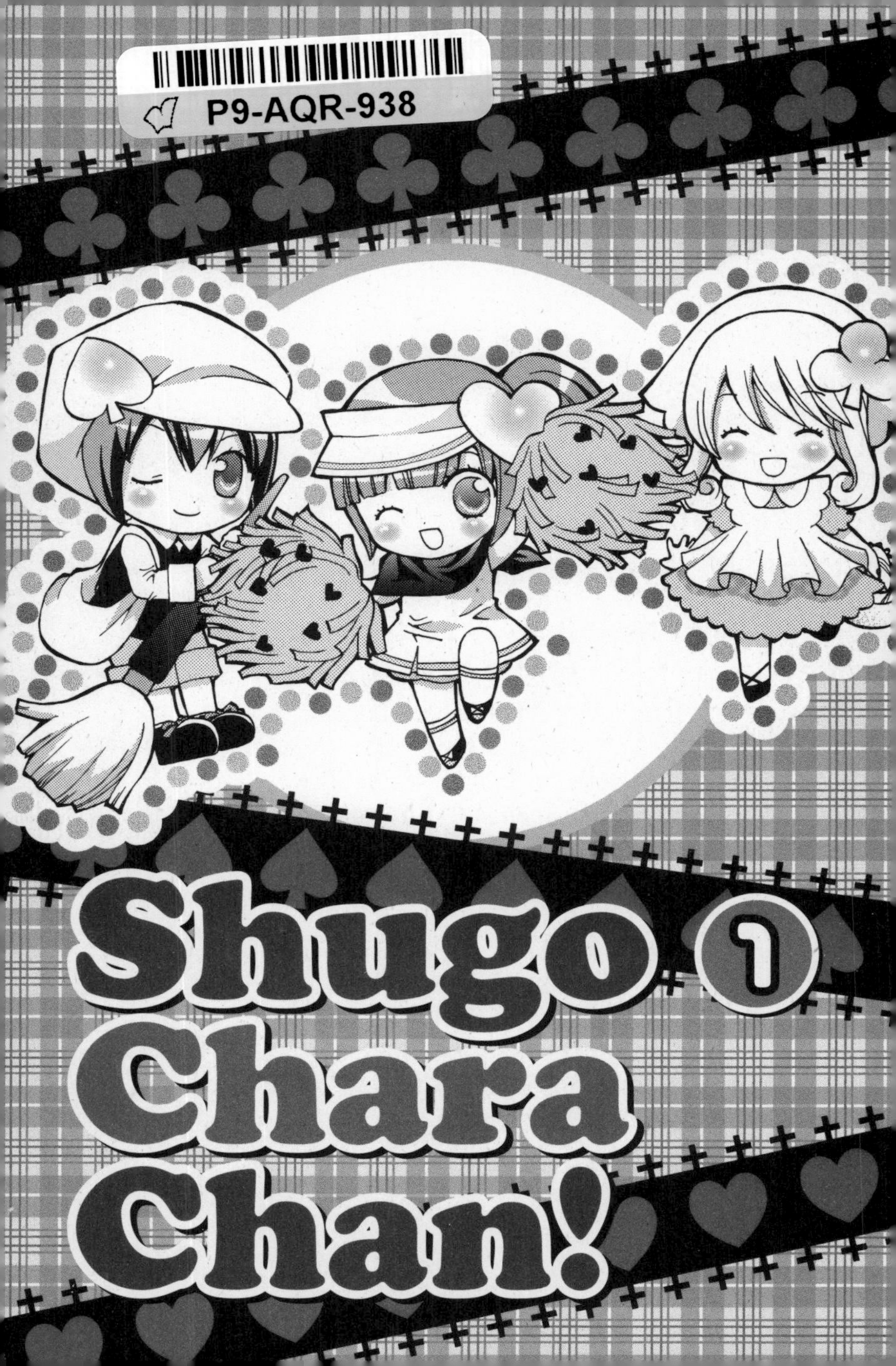
Shugo Chara Chan! 1

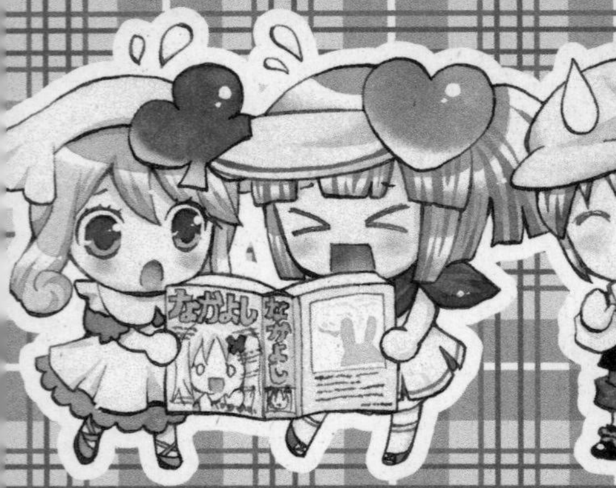
なかよし

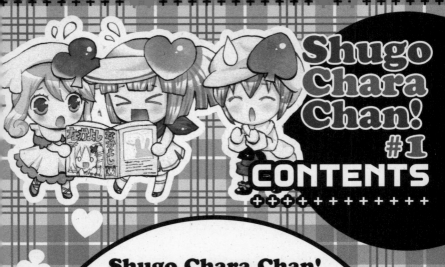

Shugo Chara Chan! #1

CONTENTS

Shugo Chara Chan!
Manga by
Naphthalene Mizushima

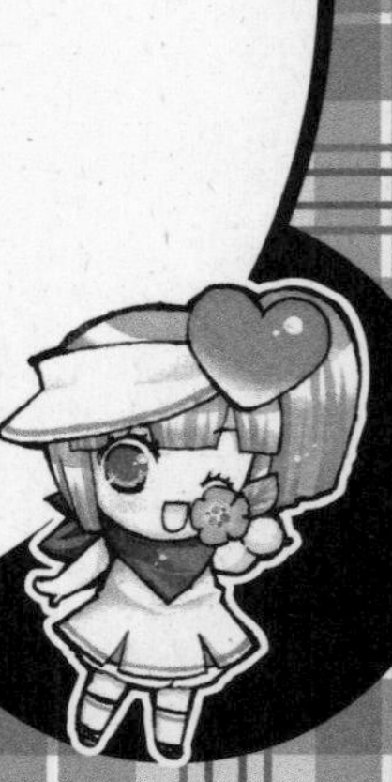

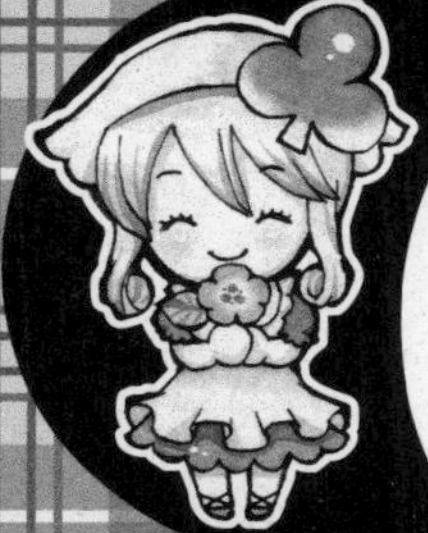

Shugo Chara Chan! Kids☆
Manga by *Kinomin*

Shugo Chara Chan! Festival

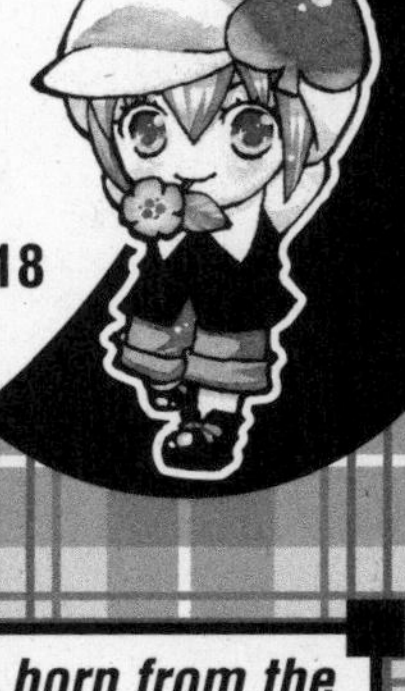

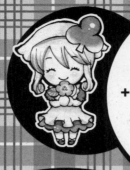

Guardian Characters are who you want to be, born from the Heart's Egg of kids. Ran, Miki, and Su are the Guardian Characters of Amu, the cool and awesome girl in grade school. There's something fun going on every day for these tiny, upbeat girls. Come take a peek!

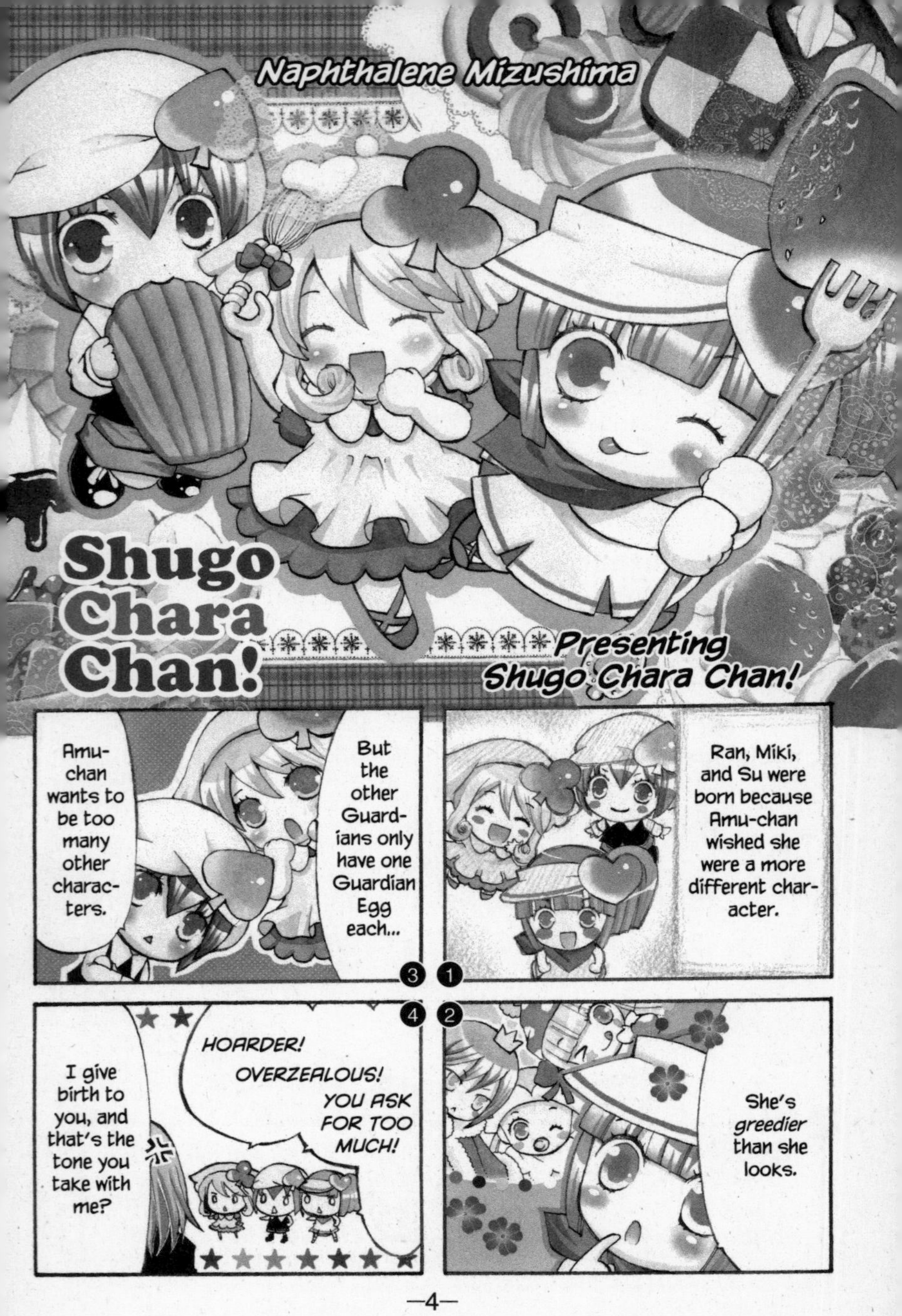
Naphthalene Mizushima
Shugo Chara Chan!
Presenting Shugo Chara Chan!
Ran, Miki, and Su were born because Amu-chan wished she were a more different character.
She's *greedier* than she looks.
Amu-chan wants to be too many other characters.
But the other Guardians only have one Guardian Egg each...
HOARDER!
OVERZEALOUS!
YOU ASK FOR TOO MUCH!
I give birth to you, and that's the tone you take with me?

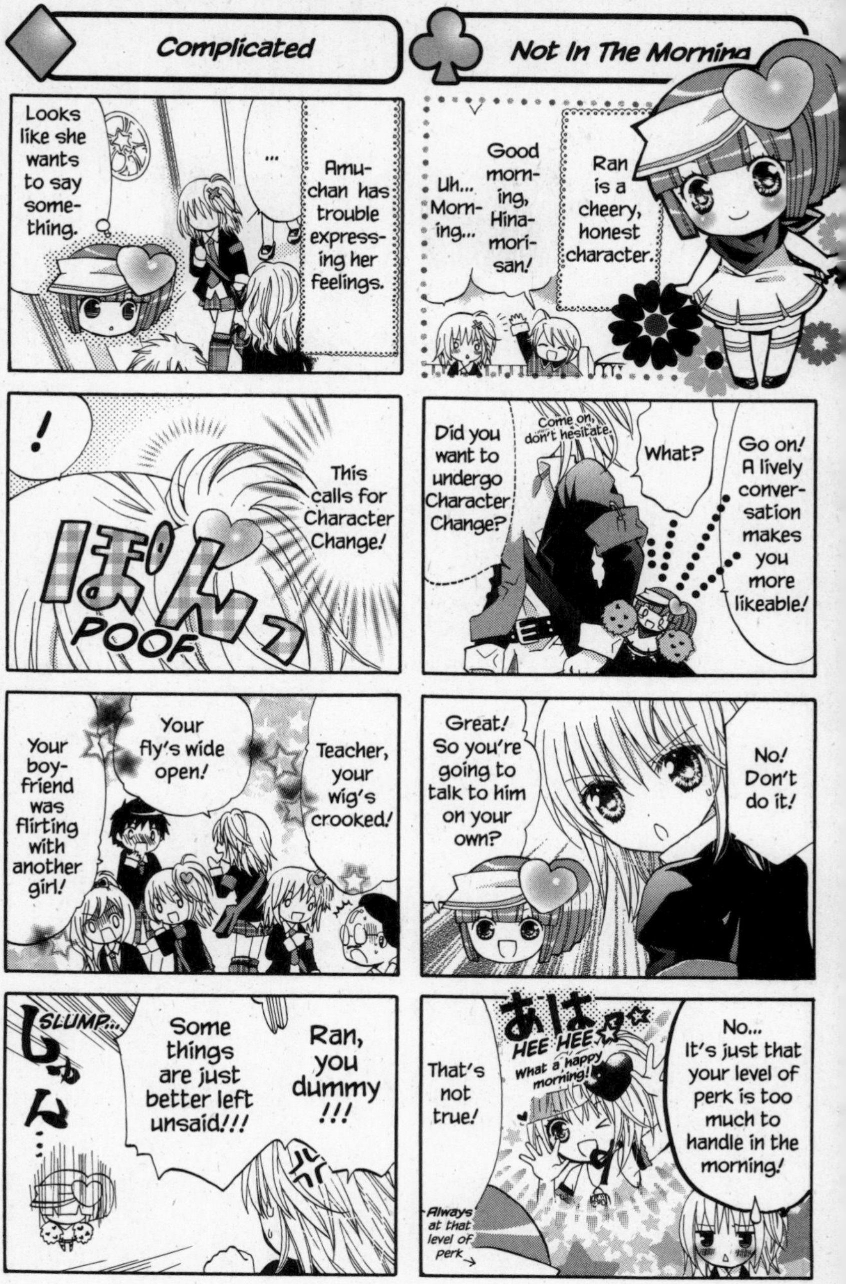
Not In The Morning
Ran is a cheery, honest character.
Good morning, Hinamori-san!
Uh... Morning...
Go on! A lively conversation makes you more likeable!
What?
Come on, don't hesitate.
Did you want to undergo Character Change?
No! Don't do it!
Great! So you're going to talk to him on your own?
No... It's just that your level of perk is too much to handle in the morning!
あは HEE HEE
what a happy morning!
That's not true!
Always at that level of perk →
Complicated
Amu-chan has trouble expressing her feelings.
...
Looks like she wants to say something.
This calls for Character Change!
!
ぽんっ POOF
Teacher, your wig's crooked!
Your fly's wide open!
Your boyfriend was flirting with another girl!
Ran, you dummy!!!
Some things are just better left unsaid!!!
しゅん... SLUMP...

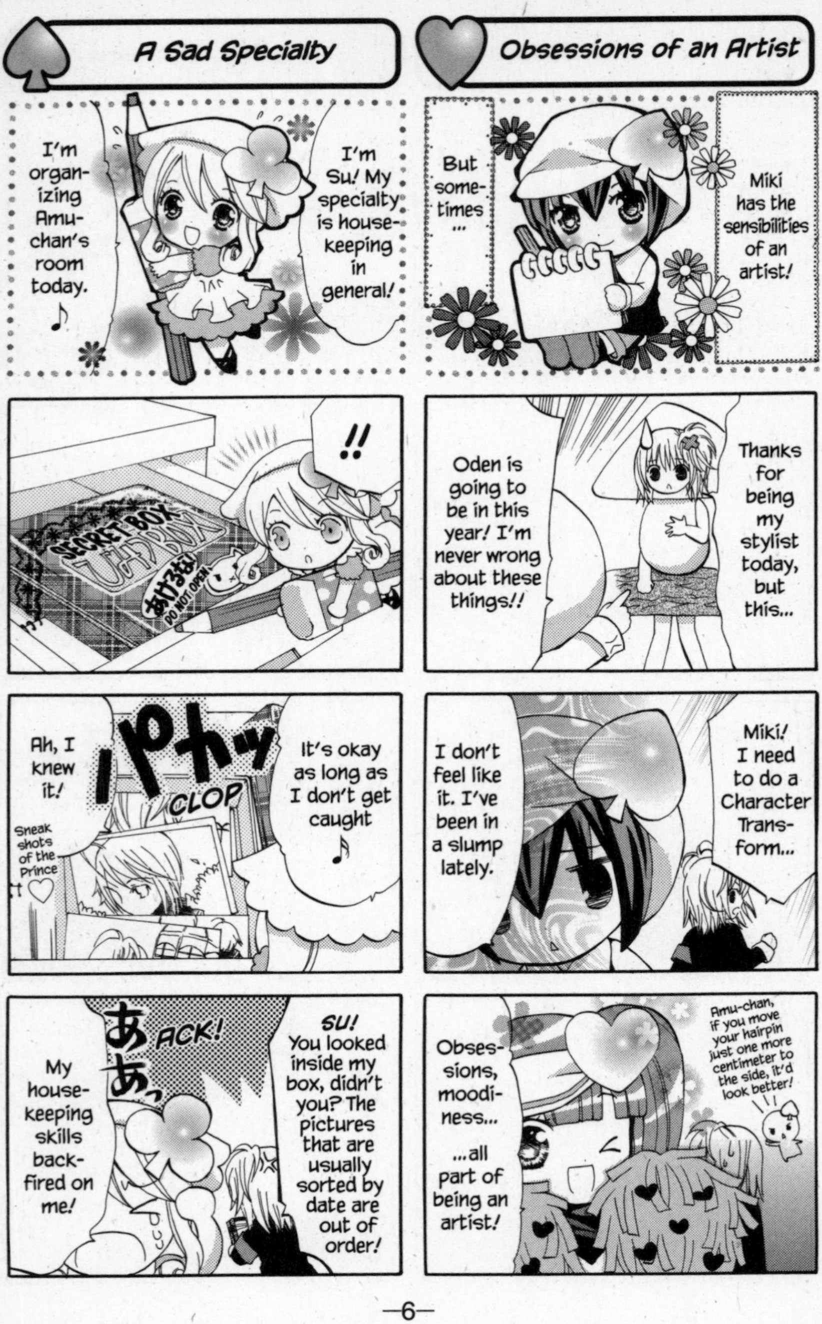

Obsessions of an Artist
Miki has the sensibilities of an artist!
But sometimes...
Thanks for being my stylist today, but this...
Oden is going to be in this year! I'm never wrong about these things!!
Miki! I need to do a Character Transform...
I don't feel like it. I've been in a slump lately.
Amu-chan, if you move your hairpin just one more centimeter to the side, it'd look better!
Obsessions, moodiness...
...all part of being an artist!
A Sad Specialty
I'm Su! My specialty is housekeeping in general!
I'm organizing Amu-chan's room today. ♪
!!
SECRET BOX
ひみつBOX
あけるな!
DO NOT OPEN
It's okay as long as I don't get caught ♪
パカッ
CLOP
Ah, I knew it!
Sneak shots of the Prince ♡
SU! You looked inside my box, didn't you? The pictures that are usually sorted by date are out of order!
ACK!
あぁっ
My housekeeping skills backfired on me!

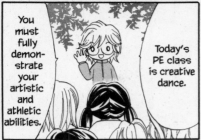

No, Not That!

CHIRP CHIRP
チュン
CHIRP CHIRP
チュン
Time to go, guys!
mmn....
Five more minutes, please...
Sleeping a sleep that knows no dawn...
Lack of sleep is bad for the complexion...
うう——ん...
MMMN
Mom, how about three more boiled eggs for breakfast?
WE'RE UP!

Good for Nothing?

Today's PE class is creative dance.
You must fully demonstrate your artistic and athletic abilities.
What? I don't have either!
This situation calls for a Character Change to--
ME! RAN!
Excuse me? This is clearly Ran's job!
You don't have any artistic abilities, Ran! No way!
You should talk, Miki! You're no athlete!
What did you say!?
DING-DONG
Um, class is over...
I did fine on my own.
Huh!?
They were arguing the whole time.

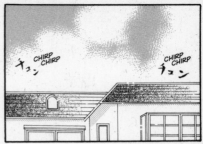

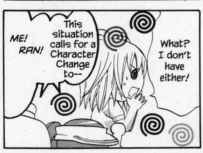

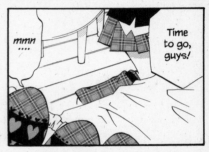

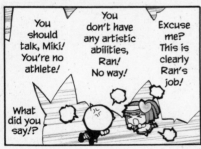

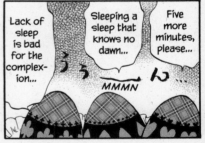

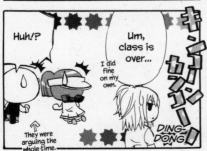

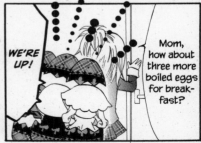

Combination

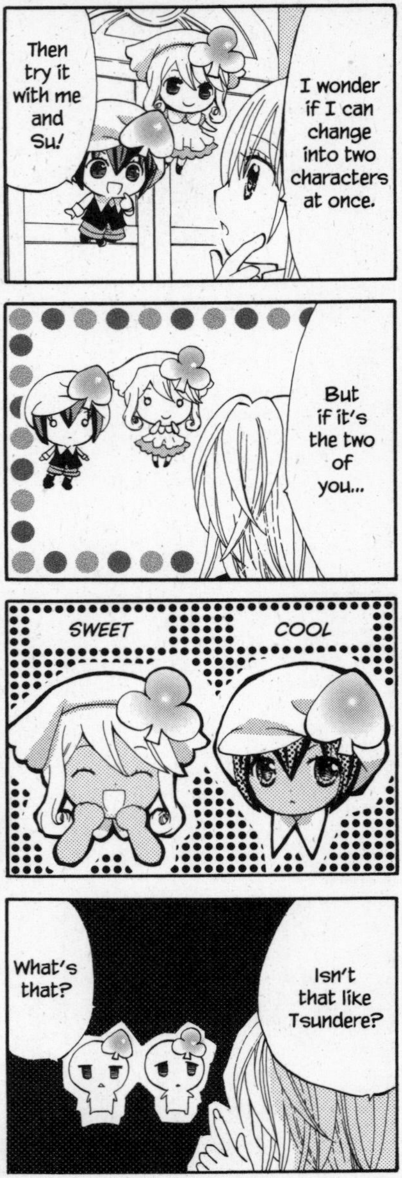
I wonder if I can change into two characters at once.
Then try it with me and Su!
But if it's the two of you...
COOL
SWEET
Isn't that like Tsundere?
What's that?

Don't Want to Admit It

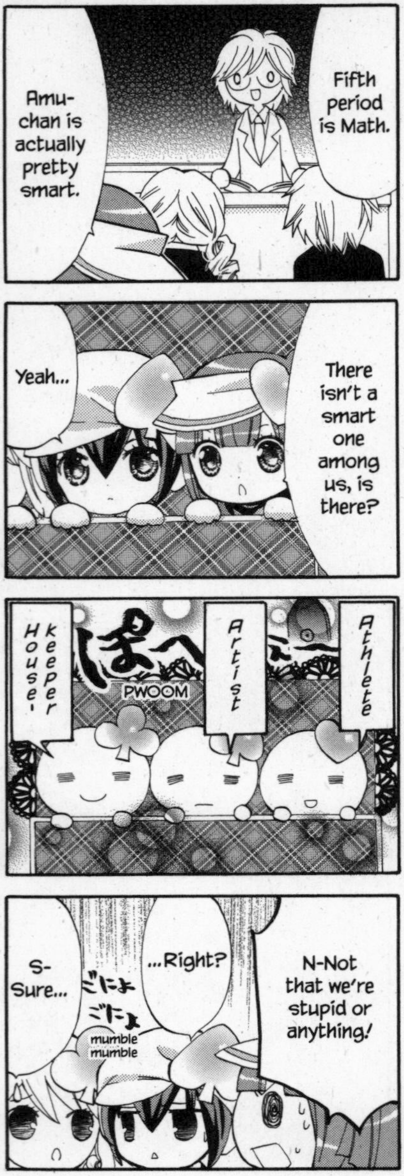
Fifth period is Math.
Amu-chan is actually pretty smart.
There isn't a smart one among us, is there?
Yeah...
Athlete
Artist
PWOOM
House-keeper
N-Not that we're stupid or anything!
...Right?
ごにょごにょ
mumble mumble
S-Sure...

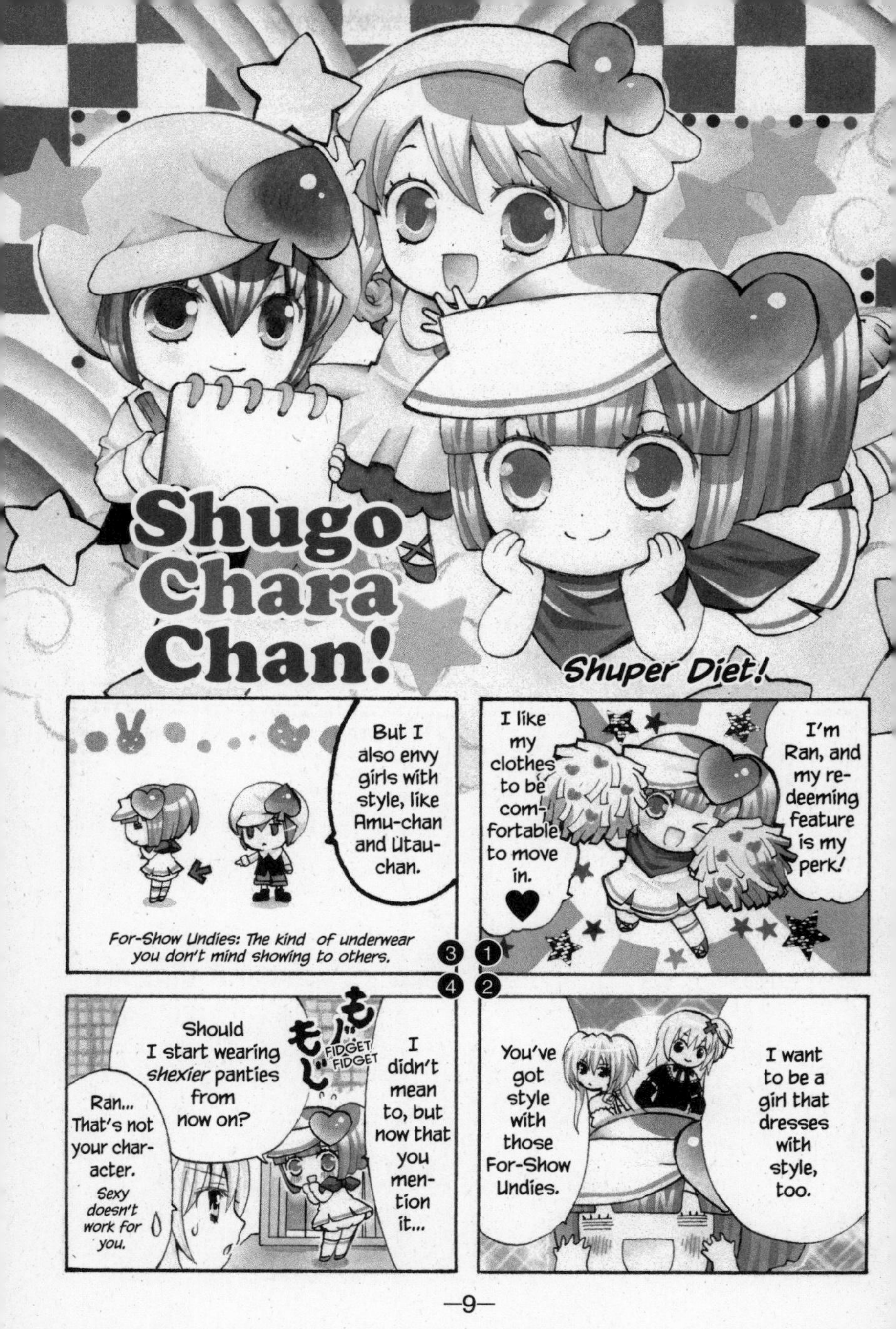
Shugo Chara Chan!
Shuper Diet!
I'm Ran, and my redeeming feature is my perk!
I like my clothes to be comfortable to move in. ♥
I want to be a girl that dresses with style, too.
You've got style with those For-Show Undies.
But I also envy girls with style, like Amu-chan and Utau-chan.
For-Show Undies: The kind of underwear you don't mind showing to others.
I didn't mean to, but now that you mention it...
もじもじ
FIDGET FIDGET
Should I start wearing *shexier* panties from now on?
Ran... That's not your character.
Sexy doesn't work for you.

How Miki Feels

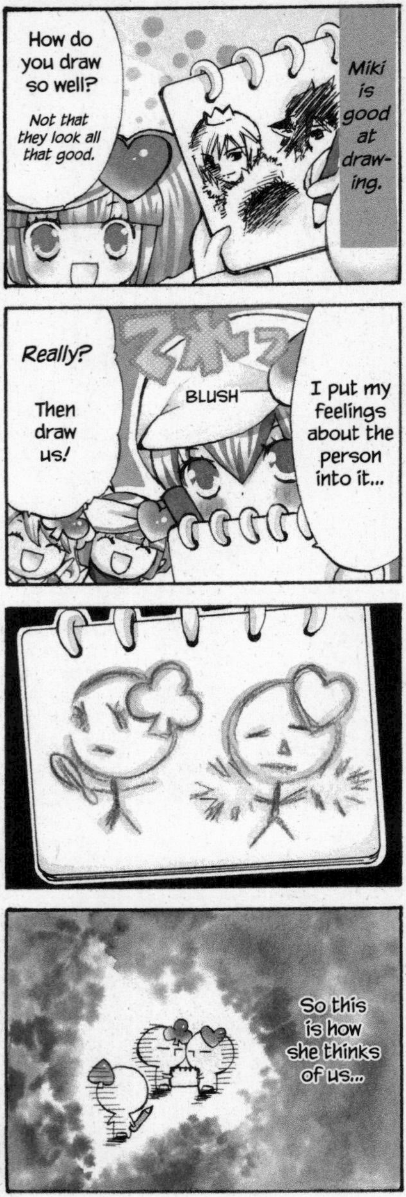
Miki is good at drawing.
How do you draw so well?
Not that they look all that good.
I put my feelings about the person into it...
BLUSH
Really?
Then draw us!
So this is how she thinks of us...

Studious

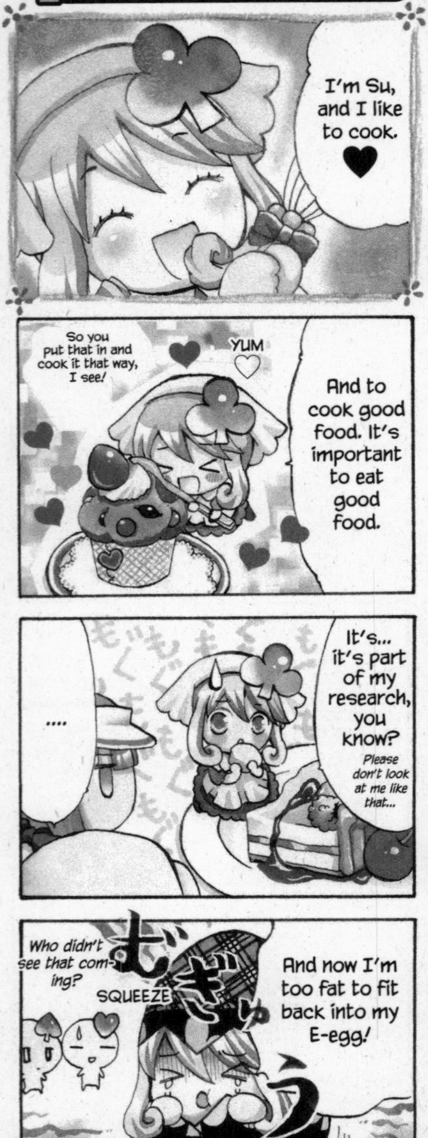
I'm Su, and I like to cook. ♥
And to cook good food. It's important to eat good food.
YUM
So you put that in and cook it that way, I see!
It's... it's part of my research, you know?
Please don't look at me like that...
....
And now I'm too fat to fit back into my E-egg!
SQUEEZE
Who didn't see that coming?

Not What I Wanted

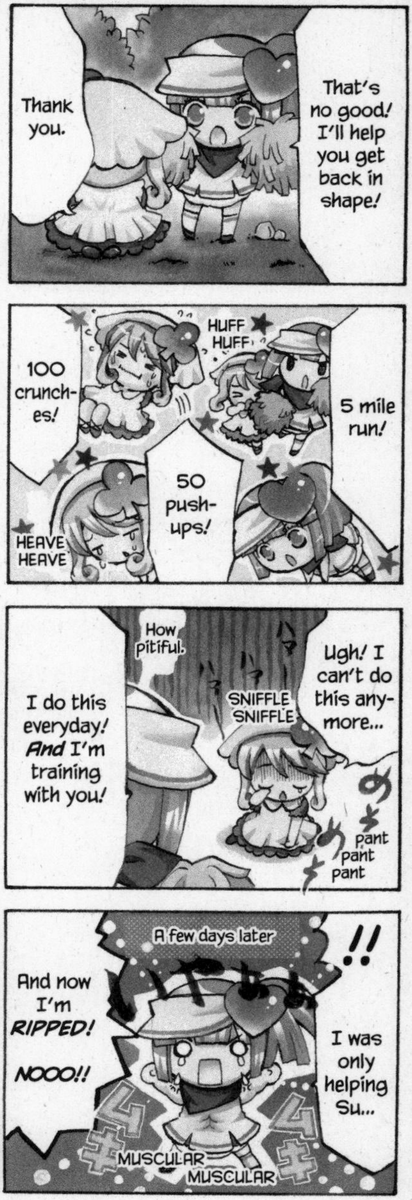
That's no good! I'll help you get back in shape!
Thank you.
HUFF HUFF
5 mile run!
100 crunches!
50 push-ups!
HEAVE HEAVE
Ugh! I can't do this any-more...
SNIFFLE SNIFFLE
How pitiful.
I do this everyday! *And* I'm training with you!
pant pant pant
!!
A few days later
I was only helping Su...
And now I'm *RIPPED!*
NOOO!!
MUSCULAR MUSCULAR

Miki's Secret

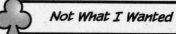

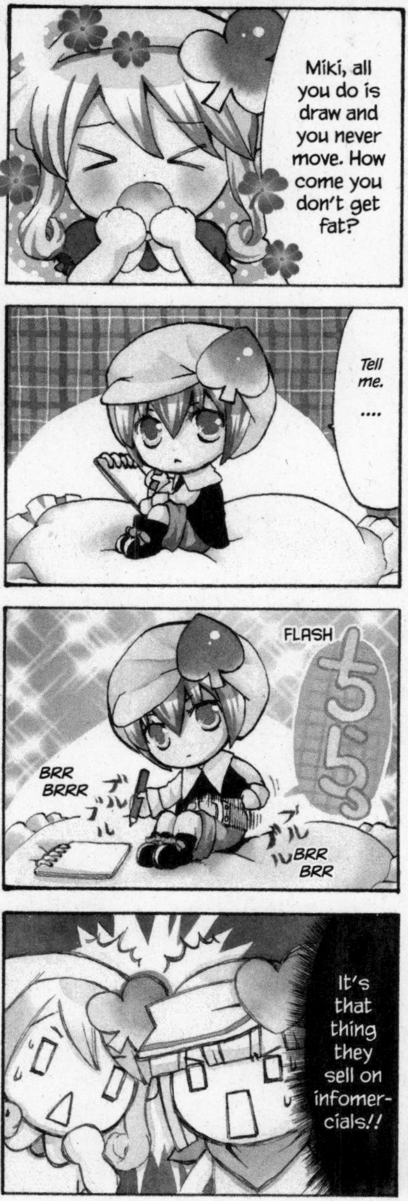
Miki, all you do is draw and you never move. How come you don't get fat?
Tell me.
....
FLASH
BRR BRR
BRR BRRR
It's that thing they sell on infomer-cials!!

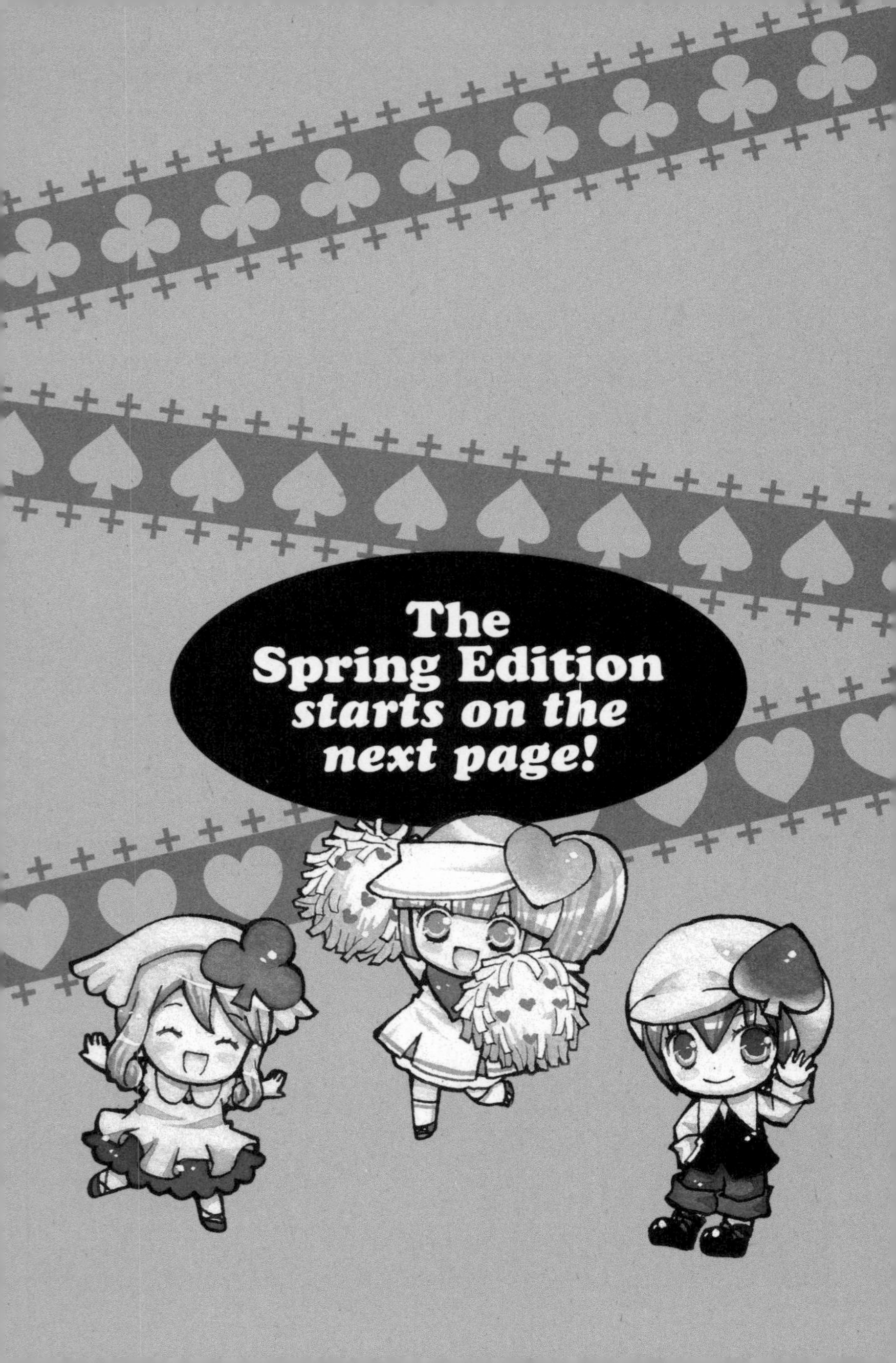
The Spring Edition starts on the next page!

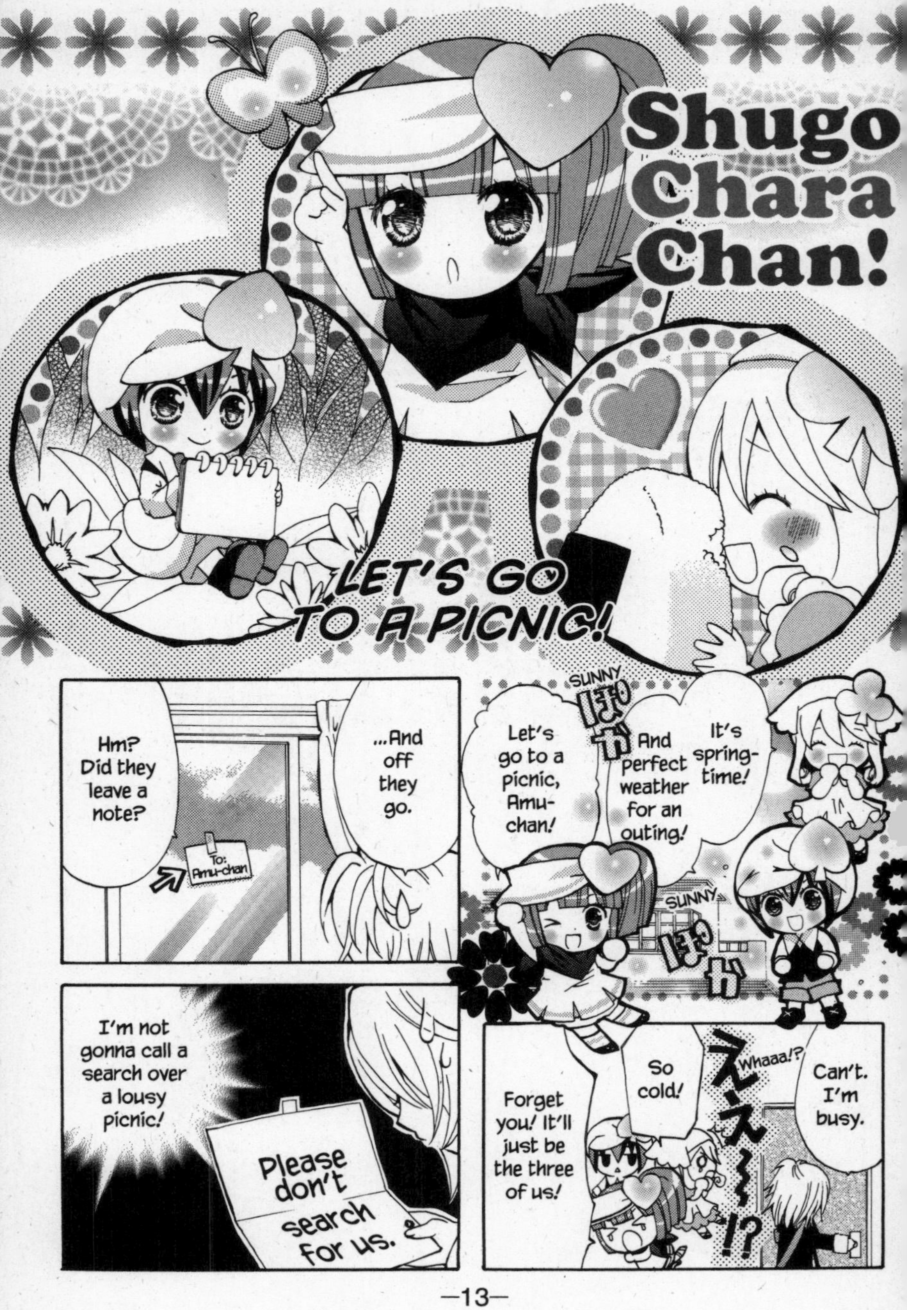
Shugo Chara Chan!
LET'S GO TO A PICNIC!
It's spring-time!
And perfect weather for an outing!
SUNNY ぽか
Let's go to a picnic, Amu-chan!
SUNNY ぽか
...And off they go.
Hm? Did they leave a note?
To: Amu-chan
Can't. I'm busy.
Whaaa!? ええ~~!?
So cold!
Forget you! It'll just be the three of us!
Please don't search for us.
I'm not gonna call a search over a lousy picnic!

Bugs!

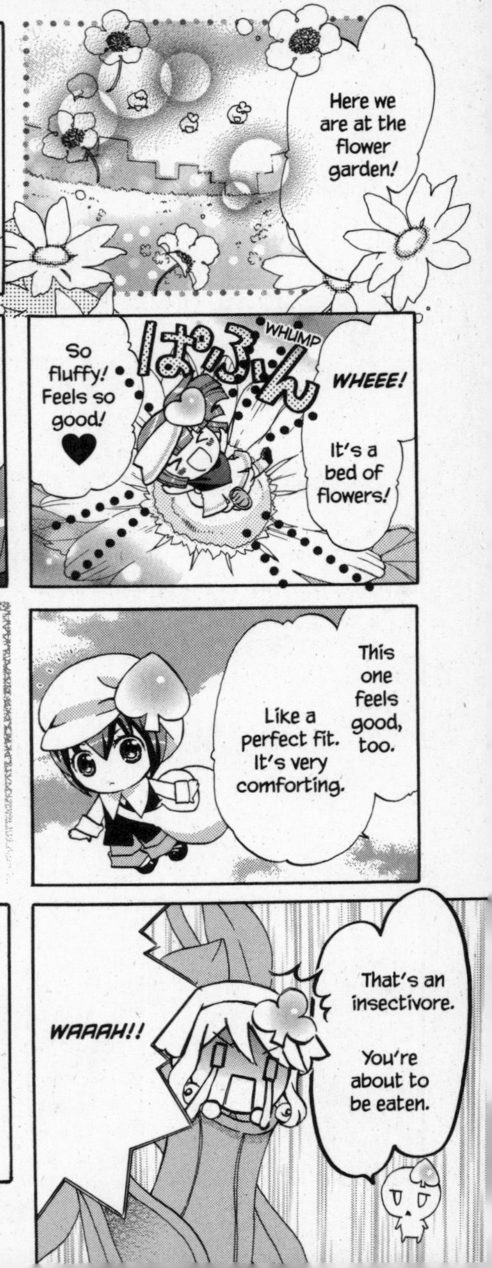
Here we are at the flower garden!
WHEEE!
It's a bed of flowers!
ぱふん
WHUMP
So fluffy! Feels so good! ♥
This one feels good, too.
Like a perfect fit. It's very comforting.
That's an insectivore.
You're about to be eaten.
WAAAH!!

Where's the Bread?

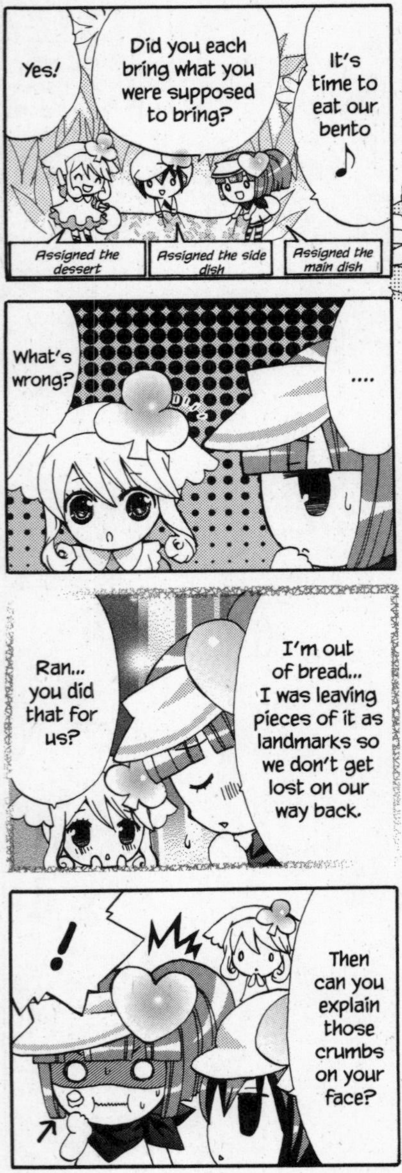
It's time to eat our bento ♪
Did you each bring what you were supposed to bring?
Yes!
Assigned the main dish
Assigned the side dish
Assigned the dessert
....
What's wrong?
I'm out of bread... I was leaving pieces of it as landmarks so we don't get lost on our way back.
Ran... you did that for us?
Then can you explain those crumbs on your face?
!

Japanese

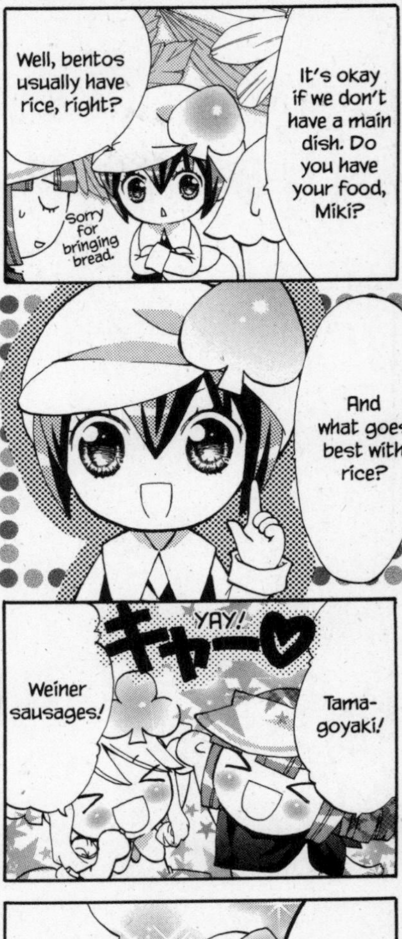
It's okay if we don't have a main dish. Do you have your food, Miki?
Well, bentos usually have rice, right?
Sorry for bringing bread.
And what goes best with rice?
Tama-goyaki!
YAY!
キャー♥
Weiner sausages!
Nothing but umeboshi, of course!
That's so mature of you!!

Extra Large

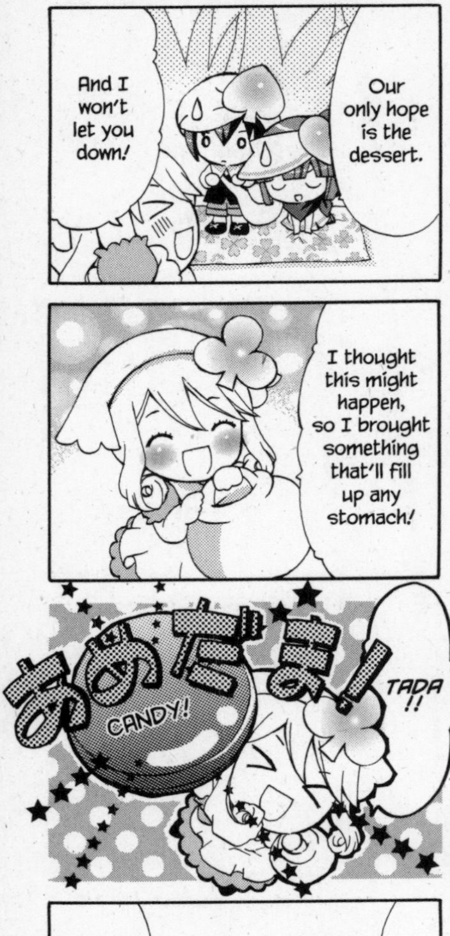
Our only hope is the dessert.
And I won't let you down!
I thought this might happen, so I brought something that'll fill up any stomach!
TADA!!
あめだま!
CANDY!
....
Not in a position to criticize
And what are we supposed to do with this?

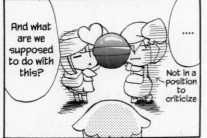

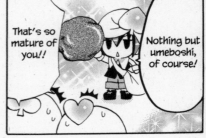

This is Perfect ♪

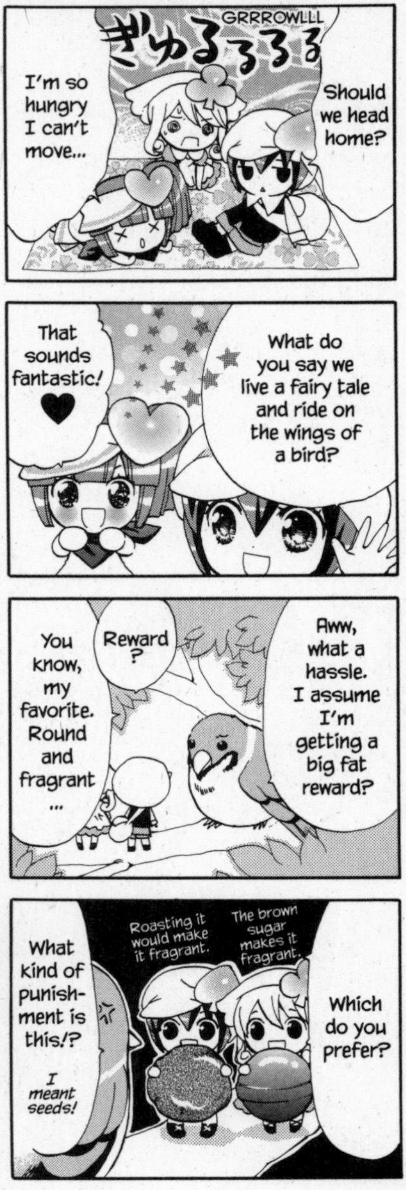
GRRROWLLL
ぎゅるるるる
Should we head home?
I'm so hungry I can't move...
What do you say we live a fairy tale and ride on the wings of a bird?
That sounds fantastic! ♥
Aww, what a hassle. I assume I'm getting a big fat reward?
Reward?
You know, my favorite. Round and fragrant ...
Which do you prefer?
The brown sugar makes it fragrant.
Roasting it would make it fragrant.
What kind of punishment is this!?
I meant seeds!

Any Bird Will Do

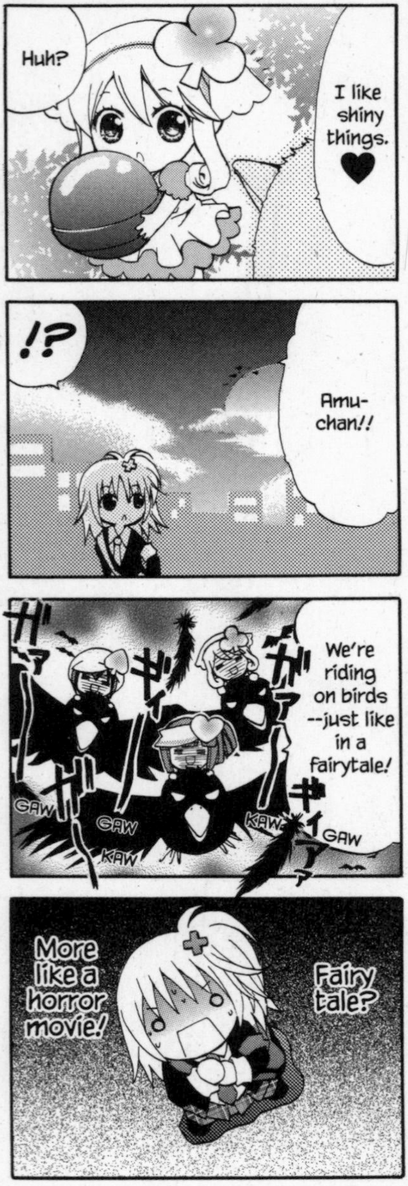
I like shiny things. ♥
Huh?
Amu-chan!!
!?
We're riding on birds --just like in a fairytale!
ギャア
ガァ
ギャア
GAW
KAW
GAW
GAW
KAW
Fairy tale?
More like a horror movie!

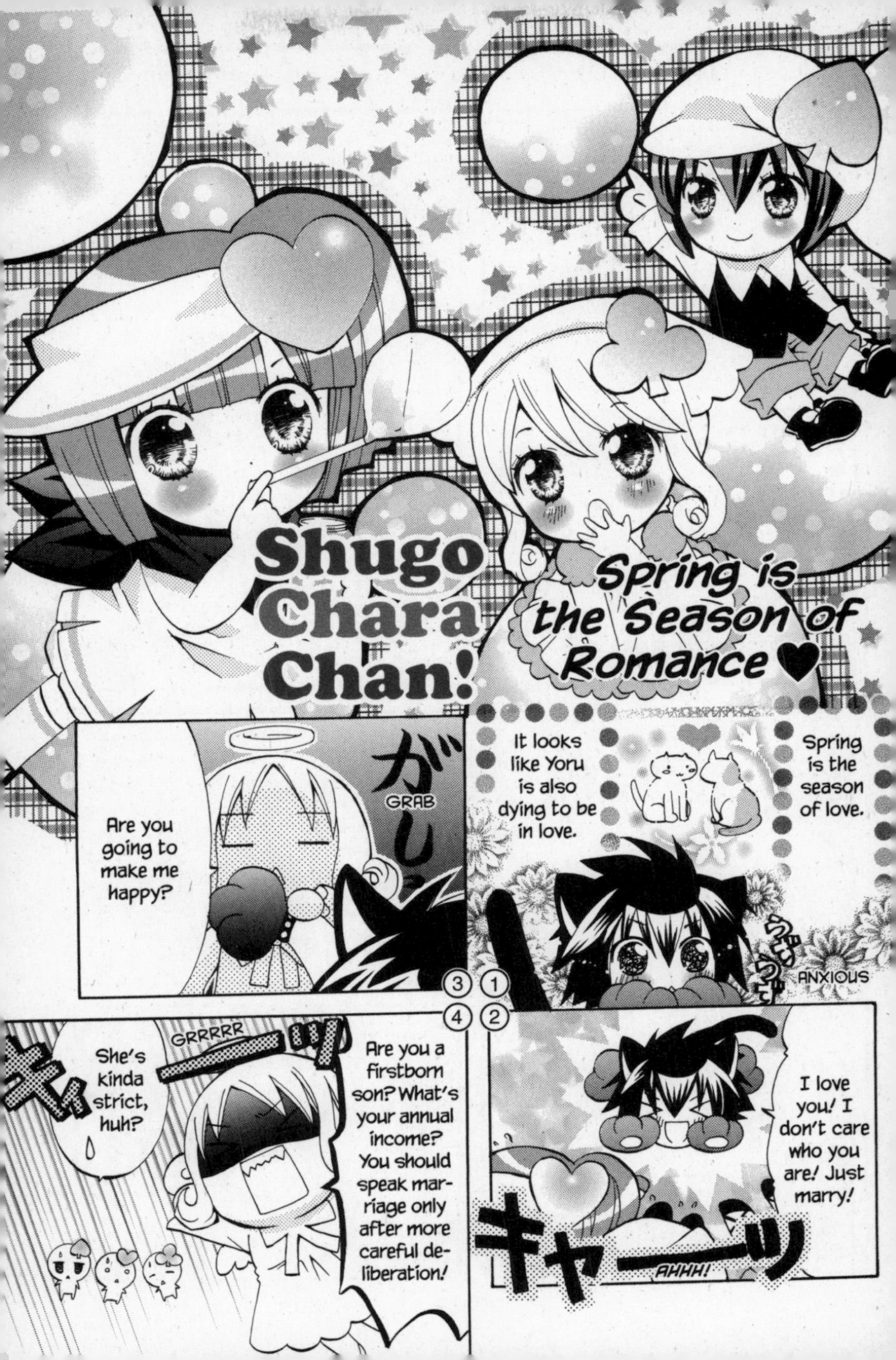
Shugo Chara Chan!
Spring is the Season of Romance♥
Spring is the season of love.
It looks like Yoru is also dying to be in love.
ANXIOUS
I love you! I don't care who you are! Just marry!
キャーーッ
AHHH!
がしっ
GRAB
Are you going to make me happy?
Are you a firstborn son? What's your annual income? You should speak marriage only after more careful deliberation!
GRRRRR
She's kinda strict, huh?

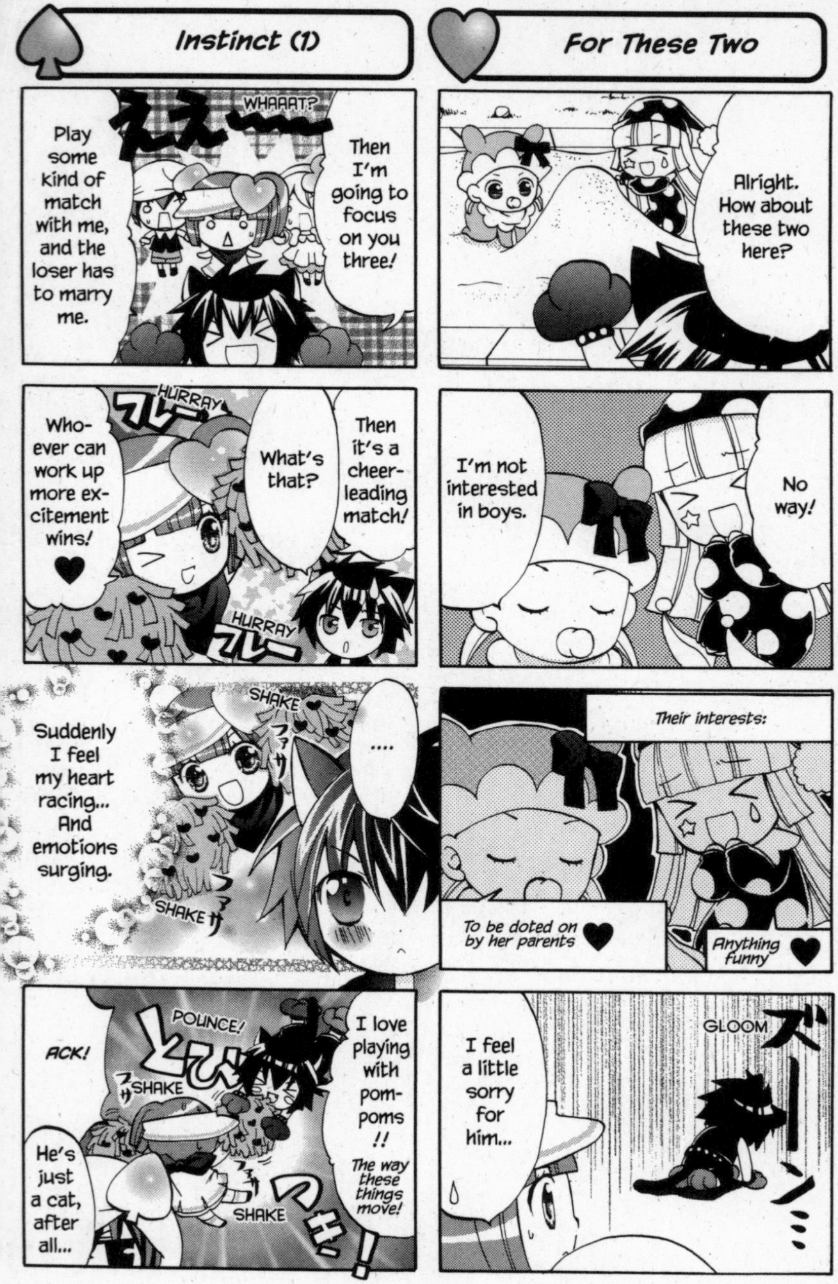
For These Two
Alright. How about these two here?
No way!
I'm not interested in boys.
Their interests:
Anything funny ♥
To be doted on by her parents ♥
GLOOM
I feel a little sorry for him...
Instinct (1)
Then I'm going to focus on you three!
WHAAAT?
Play some kind of match with me, and the loser has to marry me.
Then it's a cheerleading match!
What's that?
HURRAY
Whoever can work up more excitement wins! ♥
HURRAY
....
SHAKE
Suddenly I feel my heart racing... And emotions surging.
SHAKE
I love playing with pom-poms!!
The way these things move!
POUNCE!
ACK!
SHAKE
SHAKE
He's just a cat, after all...

That's What You Choose!?

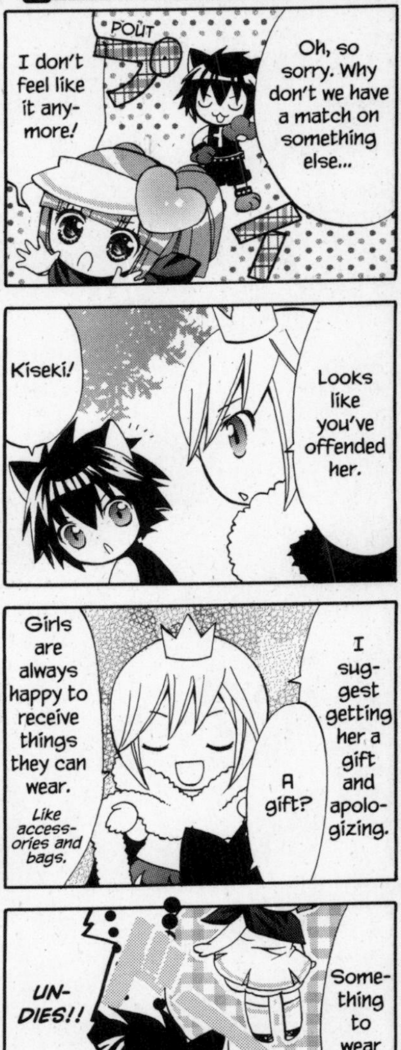
Oh, so sorry. Why don't we have a match on something else...
POUT
I don't feel like it anymore!
Looks like you've offended her.
Kiseki!
I suggest getting her a gift and apologizing.
A gift?
Girls are always happy to receive things they can wear.
Like accessories and bags.
Something to wear...
UN-DIES!!

Ruined

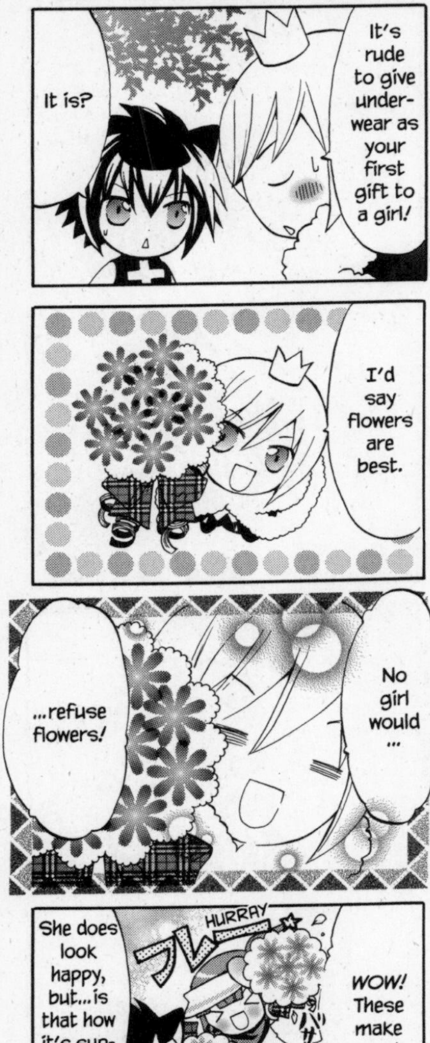
It's rude to give underwear as your first gift to a girl!
It is?
I'd say flowers are best.
No girl would...
...refuse flowers!
HURRAY
WOW! These make great pom-poms!
SHAKE
SHAKE
She does look happy, but...is that how it's supposed to be?
...

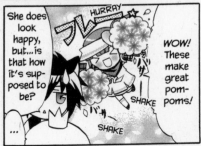

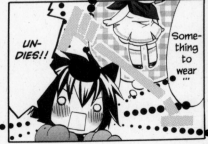

Rival for Su?

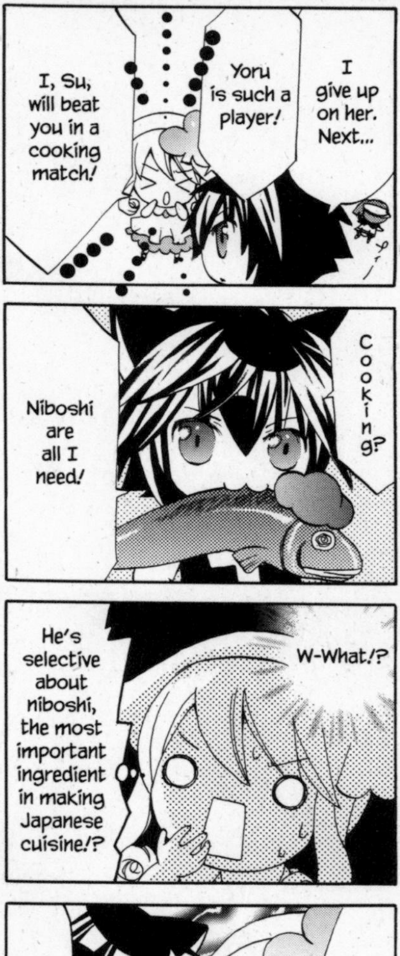
I give up on her. Next...
Yoru is such a player!
I, Su, will beat you in a cooking match!
Cooking?
Niboshi are all I need!
W-What!?
He's selective about niboshi, the most important ingredient in making Japanese cuisine!?
A formidable foe...
Fired up
バチッ
SPARK
Who? Me?

Imagination

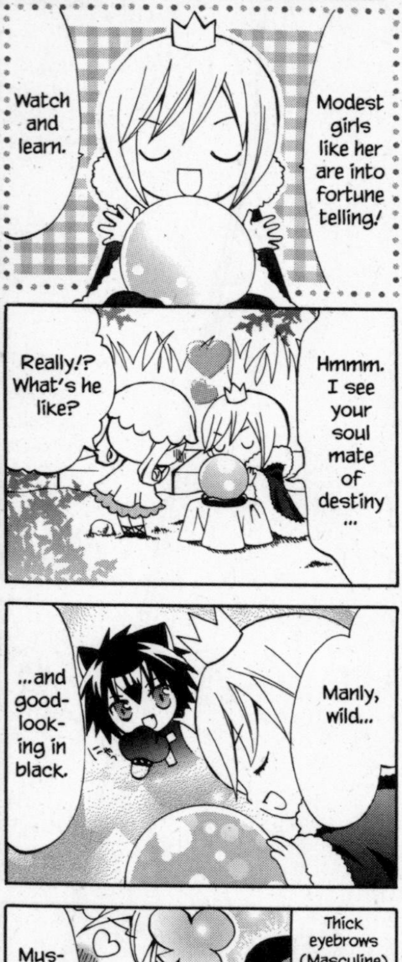
Modest girls like her are into fortune telling!
Watch and learn.
Hmmm. I see your soul mate of destiny...
Really!? What's he like?
Manly, wild...
...and good-looking in black.
Thick eyebrows (Masculine)
Muscles... ♥
Ripped (Wild)
Tanned (Good-looking in black)
Muscles!?

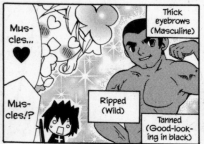

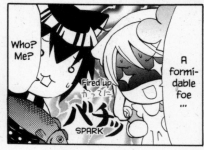

Instinct (2)

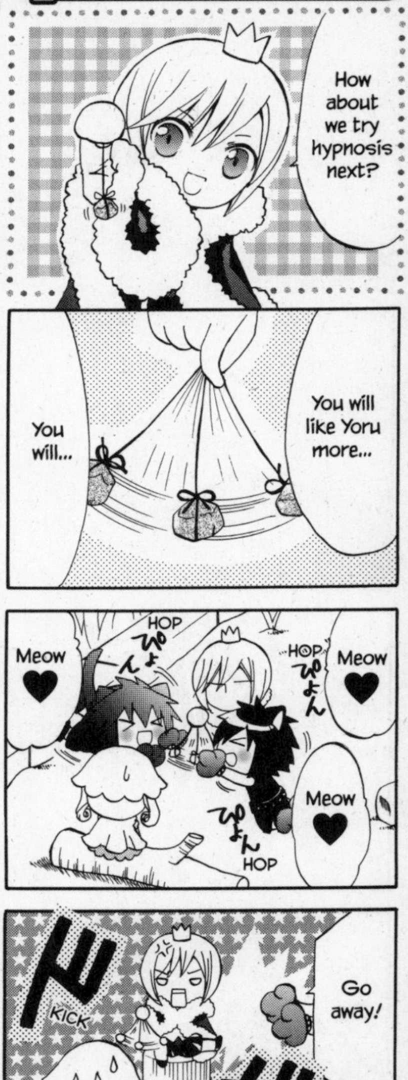
How about we try hypnosis next?
You will like Yoru more...
You will...
Meow ♥
HOP
ぴょん
Meow ♥
HOP
ぴょん
Meow ♥
ぴょん
HOP
Go away!
ド
KICK
ガッ

Think Before You Move

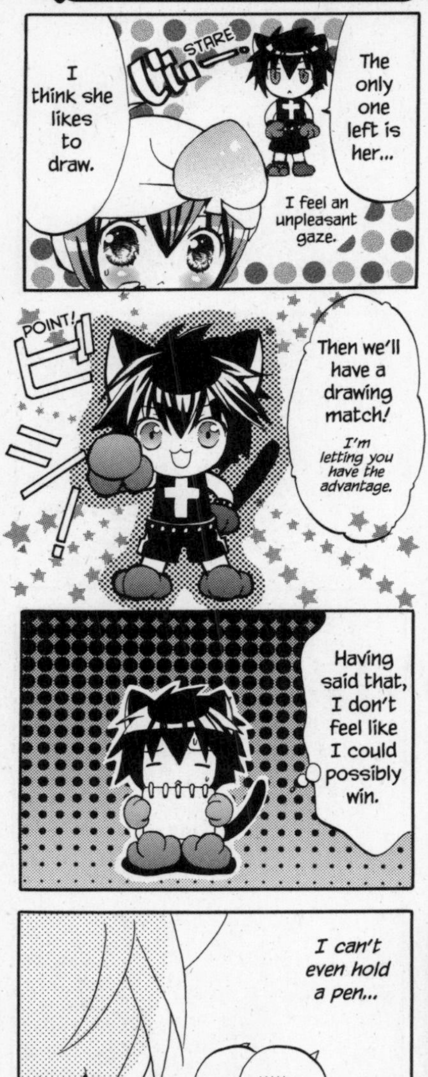
The only one left is her...
STARE
I think she likes to draw.
I feel an unpleasant gaze.
Then we'll have a drawing match!
I'm letting you have the advantage.
POINT!
Having said that, I don't feel like I could possibly win.
I can't even hold a pen...

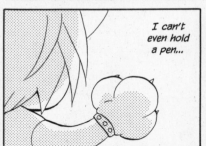

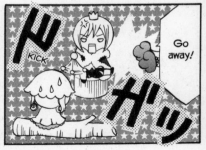

Ulterior Motive

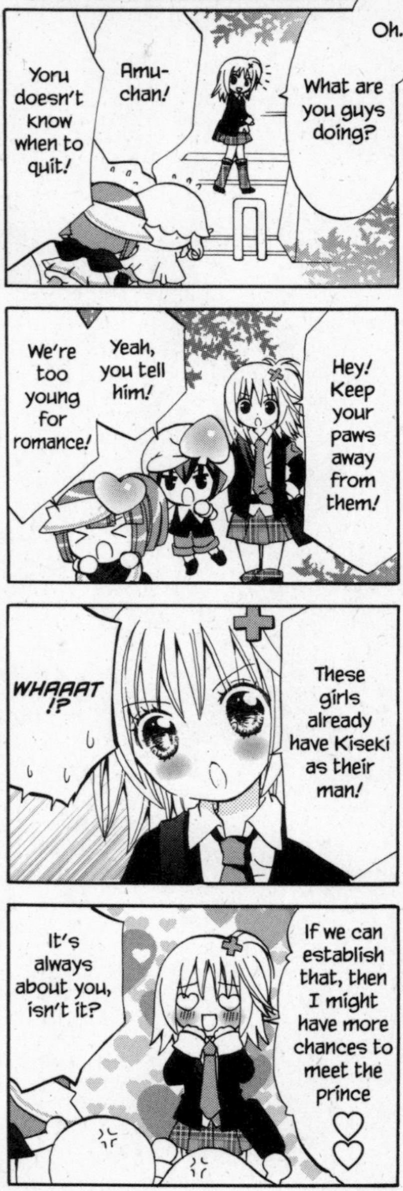
Oh.
What are you guys doing?
Amu-chan!
Yoru doesn't know when to quit!
Hey! Keep your paws away from them!
Yeah, you tell him!
We're too young for romance!
These girls already have Kiseki as their man!
WHAAAT!?
If we can establish that, then I might have more chances to meet the prince ♡♡
It's always about you, isn't it?

The Truth

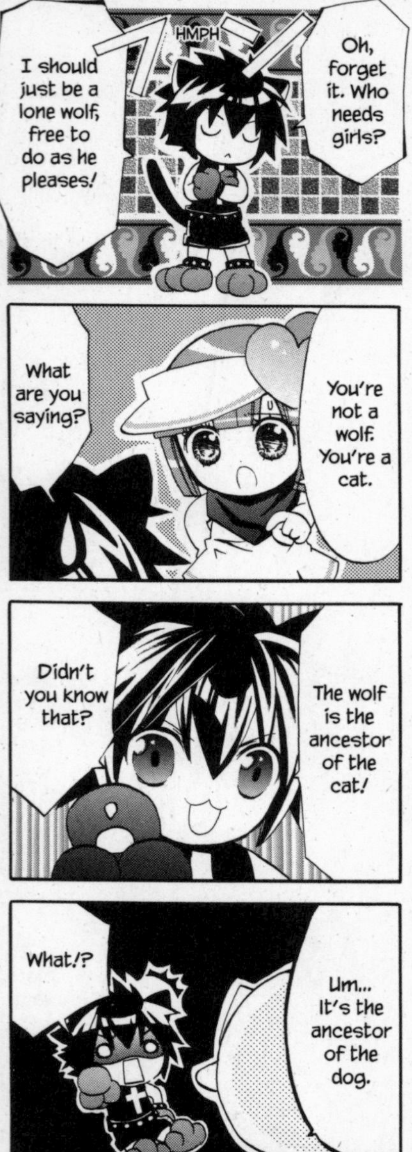
Oh, forget it. Who needs girls?
HMPH
I should just be a lone wolf, free to do as he pleases!
You're not a wolf. You're a cat.
What are you saying?
The wolf is the ancestor of the cat!
Didn't you know that?
Um... It's the ancestor of the dog.
What!?

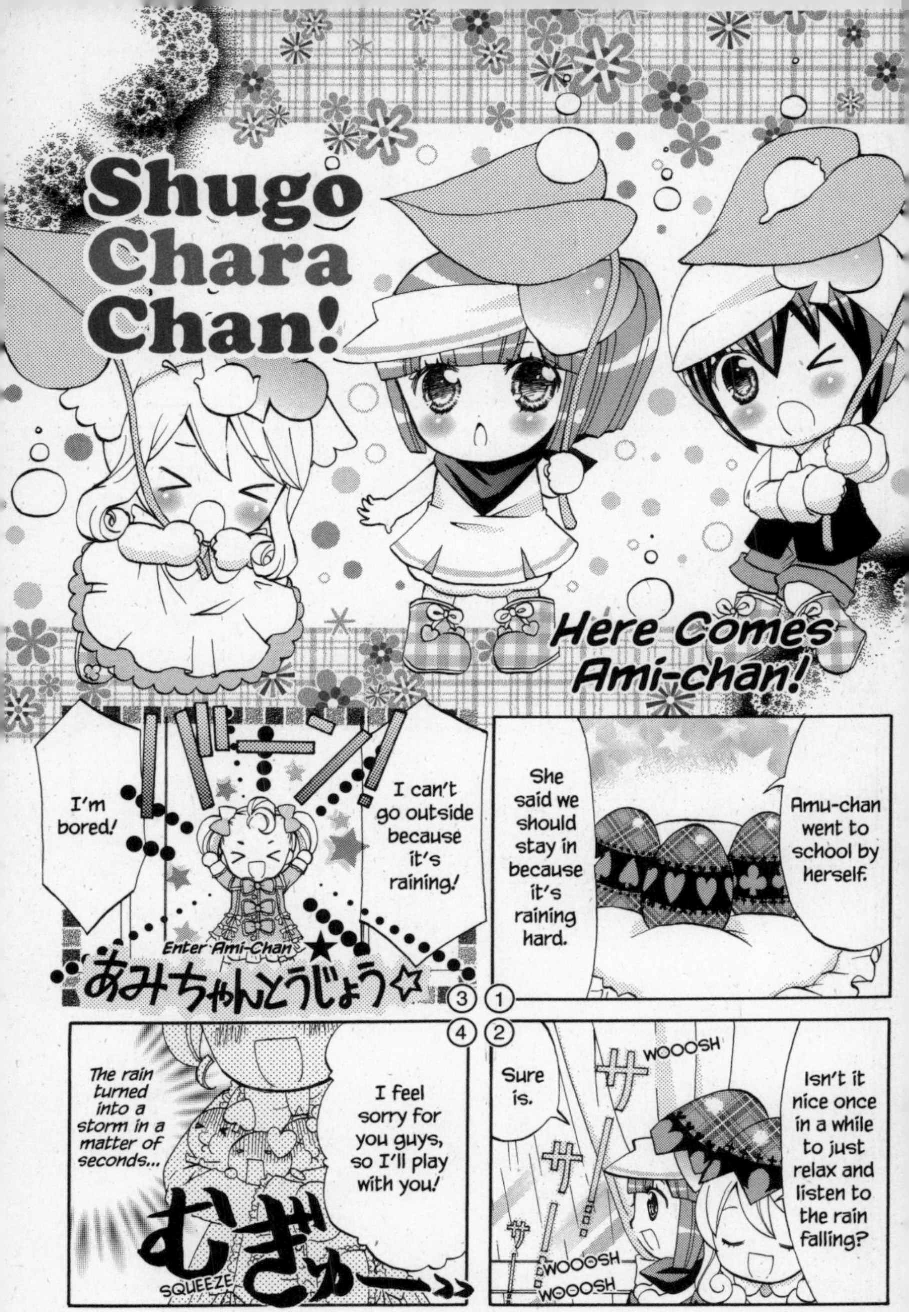
Shugo Chara Chan!
Here Comes Ami-chan!
1
Amu-chan went to school by herself.
She said we should stay in because it's raining hard.
2
Isn't it nice once in a while to just relax and listen to the rain falling?
Sure is.
WOOOSH
WOOOSH
WOOOSH
3
I can't go outside because it's raining!
I'm bored!
Enter Ami-Chan★
あみちゃんとうじょう☆
4
I feel sorry for you guys, so I'll play with you!
The rain turned into a storm in a matter of seconds...
むぎゅー
SQUEEZE

Gotcha

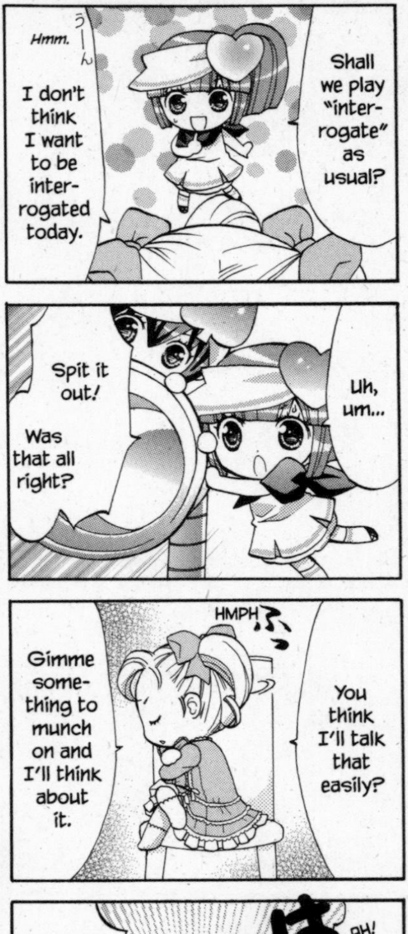

Shall we play "inter-rogate" as usual?
うーん
Hmm.
I don't think I want to be inter-rogated today.
Uh, um...
Spit it out!
Was that all right?
ふっ
HMPH
You think I'll talk that easily?
Gimme some-thing to munch on and I'll think about it.
はっ
AH!
IT'S 10 O'CLOCK!
TIME FOR HER 10 O'CLOCK SNACK!

Shifting the Blame

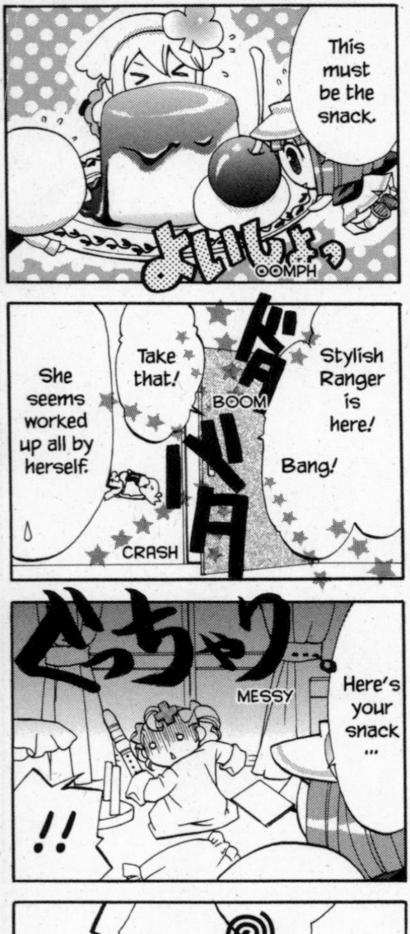

This must be the snack.
よいしょっ
OOMPH
Stylish Ranger is here!
Bang!
BOOM
Take that!
CRASH
She seems worked up all by herself.
Here's your snack...
ごっちゃり...
MESSY
!!
Detec-tive! There's been a robbery!
Looks like they trashed the room!
YOU did it!!

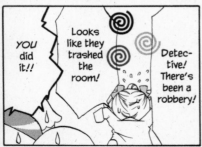

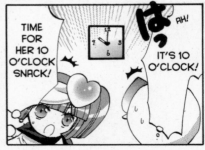

To the Stomach

OKAY! Now that my stomach is full...
...let's look for clues to solve our case.
Hmmm.
So this is the kind of book Onee-chan reads.
RUMMAGE RUMMAGE
A-ha!
Lip gloss! She's so grown up!
RUMMAGE
RUMMAGE
She's like a mother who enters her daughter's room in the name of cleaning up, but is really reading her diary.
WHOA!
Now this is a good clue. ♪
Must confiscate! ♥
You're STILL eating?
Nighttime munchies

Please Don't

Next, let's play "locked-room murder."
Not sure about this, but...
Yay ...
Makes me nervous...
IN
FIRST, we lock the three of you in a drawer...
NEXT, we leave you there for about a WEEK.
Then you grow hungry, which makes you FIGHT.
See? A locked-room murder made easy! ♪
How scary!
SHUDDER
Don't make it sound like a recipe for a meal!
SHUDDER

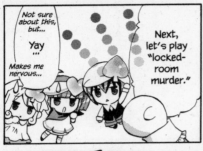

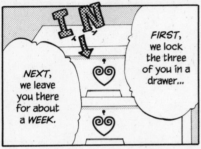

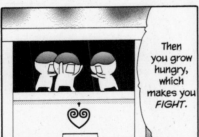

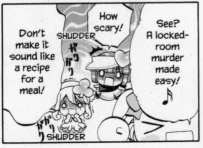

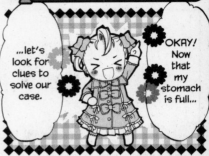

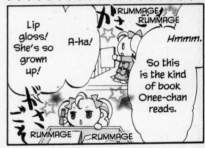

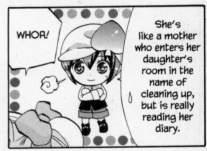

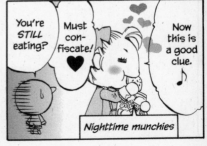

Made for Cheap ♪

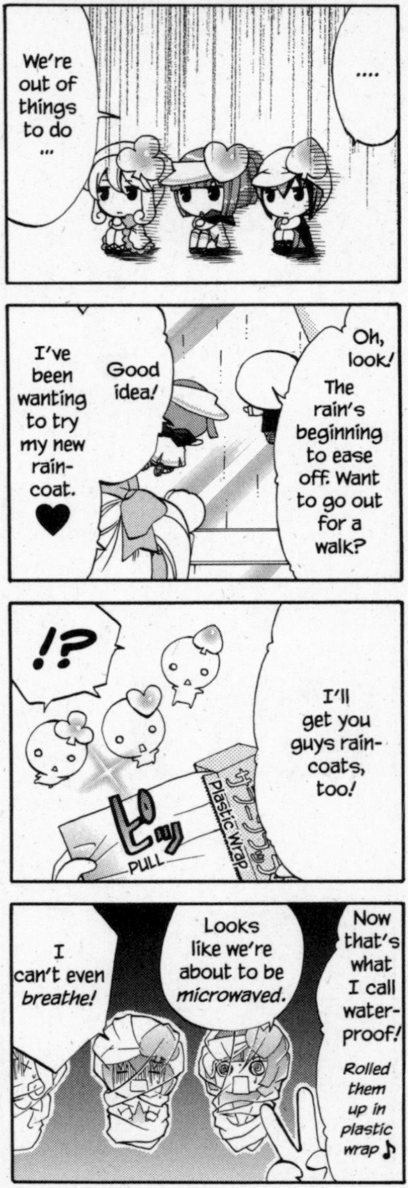
....
We're out of things to do ...
Oh, look! The rain's beginning to ease off. Want to go out for a walk?
Good idea!
I've been wanting to try my new raincoat. ♥
I'll get you guys raincoats, too!
Plastic Wrap
PULL
!?
Now that's what I call waterproof!
Rolled them up in plastic wrap ♪
Looks like we're about to be microwaved.
I can't even breathe!

Premonition

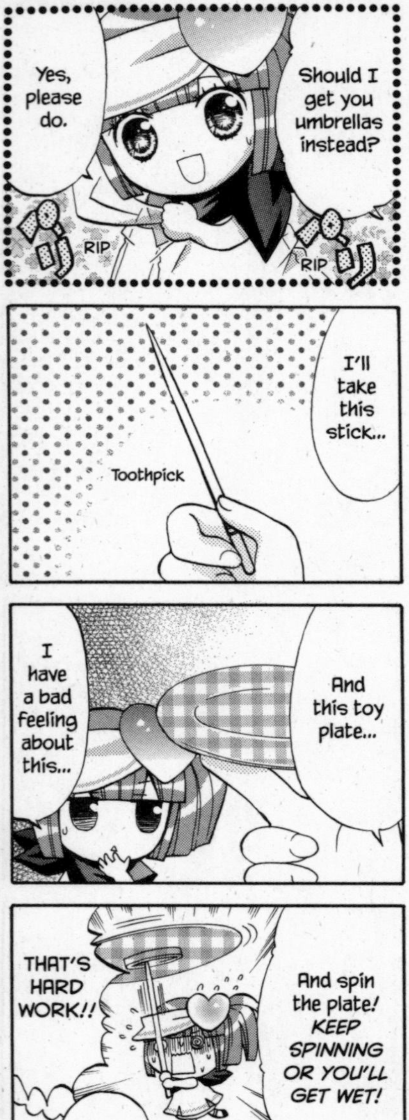
Should I get you umbrellas instead?
Yes, please do.
RIP
RIP
I'll take this stick...
Toothpick
And this toy plate...
I have a bad feeling about this...
And spin the plate! KEEP SPINNING OR YOU'LL GET WET!
THAT'S HARD WORK!!

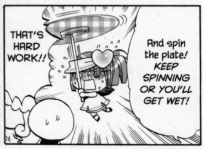

A Frightening Thing to Say

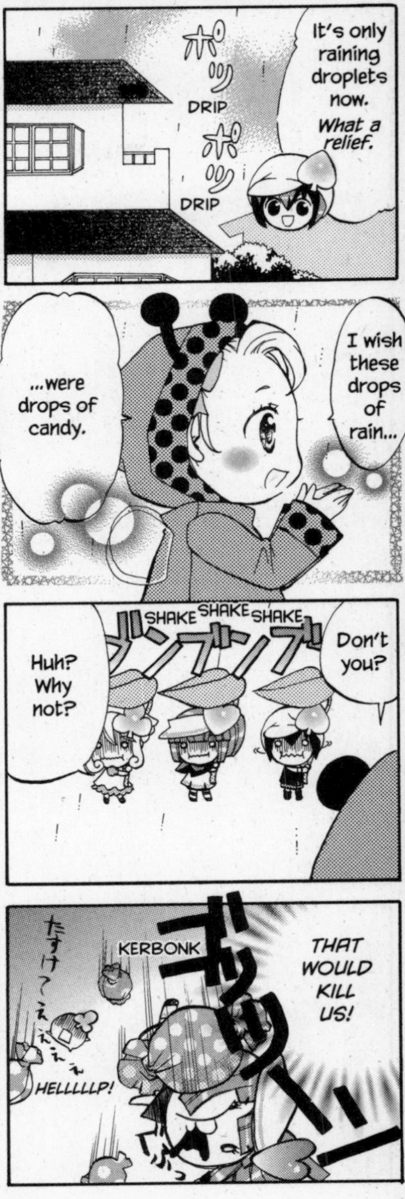
It's only raining droplets now. What a relief.
ポツ DRIP
ポツ DRIP
I wish these drops of rain...
...were drops of candy.
Don't you?
SHAKE SHAKE SHAKE
Huh? Why not?
THAT WOULD KILL US!
KERBONK
たすけてぇぇぇ
HELLLLLP!

Home Sweet Home

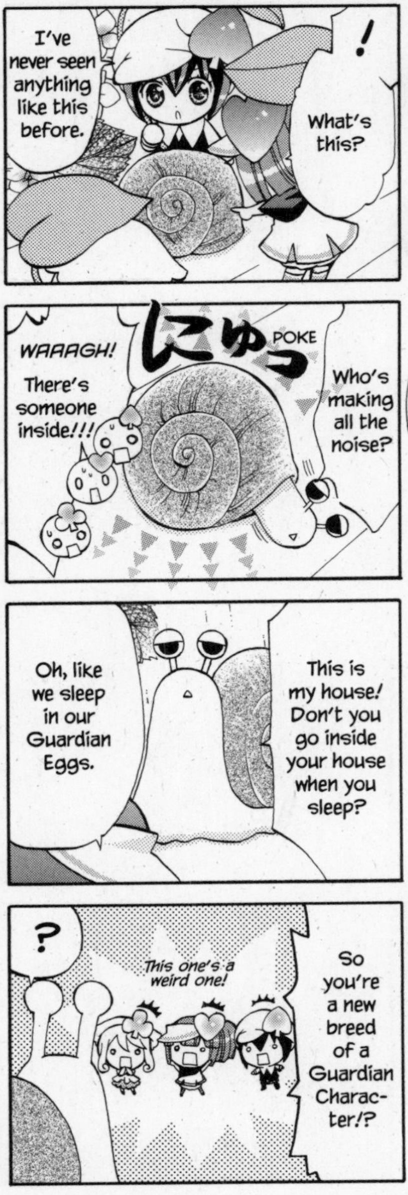
!
What's this?
I've never seen anything like this before.
Who's making all the noise?
にゅっ POKE
WAAAGH! There's someone inside!!!
This is my house! Don't you go inside your house when you sleep?
Oh, like we sleep in our Guardian Eggs.
So you're a new breed of a Guardian Character!?
This one's a weird one!
?

Get This Thing Off of Me

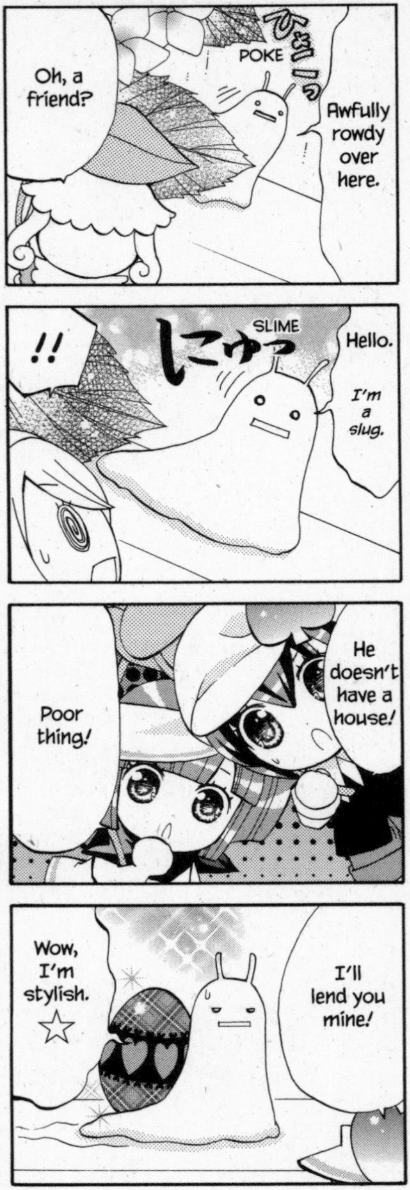
Awfully rowdy over here.
POKE
Oh, a friend?
Hello.
I'm a slug.
SLIME
にゅっ
!!
He doesn't have a house!
Poor thing!
I'll lend you mine!
Wow, I'm stylish. ☆

Thanks for Everything

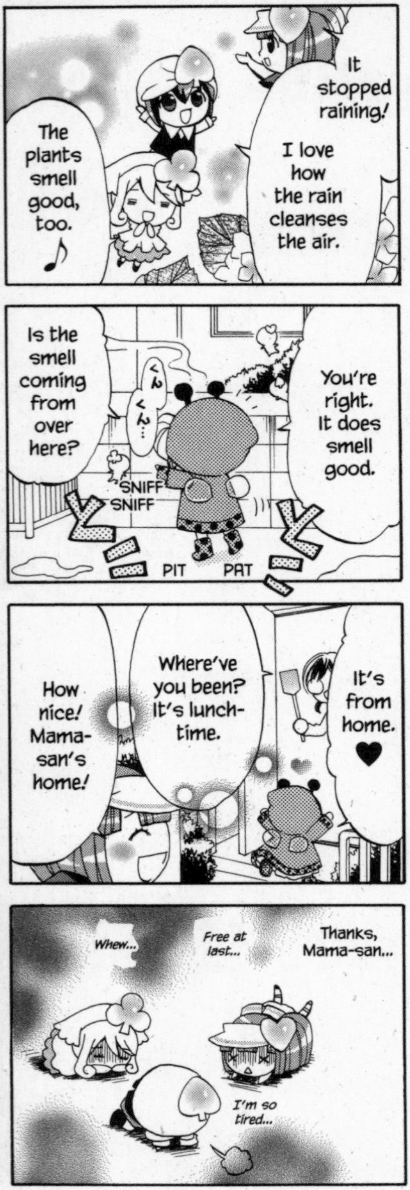
It stopped raining!
I love how the rain cleanses the air.
The plants smell good, too. ♪
You're right. It does smell good.
Is the smell coming from over here?
くん くん…
SNIFF SNIFF
PIT PAT
It's from home. ♥
Where've you been? It's lunch-time.
How nice! Mama-san's home!
Thanks, Mama-san...
Free at last...
Whew...
I'm so tired...

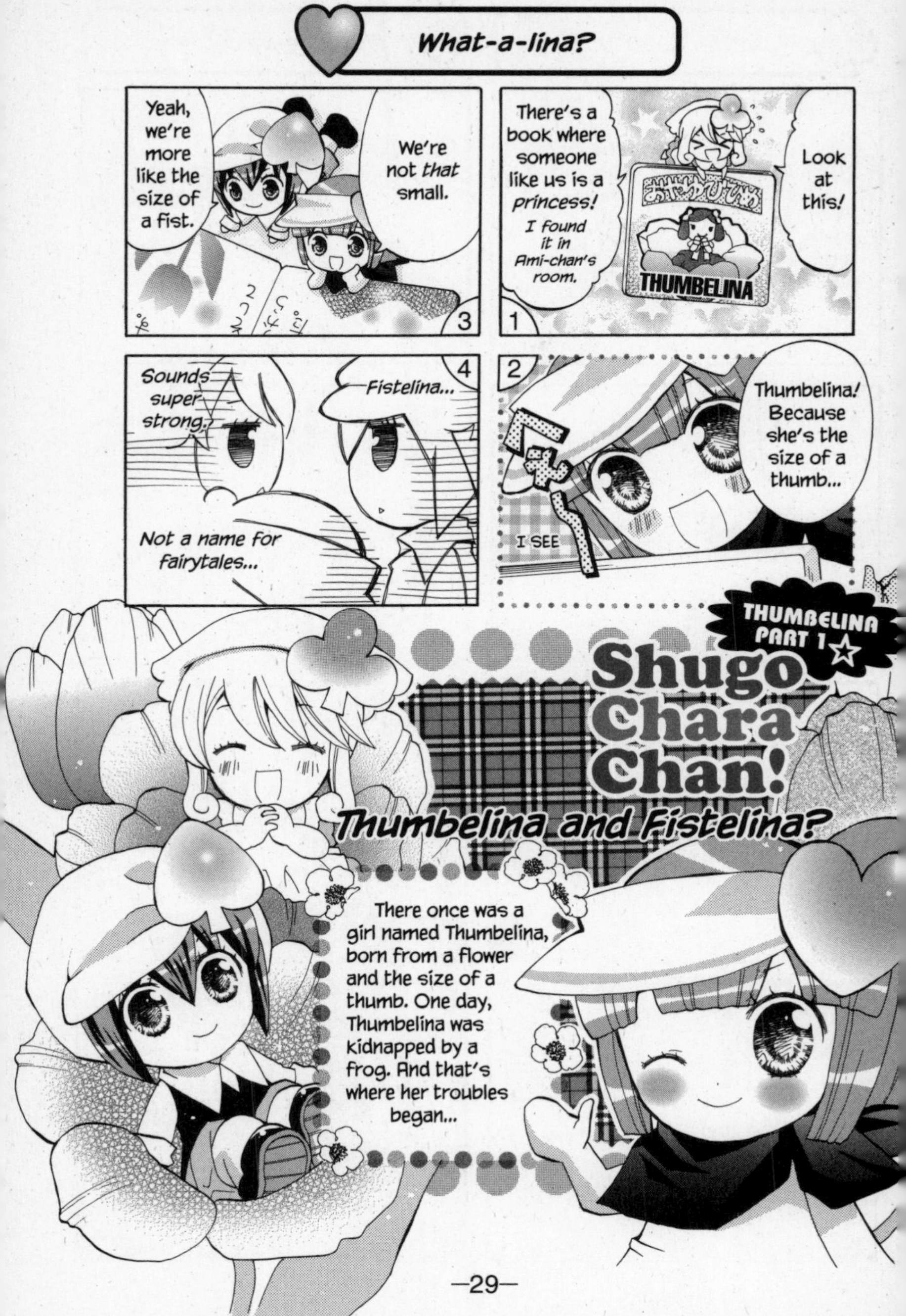
What-a-lina?
Look at this!
There's a book where someone like us is a princess!
I found it in Ami-chan's room.
おやゆびひめ
THUMBELINA
Thumbelina! Because she's the size of a thumb...
I SEE
We're not that small.
Yeah, we're more like the size of a fist.
Fistelina...
Sounds super strong.
Not a name for fairytales...
THUMBELINA PART 1☆
Shugo Chara Chan!
Thumbelina and Fistelina?
There once was a girl named Thumbelina, born from a flower and the size of a thumb. One day, Thumbelina was kidnapped by a frog. And that's where her troubles began...

Winners and Losers

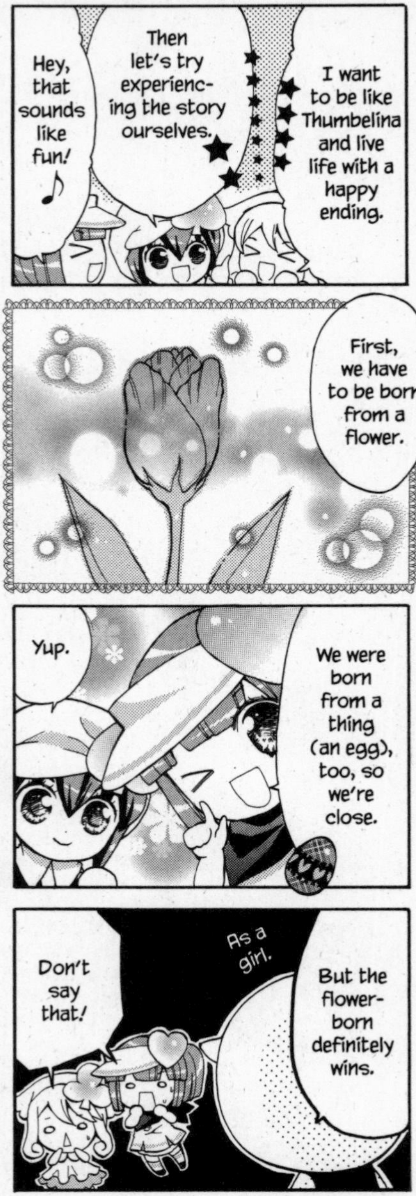
I want to be like Thumbelina and live life with a happy ending.
Then let's try experiencing the story ourselves.
Hey, that sounds like fun! ♪
First, we have to be born from a flower.
We were born from a thing (an egg), too, so we're close.
Yup.
But the flower-born definitely wins.
As a girl.
Don't say that!

The Reality

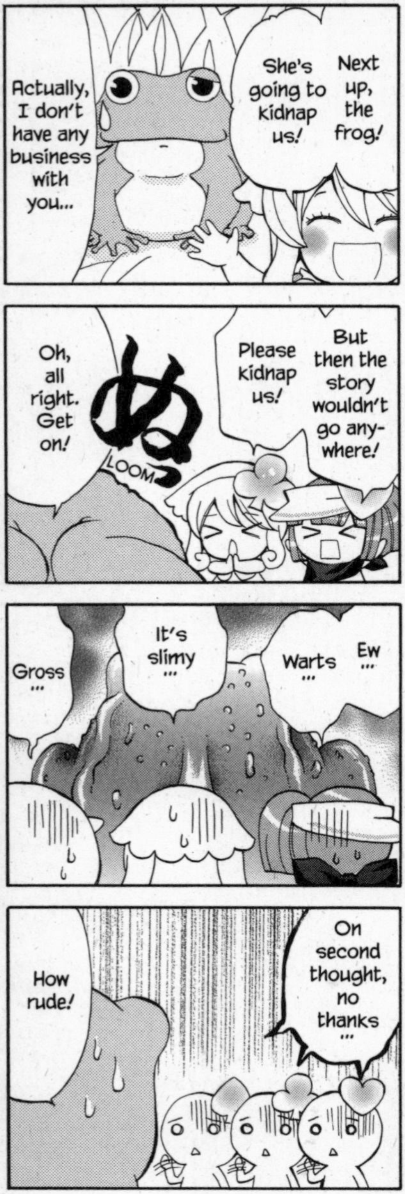
Next up, the frog!
She's going to kidnap us!
Actually, I don't have any business with you...
But then the story wouldn't go anywhere!
Please kidnap us!
ぬ
LOOM
Oh, all right. Get on!
Ew ...
Warts ...
It's slimy ...
Gross ...
On second thought, no thanks ...
How rude!

A Completely Different Danger

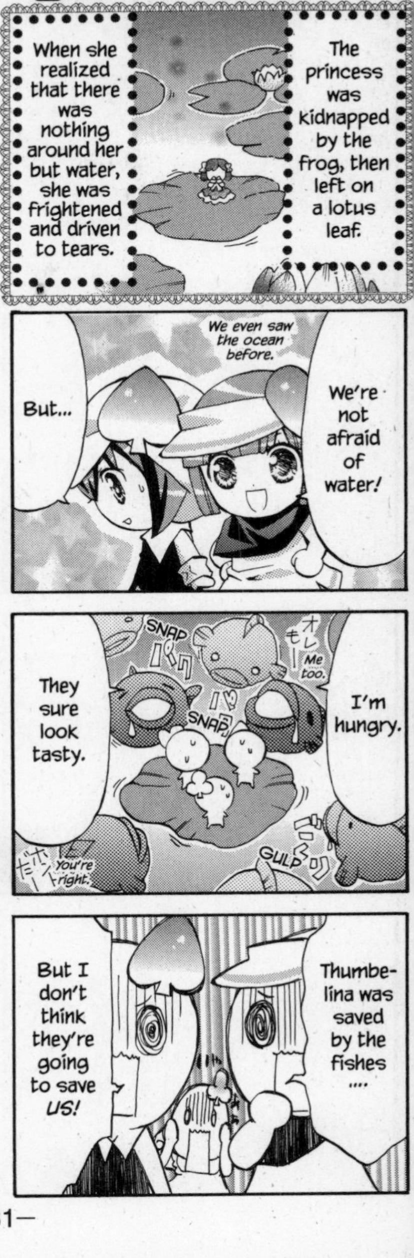
The princess was kidnapped by the frog, then left on a lotus leaf.
When she realized that there was nothing around her but water, she was frightened and driven to tears.
We're not afraid of water!
We even saw the ocean before.
But...
I'm hungry.
Me too.
SNAP
SNAP
They sure look tasty.
You're right.
GULP
Thumbelina was saved by the fishes ....
But I don't think they're going to save US!

So True

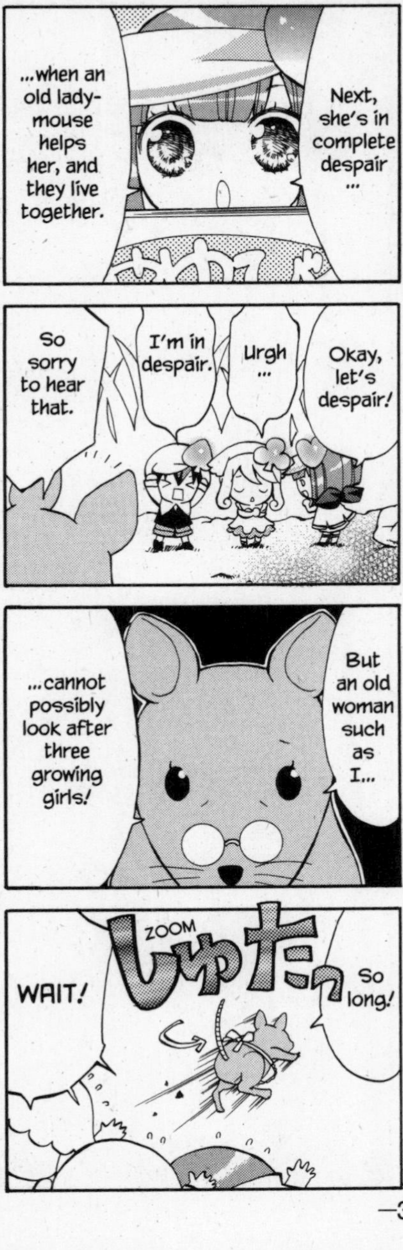
Next, she's in complete despair ...
...when an old lady-mouse helps her, and they live together.
Okay, let's despair!
Urgh ...
I'm in despair.
So sorry to hear that.
But an old woman such as I...
...cannot possibly look after three growing girls!
So long!
ZOOM
しゅたっ
WAIT!

Home Cooking

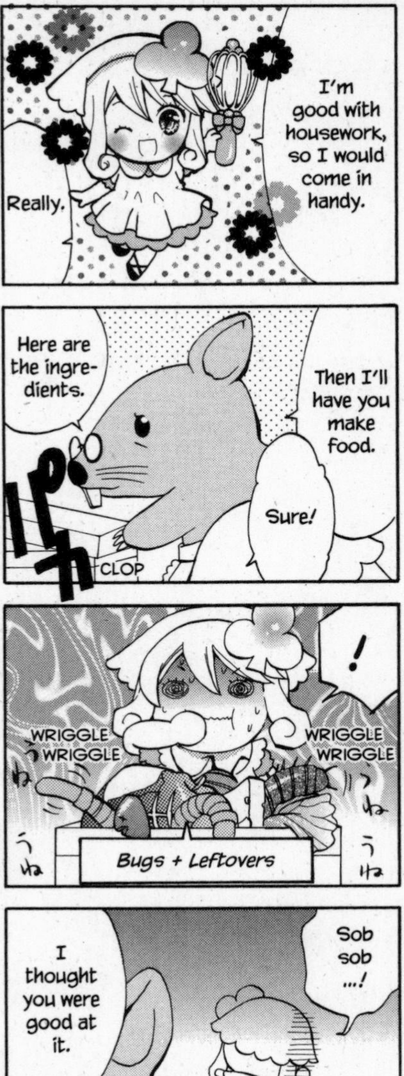
I'm good with housework, so I would come in handy.
Really.
Then I'll have you make food.
Sure!
Here are the ingredients.
CLOP
!
WRIGGLE WRIGGLE
WRIGGLE WRIGGLE
Bugs + Leftovers
Sob sob ...!
I thought you were good at it.

Not-So-Lifelike

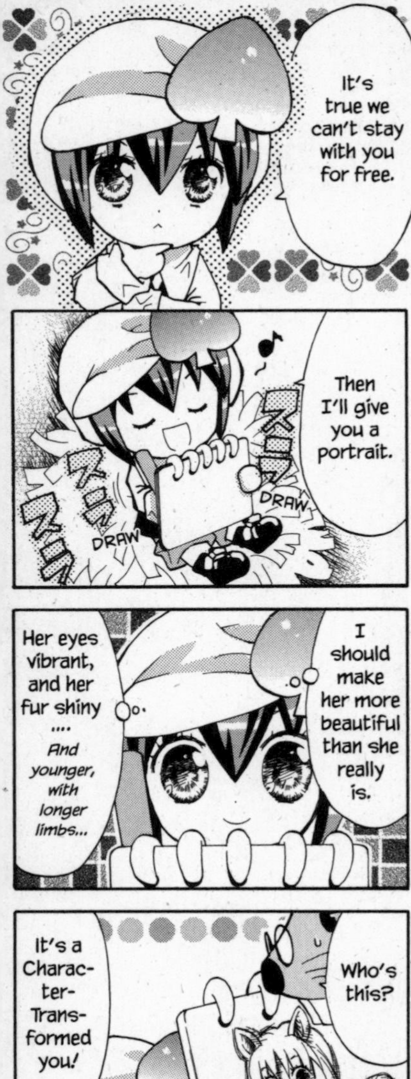
It's true we can't stay with you for free.
Then I'll give you a portrait.
DRAW
DRAW
I should make her more beautiful than she really is.
Her eyes vibrant, and her fur shiny ....
And younger, with longer limbs...
Who's this?
It's a Character-Transformed you!

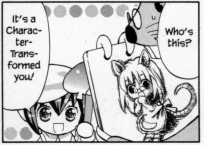

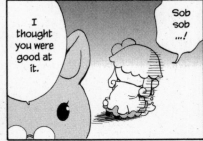

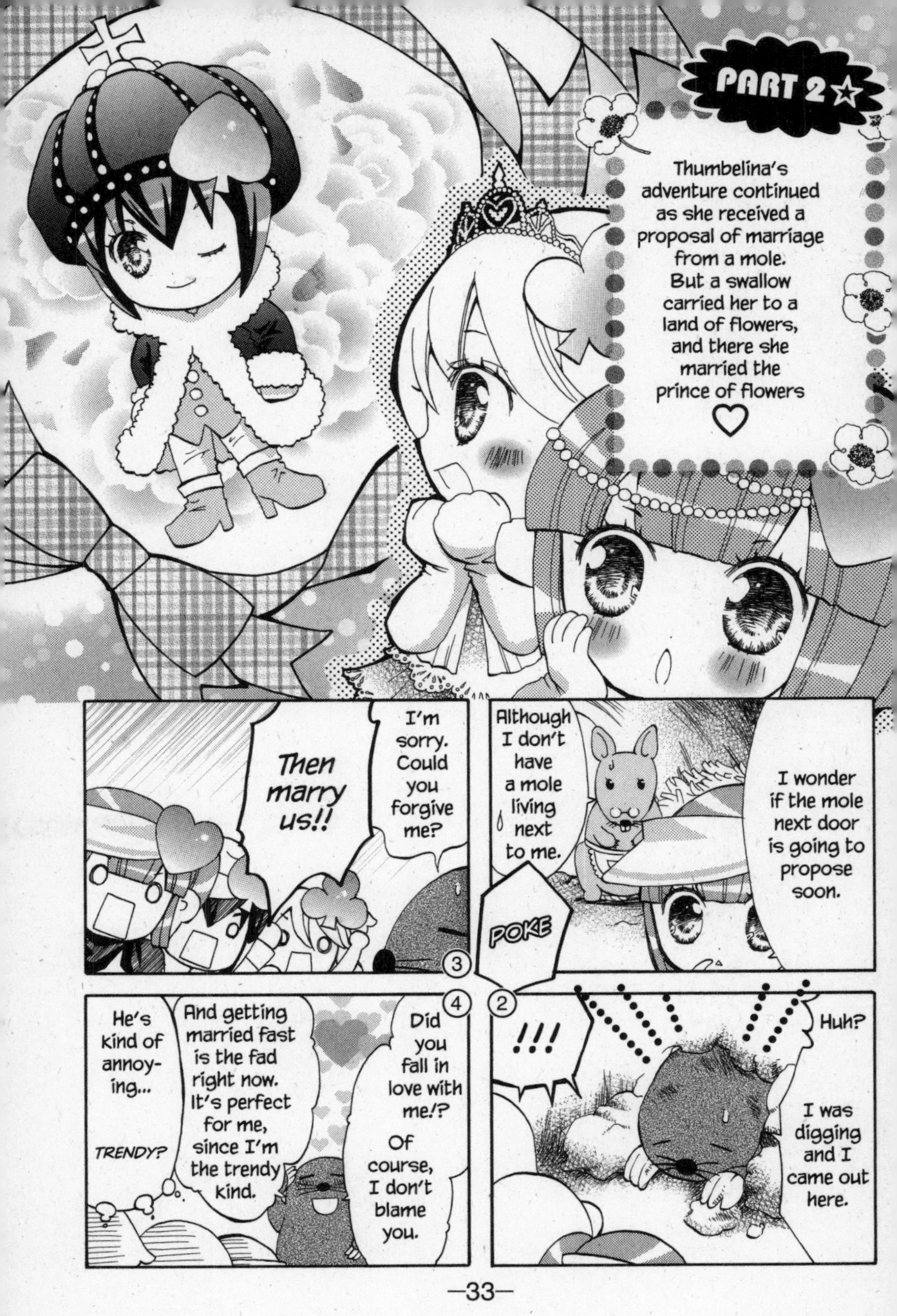

PART 2☆
Thumbelina's adventure continued as she received a proposal of marriage from a mole. But a swallow carried her to a land of flowers, and there she married the prince of flowers ♡
I wonder if the mole next door is going to propose soon.
Although I don't have a mole living next to me.
POKE
Huh?
I was digging and I came out here.
!!!
I'm sorry. Could you forgive me?
Then marry us!!
Did you fall in love with me!?
Of course, I don't blame you.
And getting married fast is the fad right now. It's perfect for me, since I'm the trendy kind.
He's kind of annoy-ing...
TRENDY?

Proposal

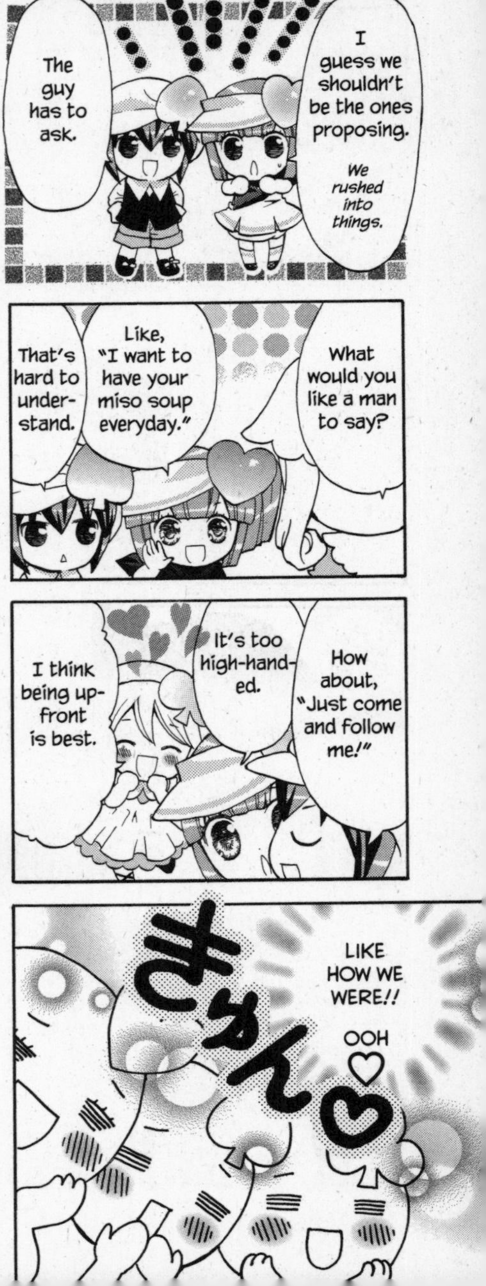
I guess we shouldn't be the ones proposing.
We rushed into things.
The guy has to ask.
What would you like a man to say?
Like, "I want to have your miso soup everyday."
That's hard to understand.
How about, "Just come and follow me!"
It's too high-handed.
I think being up-front is best.
きゃん♡
LIKE HOW WE WERE!!
OOH ♡

Extreme

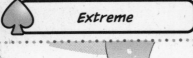

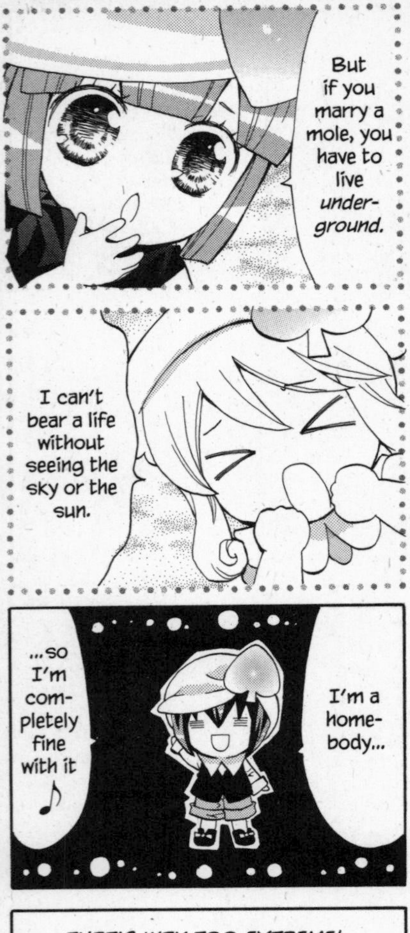
But if you marry a mole, you have to live underground.
I can't bear a life without seeing the sky or the sun.
I'm a homebody...
...so I'm completely fine with it ♪
THAT'S WAY TOO EXTREME!

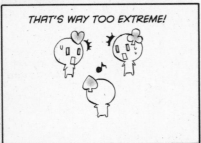

Trying to Marry for Money

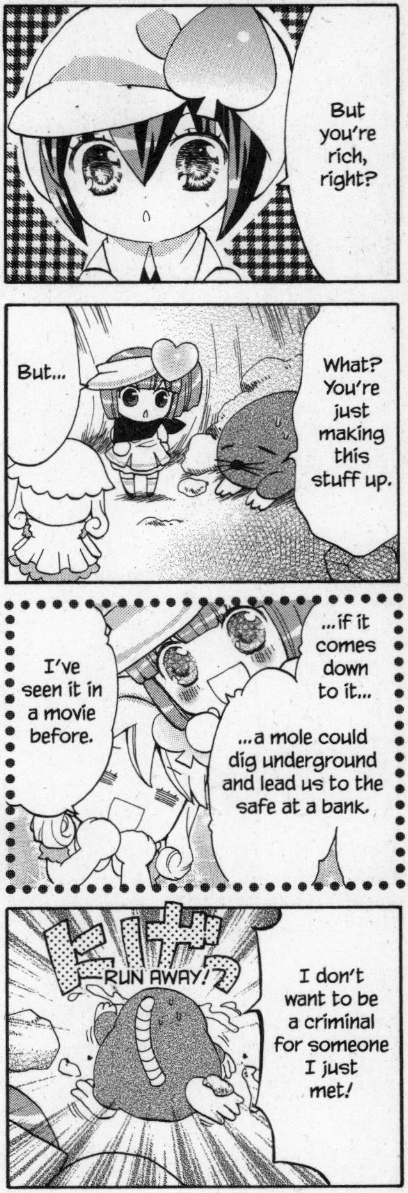

But you're rich, right?
What? You're just making this stuff up.
But...
...if it comes down to it...
...a mole could dig underground and lead us to the safe at a bank.
I've seen it in a movie before.
I don't want to be a criminal for someone I just met!
RUN AWAY!

A Better Reason

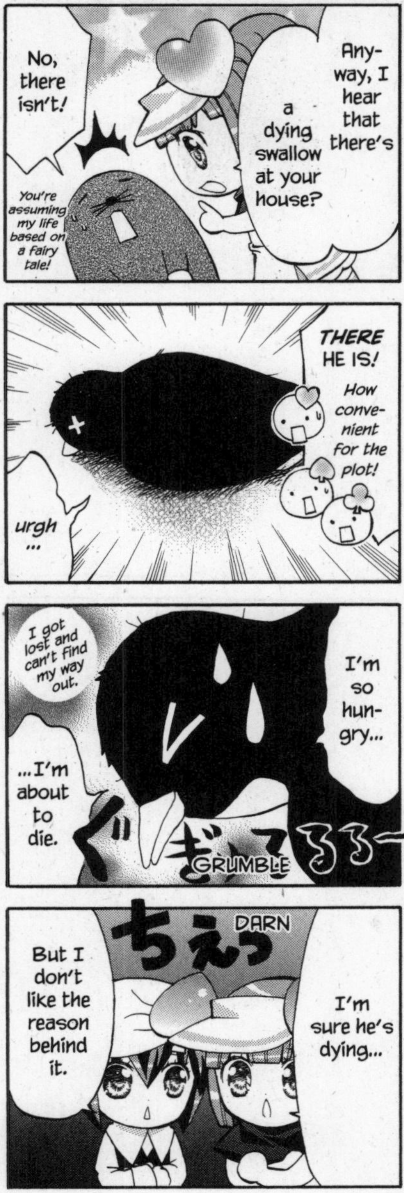

Anyway, I hear that there's a dying swallow at your house?
No, there isn't!
You're assuming my life based on a fairy tale!
THERE HE IS!
How convenient for the plot!
urgh ...
I'm so hungry...
I got lost and can't find my way out.
...I'm about to die.
GRUMBLE
DARN
I'm sure he's dying...
But I don't like the reason behind it.

There's No Place Like Home!

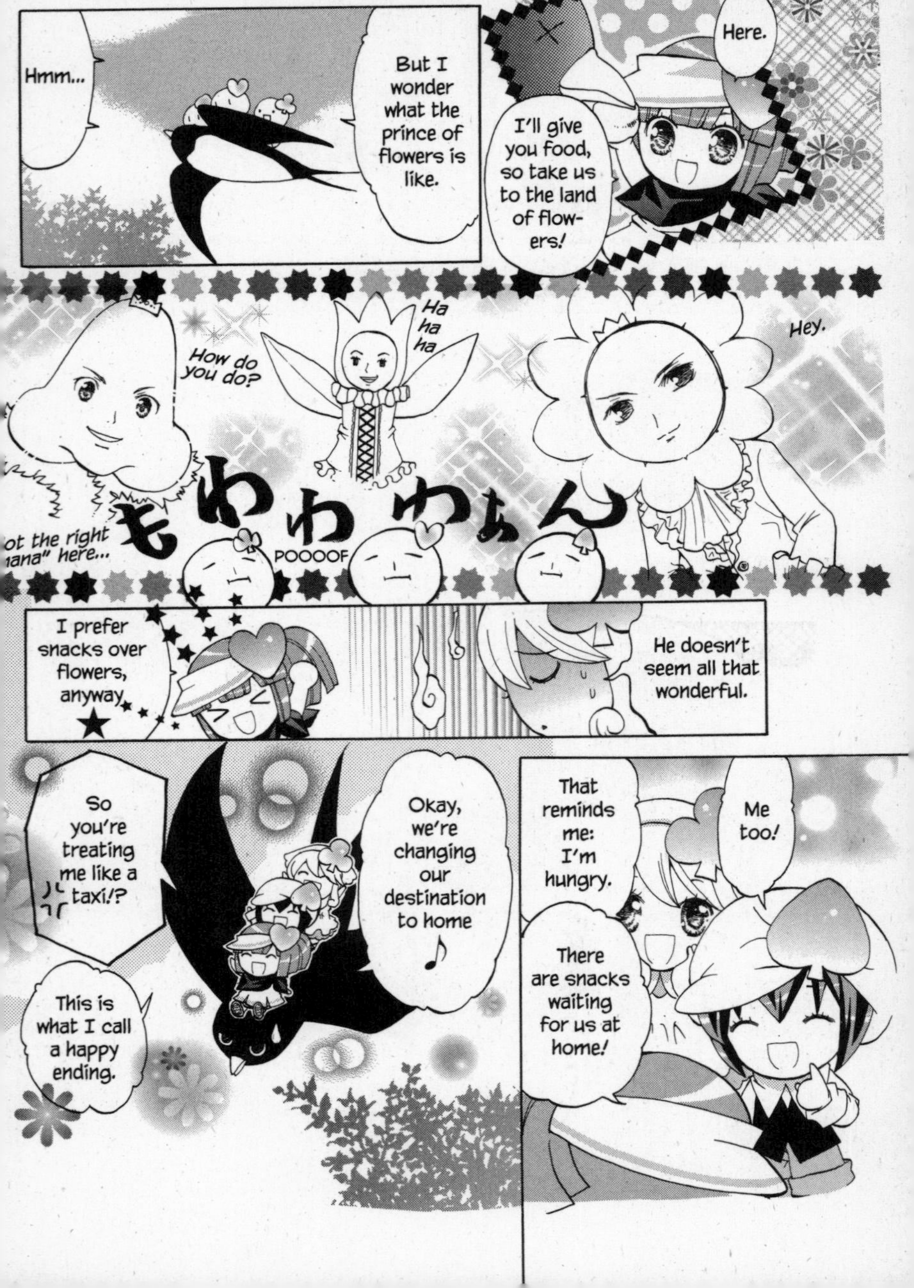
Here.
I'll give you food, so take us to the land of flowers!
But I wonder what the prince of flowers is like.
Hmm...
Hey.
Ha ha ha
How do you do?
もわゎわぁん
POOOOF
ot the right
ana" here...
He doesn't seem all that wonderful.
I prefer snacks over flowers, anyway★
Me too!
That reminds me: I'm hungry.
There are snacks waiting for us at home!
Okay, we're changing our destination to home ♪
So you're treating me like a taxi!?
This is what I call a happy ending.

It seems that there are many who think Miki is a boy. And when my former editor read the episode about Yoru searching for a bride, she thought, *"They're both boys, though!"*

I wish she would read more carefully!

I'm pretty girly and fall in love easily, you know.

You can see that in *Shugo Chara!* Volume 2.

HEE HEE

The
Summer Edition
starts on the
next page!

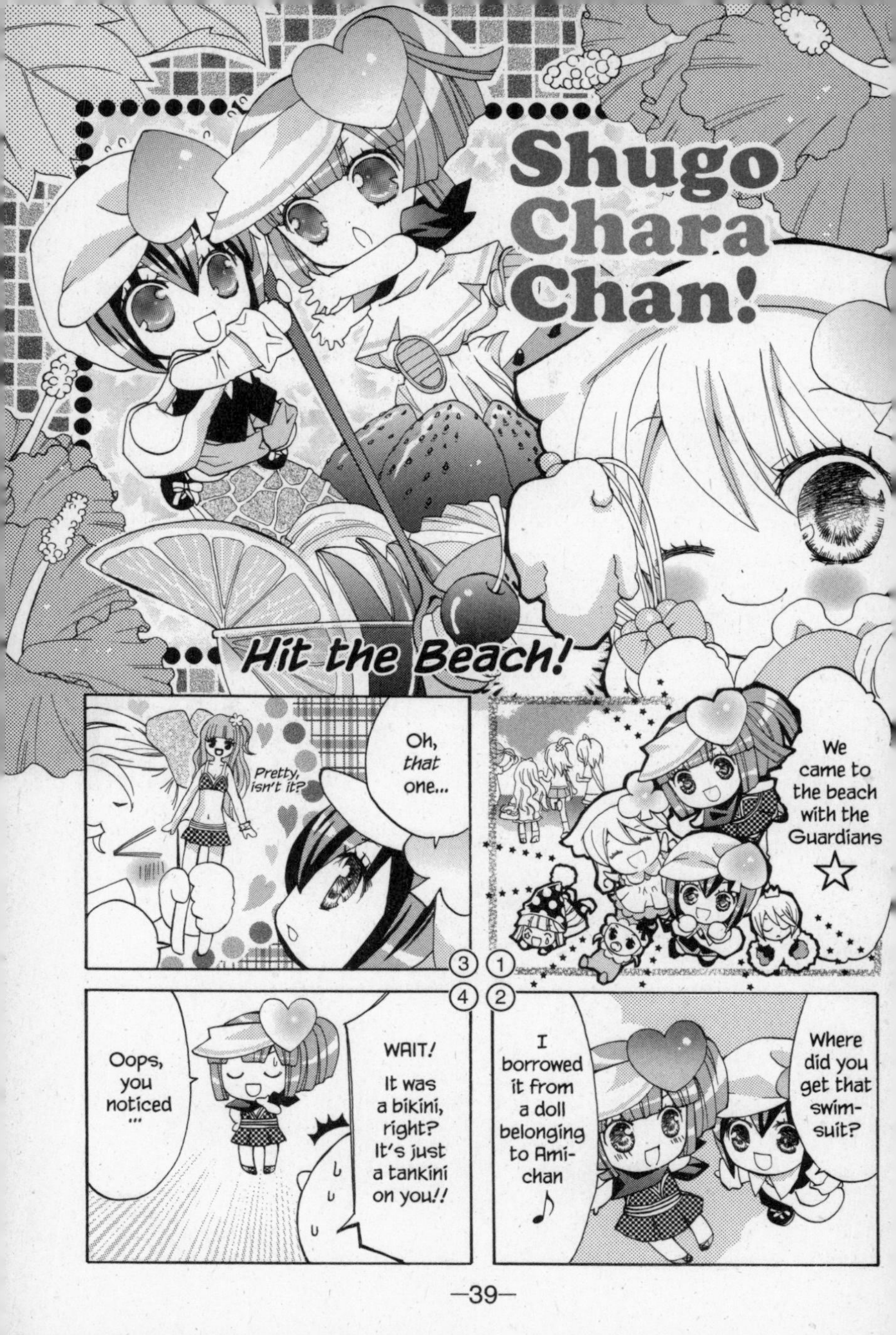
Shugo Chara Chan!
Hit the Beach!
We came to the beach with the Guardians ☆
Where did you get that swim-suit?
I borrowed it from a doll belonging to Ami-chan ♪
Oh, that one...
Pretty, isn't it?
WAIT! It was a bikini, right? It's just a tankini on you!!
Oops, you noticed ...

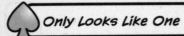

A Hot Idea?

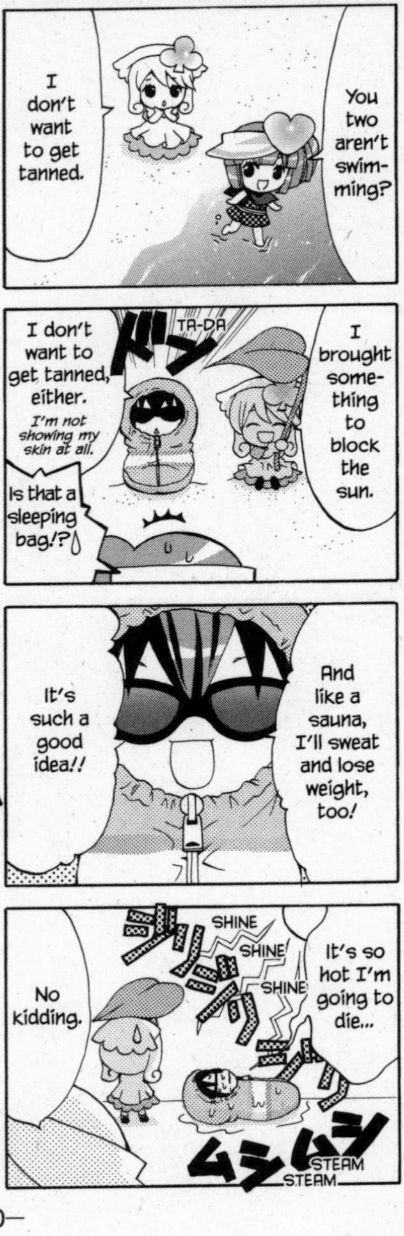
You two aren't swimming?
I don't want to get tanned.
I brought something to block the sun.
TA-DA
I don't want to get tanned, either.
I'm not showing my skin at all.
Is that a sleeping bag!?
And like a sauna, I'll sweat and lose weight, too!
It's such a good idea!!
It's so hot I'm going to die...
SHINE
SHINE
SHINE
No kidding.
STEAM
STEAM

Only Looks Like One

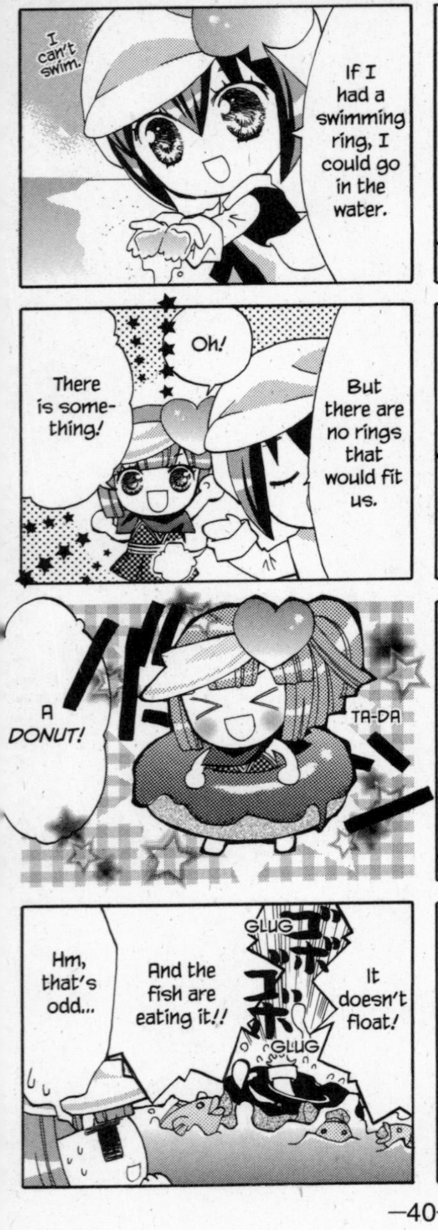
If I had a swimming ring, I could go in the water.
I can't swim.
But there are no rings that would fit us.
Oh!
There is something!
TA-DA
A DONUT!
It doesn't float!
GLUG
GLUG
And the fish are eating it!!
Hm, that's odd...

So True

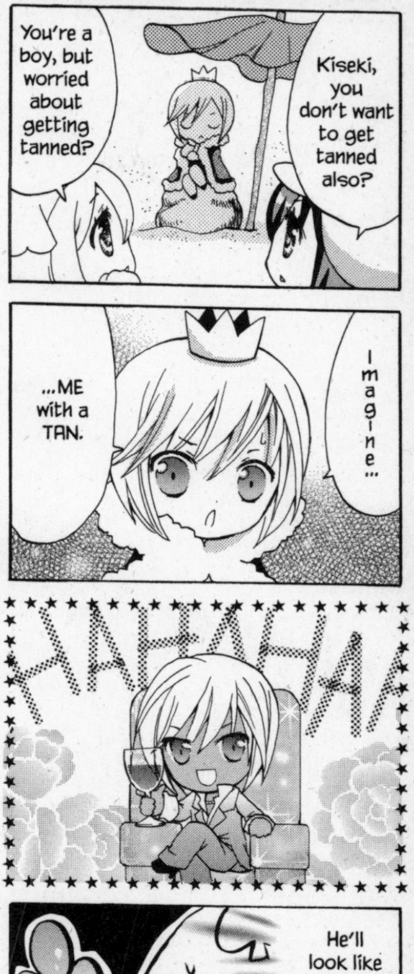
Kiseki, you don't want to get tanned also?
You're a boy, but worried about getting tanned?
Imagine...
...ME with a TAN.
HAHAHA
He'll look like a shady host!!

Su's Performance

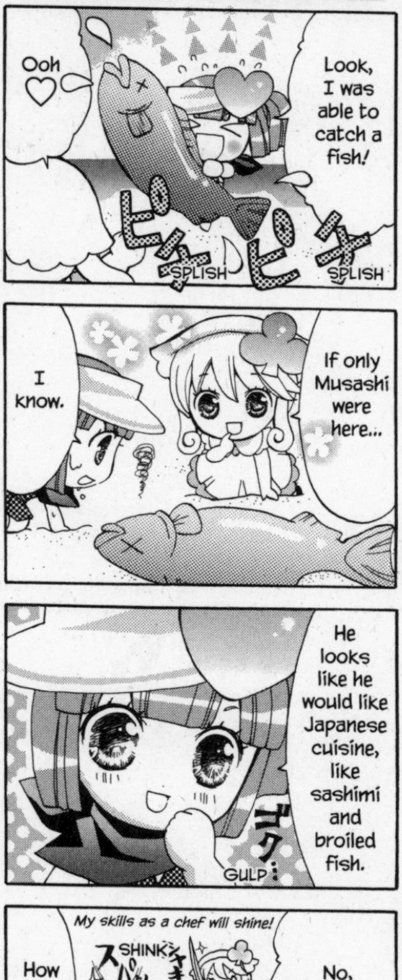
Look, I was able to catch a fish!
Ooh ♡
ピチ SPLISH
ピチ SPLISH
If only Musashi were here...
I know.
He looks like he would like Japanese cuisine, like sashimi and broiled fish.
ゴクッ GULP
No, I want to borrow his sword and do a slicing show!!
My skills as a chef will shine!
SHINK シャキーン
スパッ SLICE
スパッ SLICE
ドーーン! TA DA!
How manly!

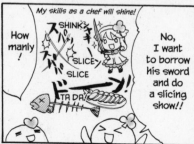

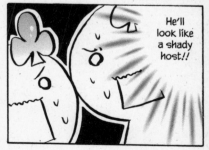

Won't Come Out

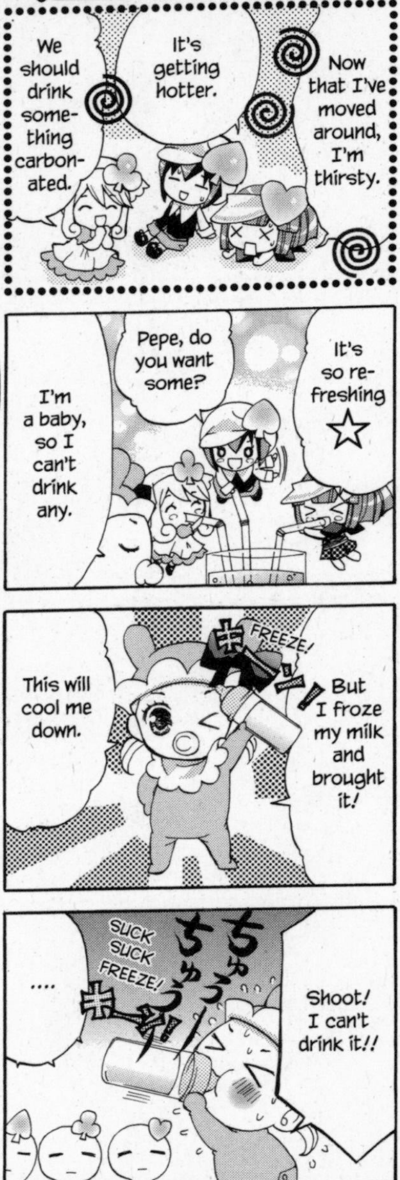
Now that I've moved around, I'm thirsty.
It's getting hotter.
We should drink something carbonated.
It's so refreshing ☆
Pepe, do you want some?
I'm a baby, so I can't drink any.
But I froze my milk and brought it!
FREEZE!
This will cool me down.
Shoot! I can't drink it!!
ちゅうちゅう
SUCK SUCK FREEZE!
....

Playing Alone

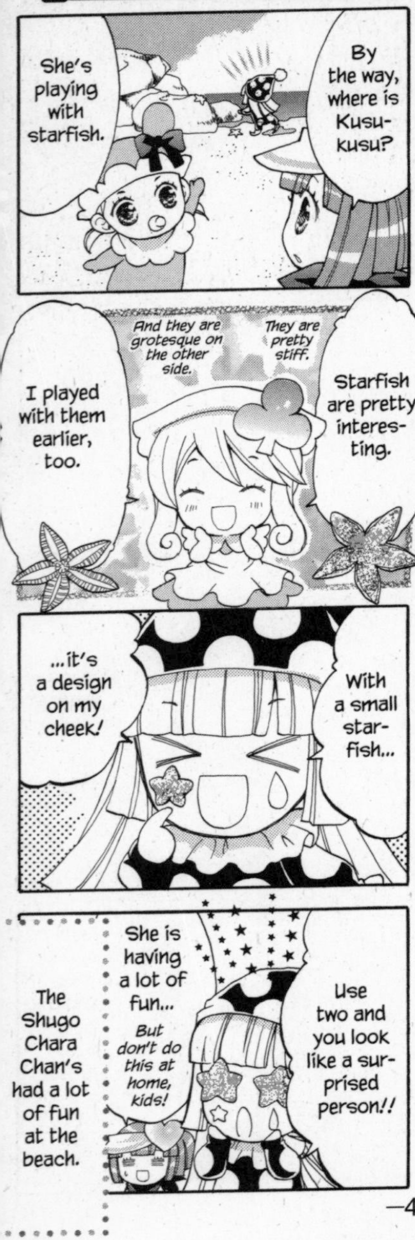
By the way, where is Kusukusu?
She's playing with starfish.
Starfish are pretty interesting.
They are pretty stiff.
And they are grotesque on the other side.
I played with them earlier, too.
With a small starfish...
...it's a design on my cheek!
Use two and you look like a surprised person!!
She is having a lot of fun...
But don't do this at home, kids!
The Shugo Chara Chan's had a lot of fun at the beach.

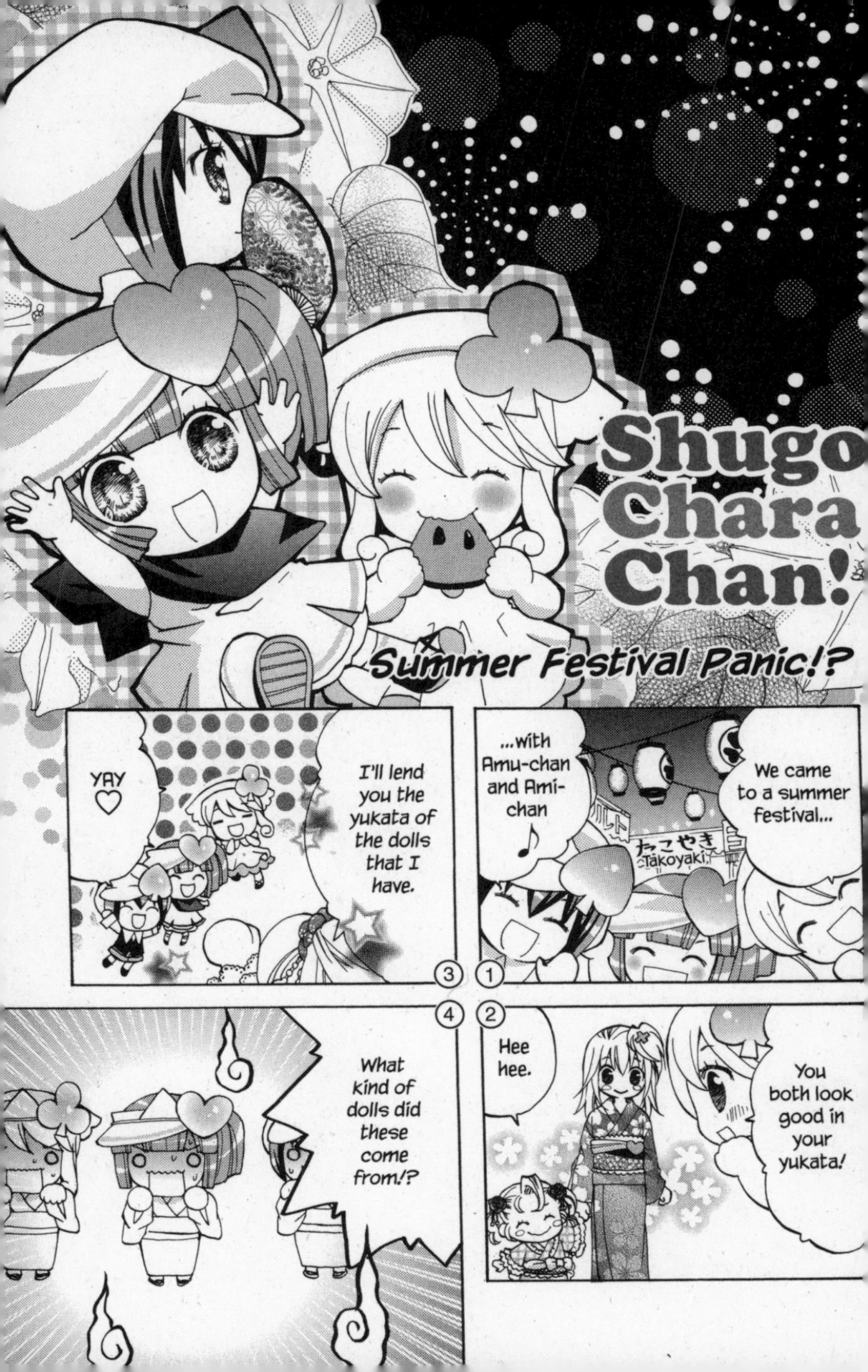
Shugo Chara Chan!
Summer Festival Panic!?
We came to a summer festival...
...with Amu-chan and Ami-chan ♪
たこやき
Takoyaki
You both look good in your yukata!
Hee hee.
I'll lend you the yukata of the dolls that I have.
YAY ♡
What kind of dolls did these come from!?

Aim and Aim

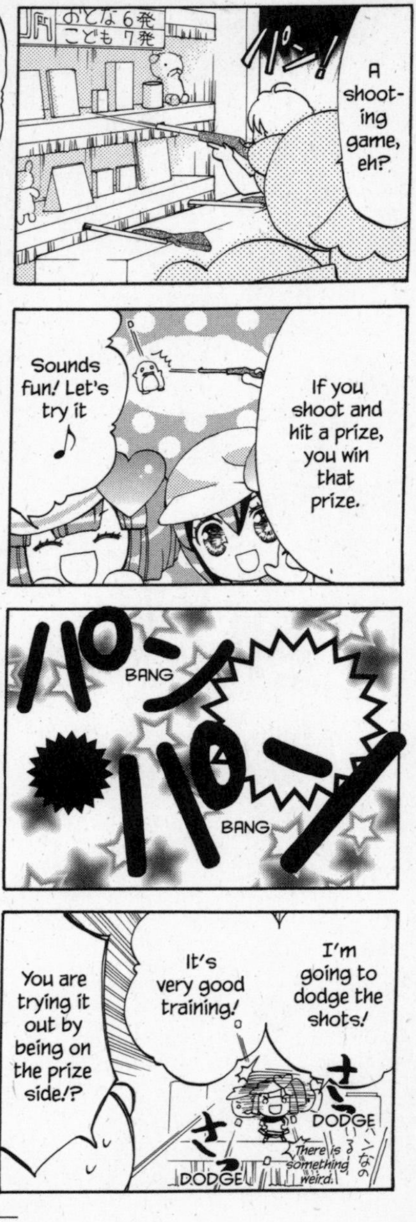
おとな 6発
こども 7発
パン!
A shooting game, eh?
If you shoot and hit a prize, you win that prize.
Sounds fun! Let's try it ♪
パーン
BANG
パーン
BANG
I'm going to dodge the shots!
It's very good training!
You are trying it out by being on the prize side!?
さっ
DODGE
さっ
DODGE
ヘンなのいる
There is something weird.

Scheming

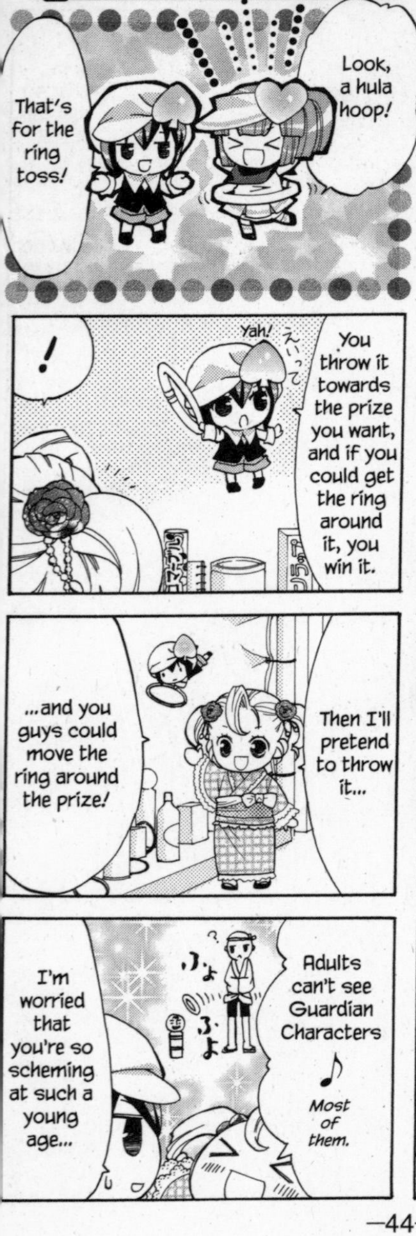
Look, a hula hoop!
That's for the ring toss!
You throw it towards the prize you want, and if you could get the ring around it, you win it.
えいっ
Yah!
!
Then I'll pretend to throw it...
...and you guys could move the ring around the prize!
Adults can't see Guardian Characters ♪
Most of them.
ふよ
ふよ
I'm worried that you're so scheming at such a young age...

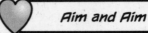

Natural Attraction

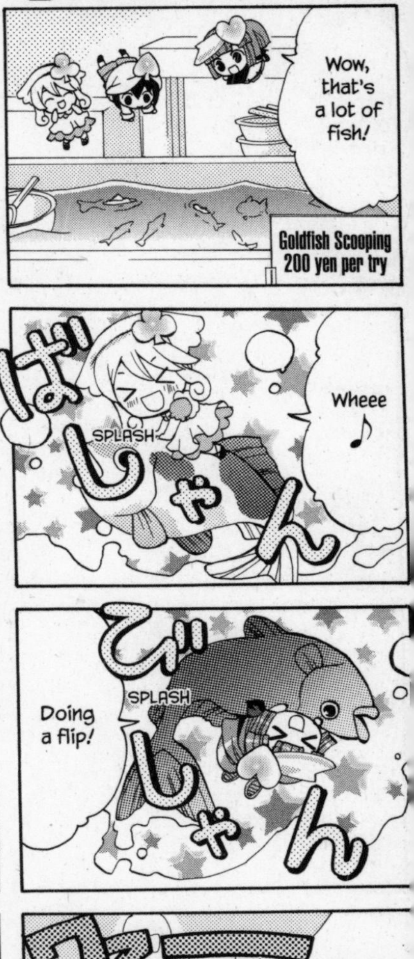
Wow, that's a lot of fish!
Goldfish Scooping
200 yen per try
Wheee ♪
ばしゃん
SPLASH
びしゃん
SPLASH
Doing a flip!
Why are there so many people now!?
ワァー
OOOOOH
すご――!!
How amazing!
OWNER

Its Original Use

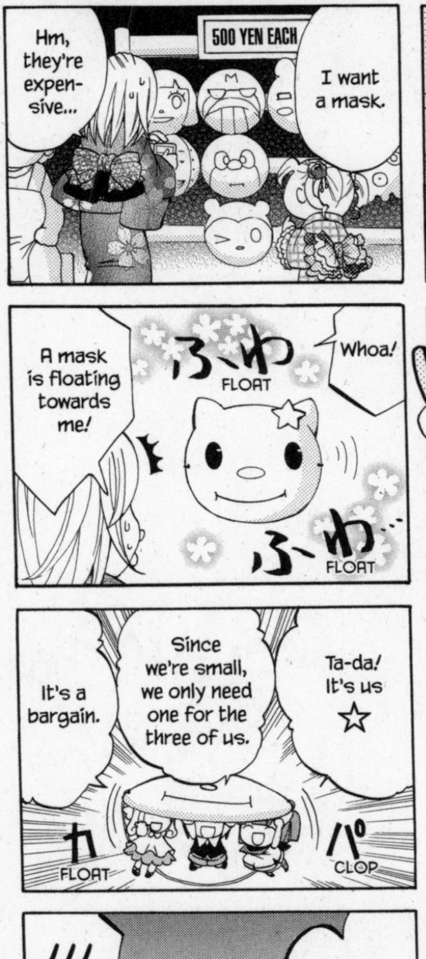
I want a mask.
500 YEN EACH
Hm, they're expensive...
Whoa!
ふわ
FLOAT
ふわ…
FLOAT
A mask is floating towards me!
Ta-da! It's us ☆
Since we're small, we only need one for the three of us.
It's a bargain.
パ
CLOP
カ
FLOAT
But it's not a mask anymore.
It hides your whole body.
!!!

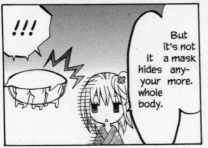

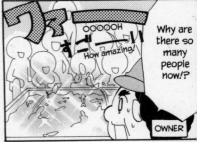

Ran's Fantasy

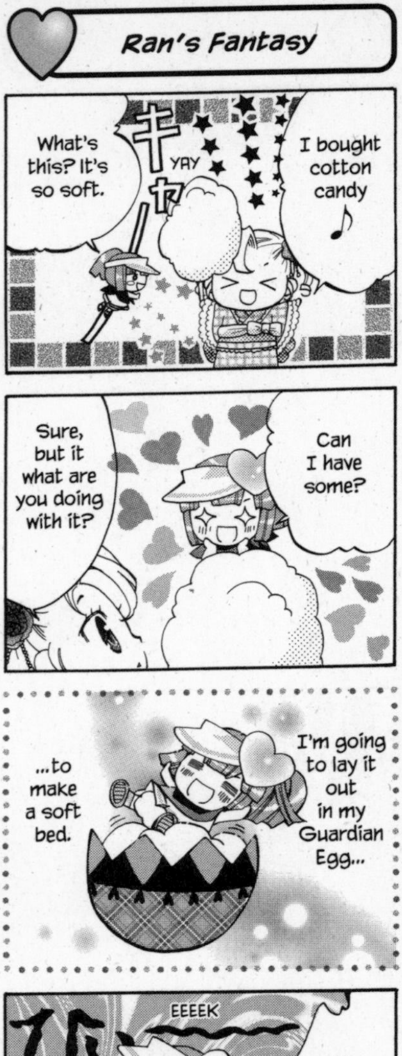

I bought cotton candy ♪
キャ
YAY
What's this? It's so soft.
Can I have some?
Sure, but it what are you doing with it?
I'm going to lay it out in my Guardian Egg...
...to make a soft bed.
It's MELTING!
It's STICKY!!
EEEEK
ひ

Various Syrup

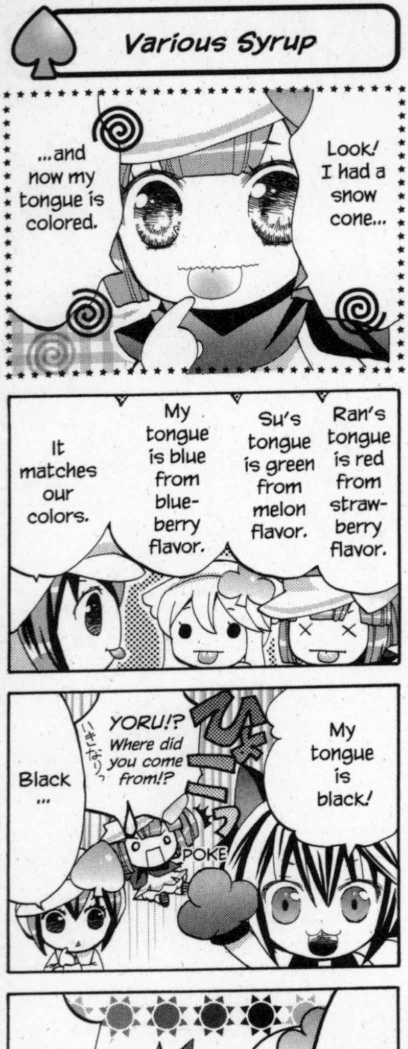

Look! I had a snow cone...
...and now my tongue is colored.
Ran's tongue is red from straw-berry flavor.
Su's tongue is green from melon flavor.
My tongue is blue from blue-berry flavor.
It matches our colors.
My tongue is black!
YORU!? Where did you come from!?
いきなり!?
POKE
Black ...
...from squid ink?
From coffee flavor !!

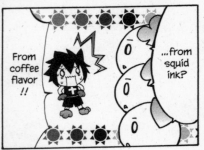

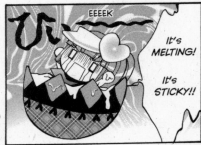

Because I'm Not Good at Exercise

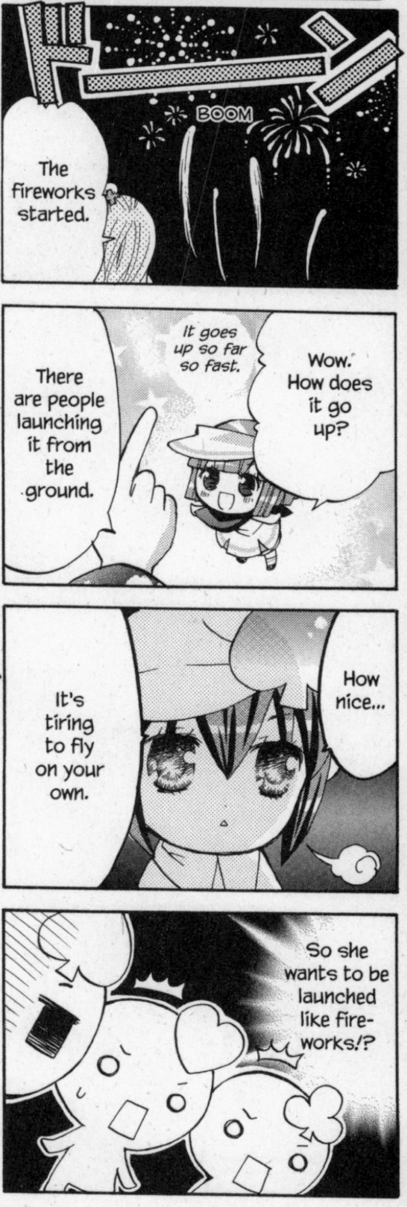
BOOM
The fireworks started.
Wow. How does it go up?
It goes up so far so fast.
There are people launching it from the ground.
How nice...
It's tiring to fly on your own.
So she wants to be launched like fireworks!?

The Real Thing Wouldn't...

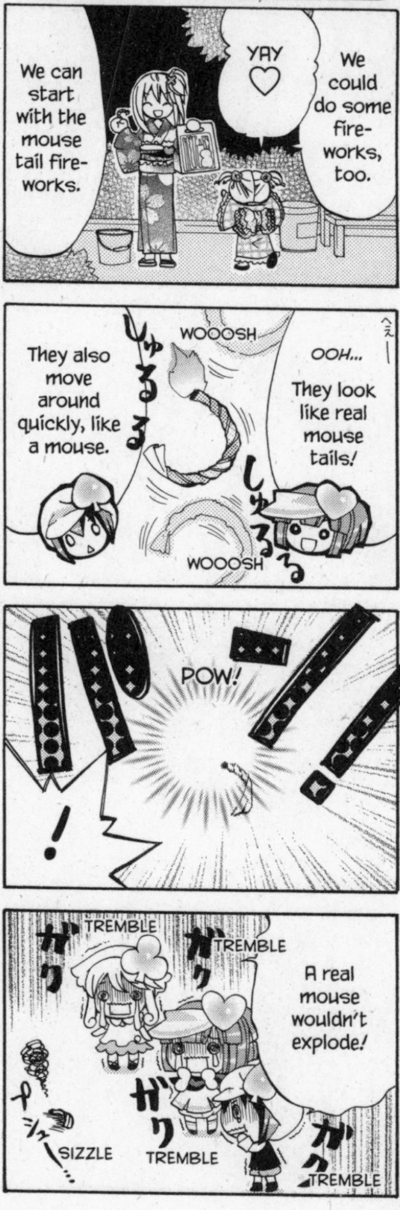
We could do some fire-works, too.
YAY ♥
We can start with the mouse tail fire-works.
へえー
OOH...
They look like real mouse tails!
WOOOSH
しゅるる
They also move around quickly, like a mouse.
しゅるるる
WOOOSH
POW!
!
TREMBLE
TREMBLE
A real mouse wouldn't explode!
SIZZLE
TREMBLE
TREMBLE

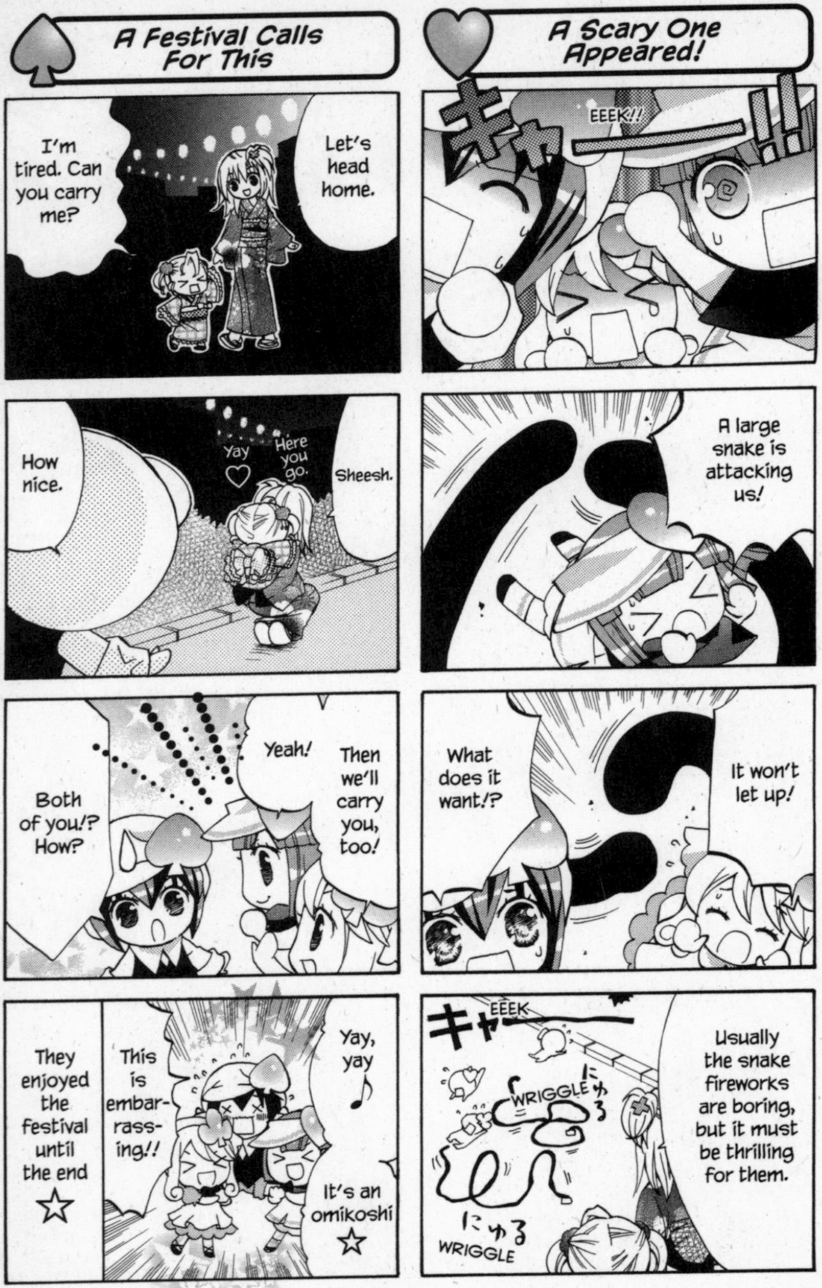
A Scary One Appeared!
キャー
EEEK!!
A large snake is attacking us!
It won't let up!
What does it want!?
キャー
EEEK
Usually the snake fireworks are boring, but it must be thrilling for them.
にゅる
WRIGGLE
にゅる
WRIGGLE
A Festival Calls For This
Let's head home.
I'm tired. Can you carry me?
Sheesh.
Here you go.
Yay ♡
How nice.
Then we'll carry you, too!
Yeah!
Both of you!? How?
Yay, yay ♪
It's an omikoshi ☆
This is embarrassing!!
They enjoyed the festival until the end ☆

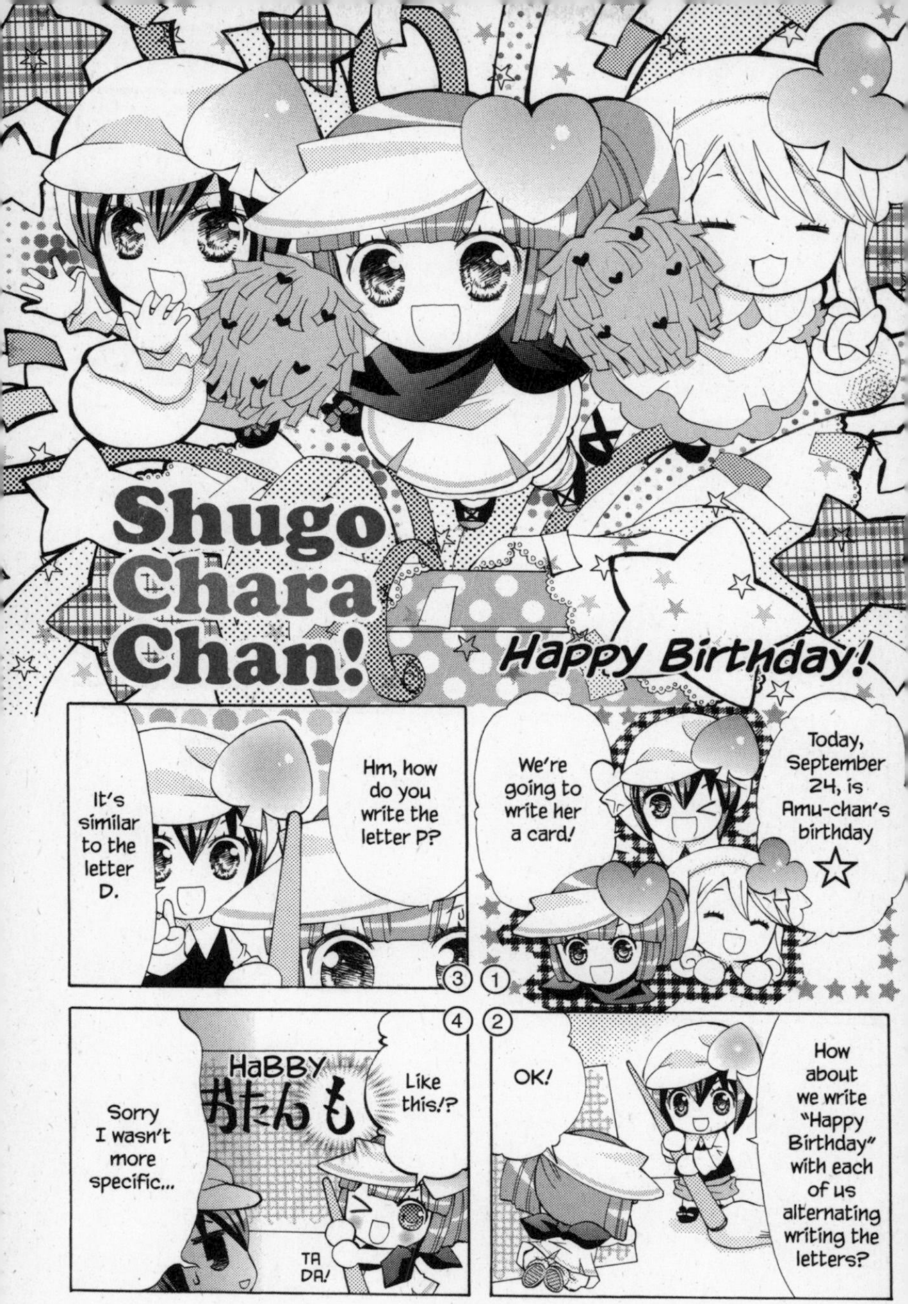

Shugo Chara Chan!
Happy Birthday!
Today, September 24, is Amu-chan's birthday ☆
We're going to write her a card!
How about we write "Happy Birthday" with each of us alternating writing the letters?
OK!
Hm, how do you write the letter P?
It's similar to the letter D.
Like this!?
HaBBY おたんも
TA DA!
Sorry I wasn't more specific...

Who's This!?

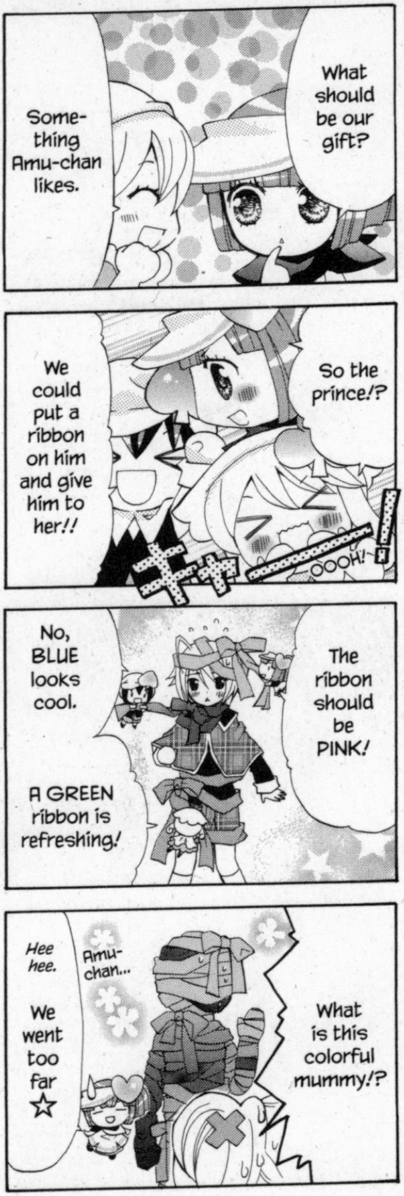
What should be our gift?
Something Amu-chan likes.
So the prince!?
We could put a ribbon on him and give him to her!!
OOOH!
The ribbon should be PINK!
No, BLUE looks cool.
A GREEN ribbon is refreshing!
What is this colorful mummy!?
Amu-chan...
Hee hee.
We went too far ☆

It's Still a Surprise

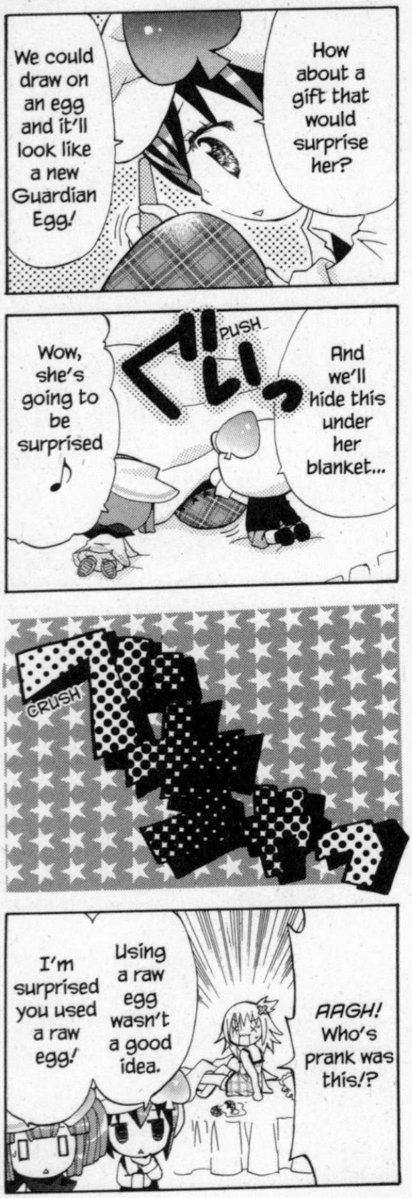
How about a gift that would surprise her?
We could draw on an egg and it'll look like a new Guardian Egg!
PUSH
And we'll hide this under her blanket...
Wow, she's going to be surprised ♪
CRUSH
AAGH! Who's prank was this!?
Using a raw egg wasn't a good idea.
I'm surprised you used a raw egg!

Ran's Hard Work

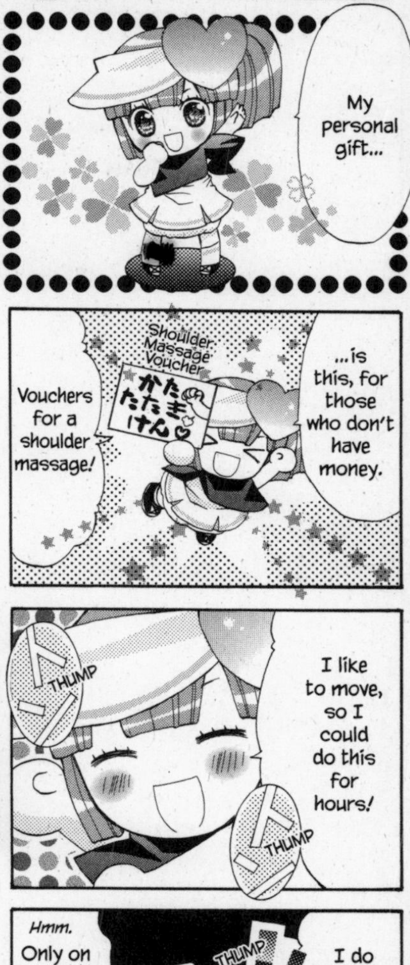
My personal gift...
...is this, for those who don't have money.
Shoulder Massage Voucher
かたたたきけん
Vouchers for a shoulder massage!
I like to move, so I could do this for hours!
THUMP
THUMP
I do a good job, right?
THUMP
THUMP
THUMP
Hmm.
Only on one side doesn't help much...

Only Good in the Beginning

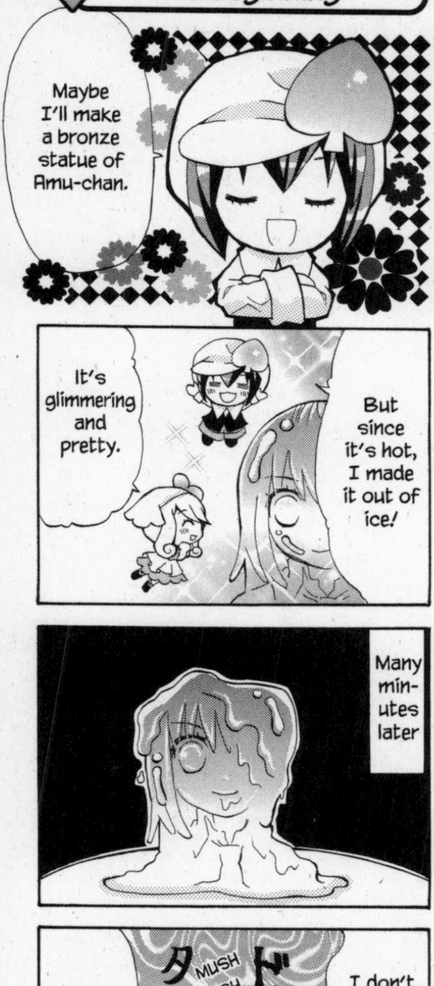
Maybe I'll make a bronze statue of Amu-chan.
But since it's hot, I made it out of ice!
It's glimmering and pretty.
Many minutes later
I don't want to see myself melt!!
ドロドロ
MUSH MUSH
タラー
MELT
It's pretty gross.

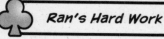

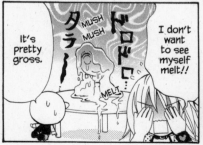

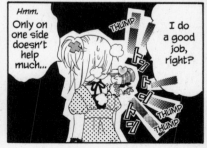

Cake Avalanche!

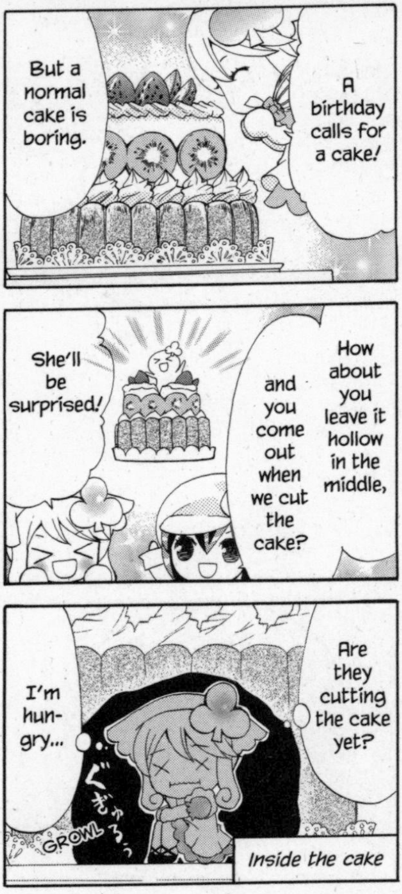
A birthday calls for a cake!
But a normal cake is boring.
How about you leave it hollow in the middle,
and you come out when we cut the cake?
She'll be surprised!
Are they cutting the cake yet?
I'm hun-gry...
ぐぎゅるっ
GROWL
Inside the cake
ずずっ
THUD
THUD
She's eating the inside!?

What Amu Wanted

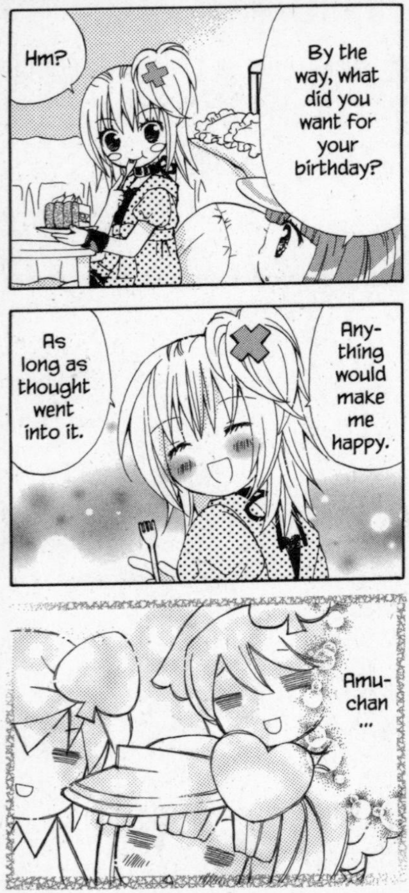
By the way, what did you want for your birthday?
Hm?
Any-thing would make me happy.
As long as thought went into it.
Amu-chan ...
I'm sur-prised you like hot things.
Did you want Tabasco to pour over your cake?
I didn't say, "hot," I said, "thought!!"

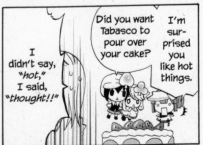

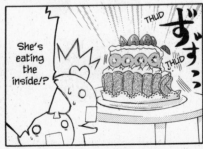

Summer is over and it's Autumn, when food tastes good! I'm jealous of the small Shugo Chara Chans, because even a small amount of sea urchin and foie gras would fill them up so fast!

I wish you would be more lady-like and want fruit or cake.
How much of a gourmet are you?

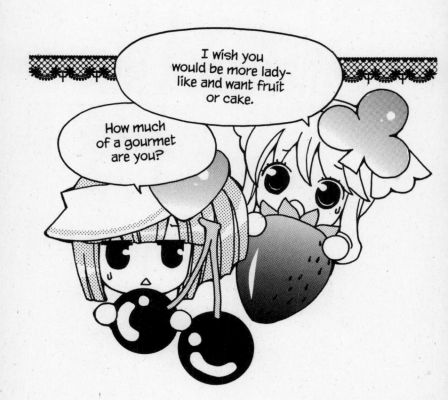

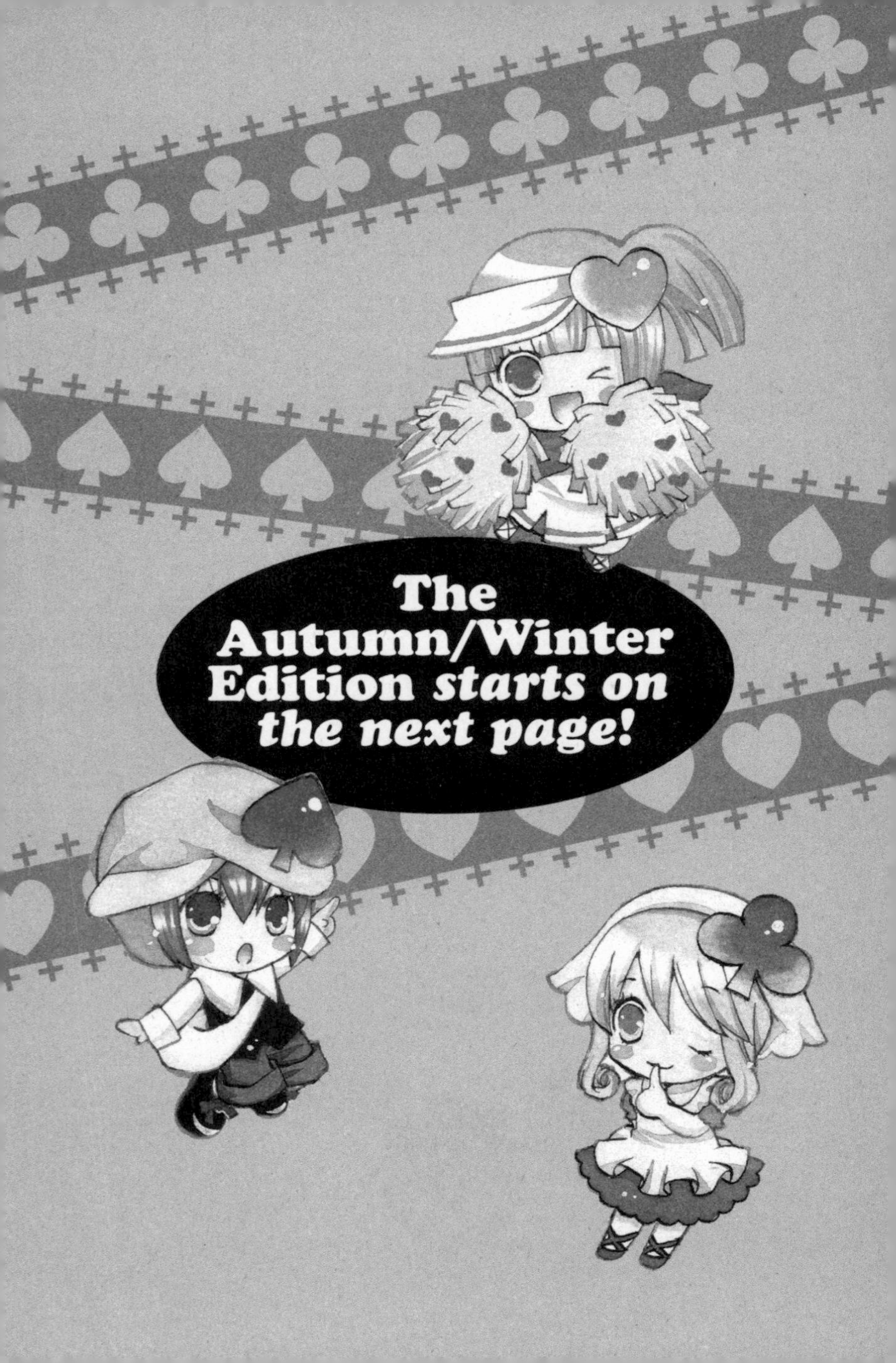
The Autumn/Winter Edition *starts on the next page!*

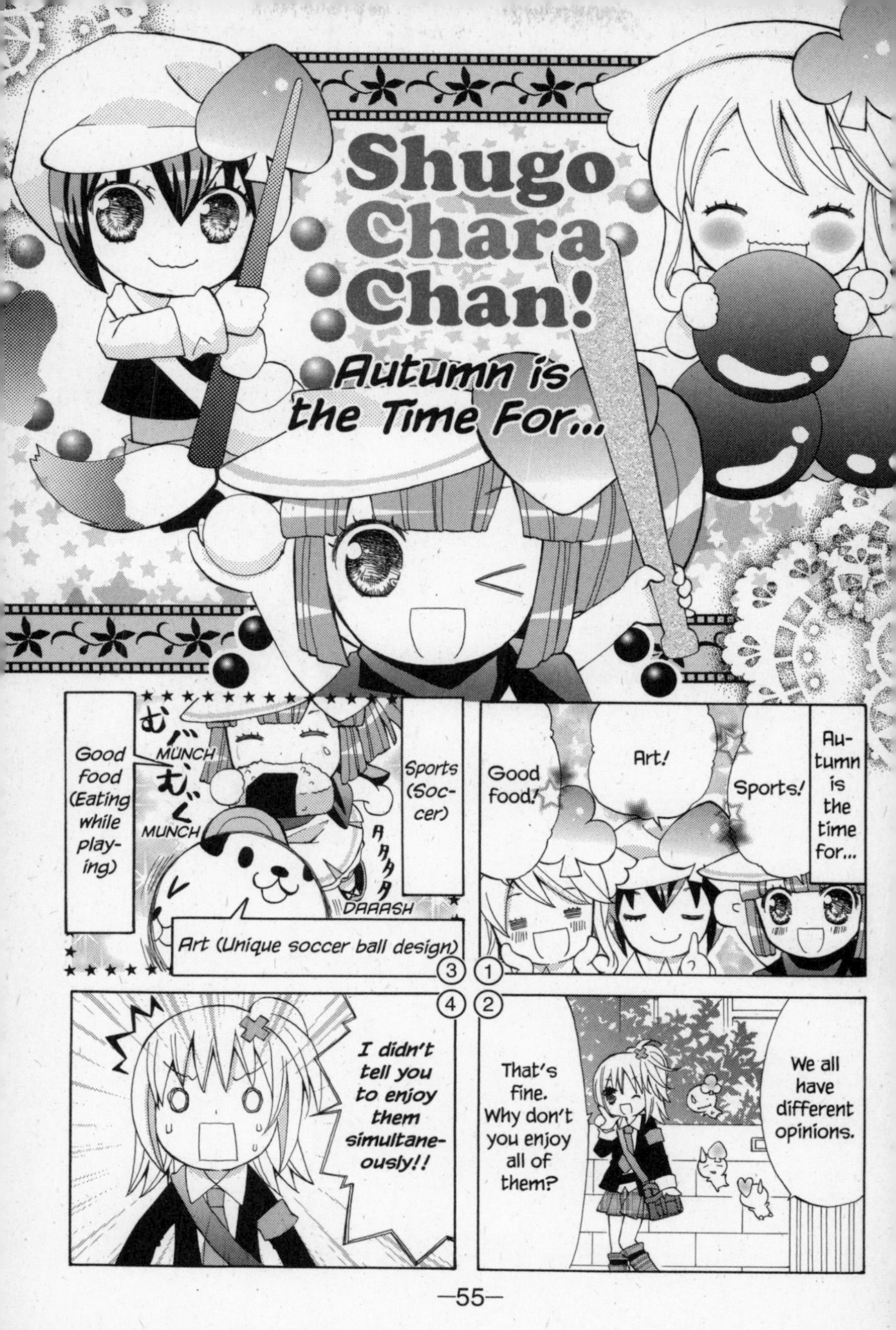
Shugo Chara Chan!
Autumn is the Time For...
Autumn is the time for...
Sports!
Art!
Good food!
We all have different opinions.
That's fine. Why don't you enjoy all of them?
Sports (Soccer)
DAAASH
Good food (Eating while playing)
MUNCH
MUNCH
Art (Unique soccer ball design)
I didn't tell you to enjoy them simultaneously!!

Cheater

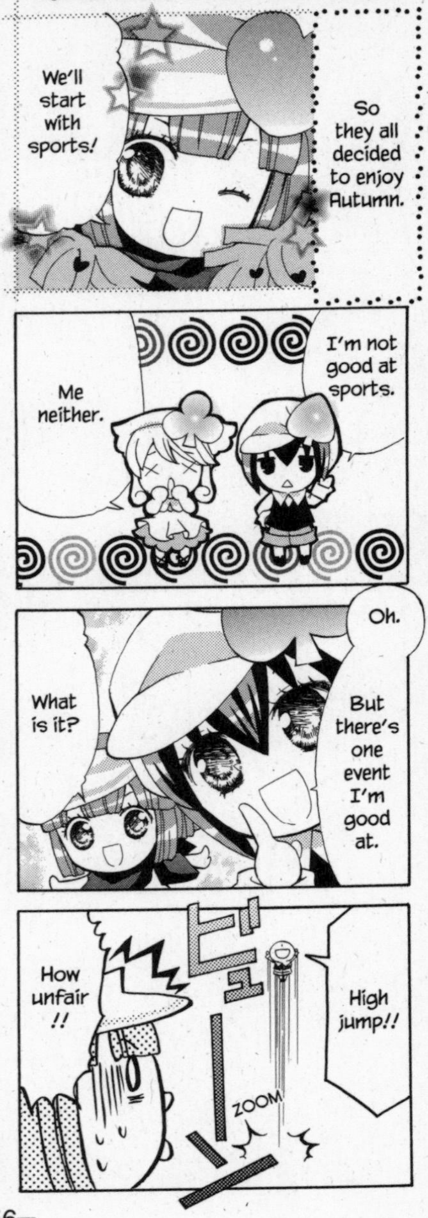

So they all decided to enjoy Autumn.
We'll start with sports!
I'm not good at sports.
Me neither.
Oh.
But there's one event I'm good at.
What is it?
High jump!!
ZOOM
How unfair!!

Header

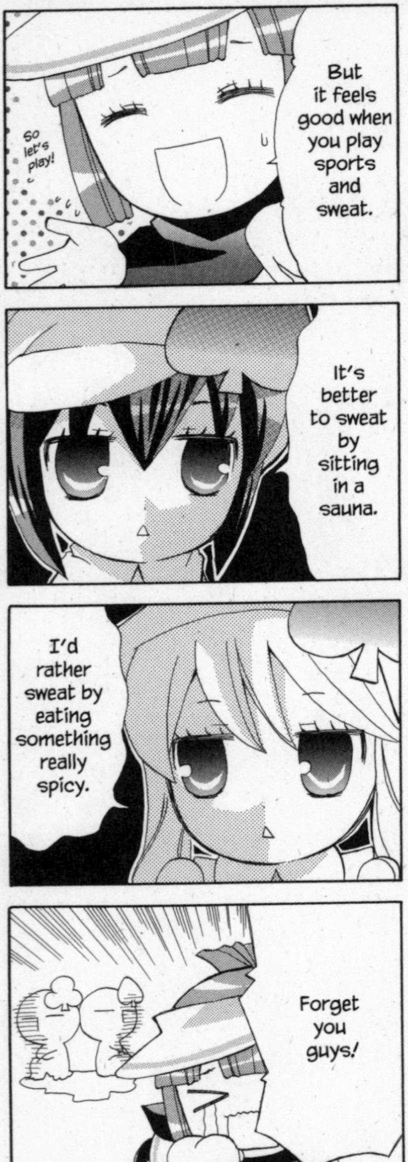

But it feels good when you play sports and sweat.
So let's play!
It's better to sweat by sitting in a sauna.
I'd rather sweat by eating something really spicy.
Forget you guys!

Inside Su's Head

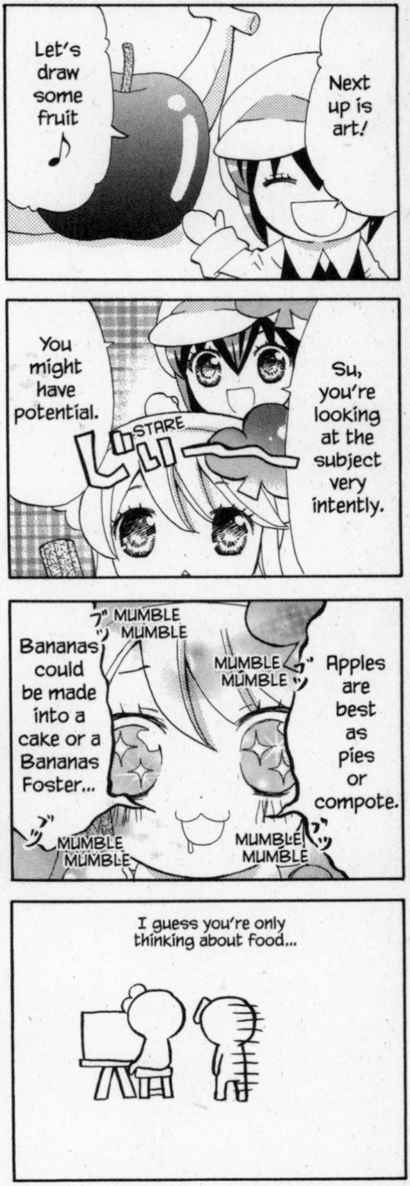

Next up is art!
Let's draw some fruit ♪
Su, you're looking at the subject very intently.
STARE
You might have potential.
MUMBLE MUMBLE
Apples are best as pies or compote.
MUMBLE MUMBLE
MUMBLE MUMBLE
Bananas could be made into a cake or a Bananas Foster...
MUMBLE MUMBLE
I guess you're only thinking about food...

Work of a Professional

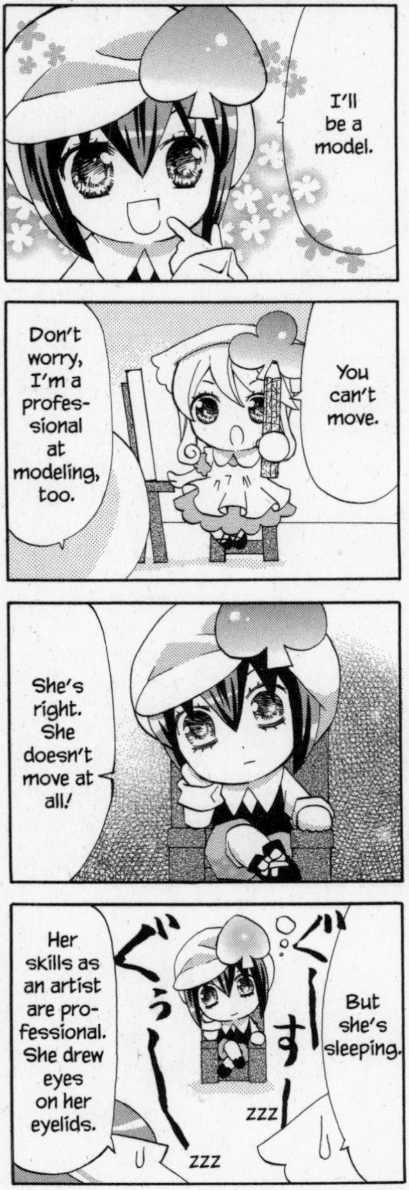

I'll be a model.
You can't move.
Don't worry, I'm a professional at modeling, too.
She's right. She doesn't move at all!
But she's sleeping.
ZZZ
Her skills as an artist are professional. She drew eyes on her eyelids.
ZZZ

Ran's Cooking

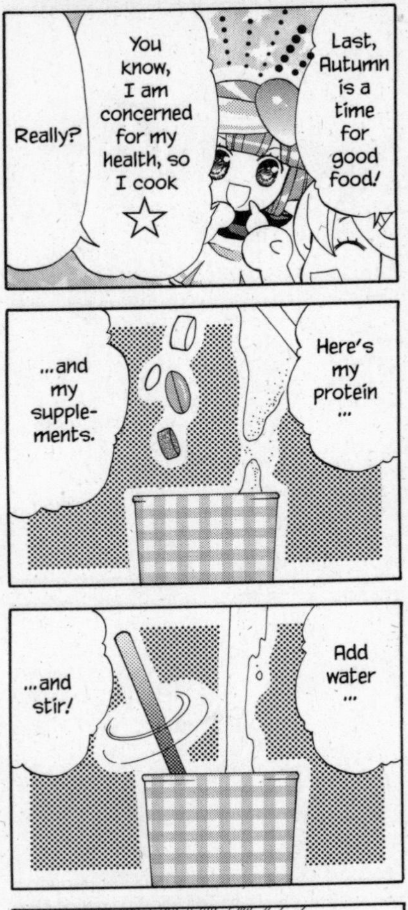
Last, Autumn is a time for good food!
You know, I am concerned for my health, so I cook ☆
Really?
Here's my protein ...
...and my supplements.
Add water ...
...and stir!
Ta-da! Lots of nutrients ♪
You don't call that cooking!

I'm Good, Right?

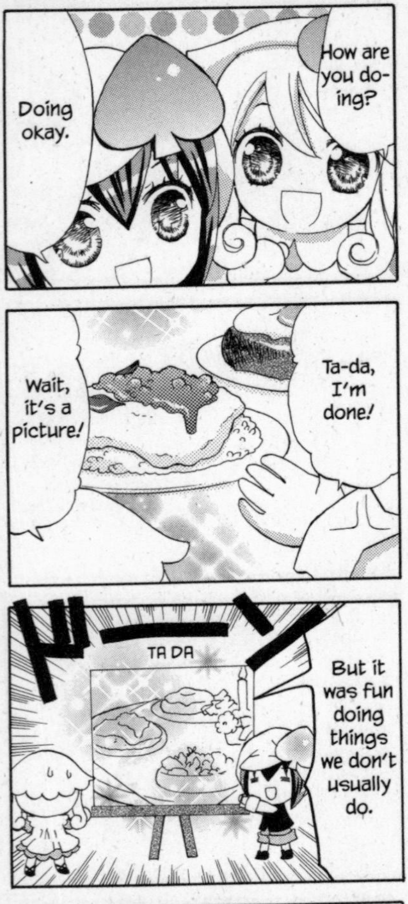
How are you doing?
Doing okay.
Ta-da, I'm done!
Wait, it's a picture!
TA DA
But it was fun doing things we don't usually do.
I wonder if that's true ...
Yeah.
We discovered something new about ourselves!
It seems like they all enjoyed Autumn.

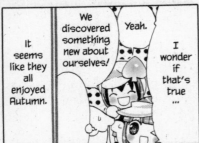

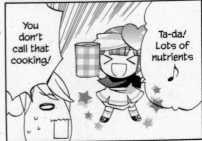

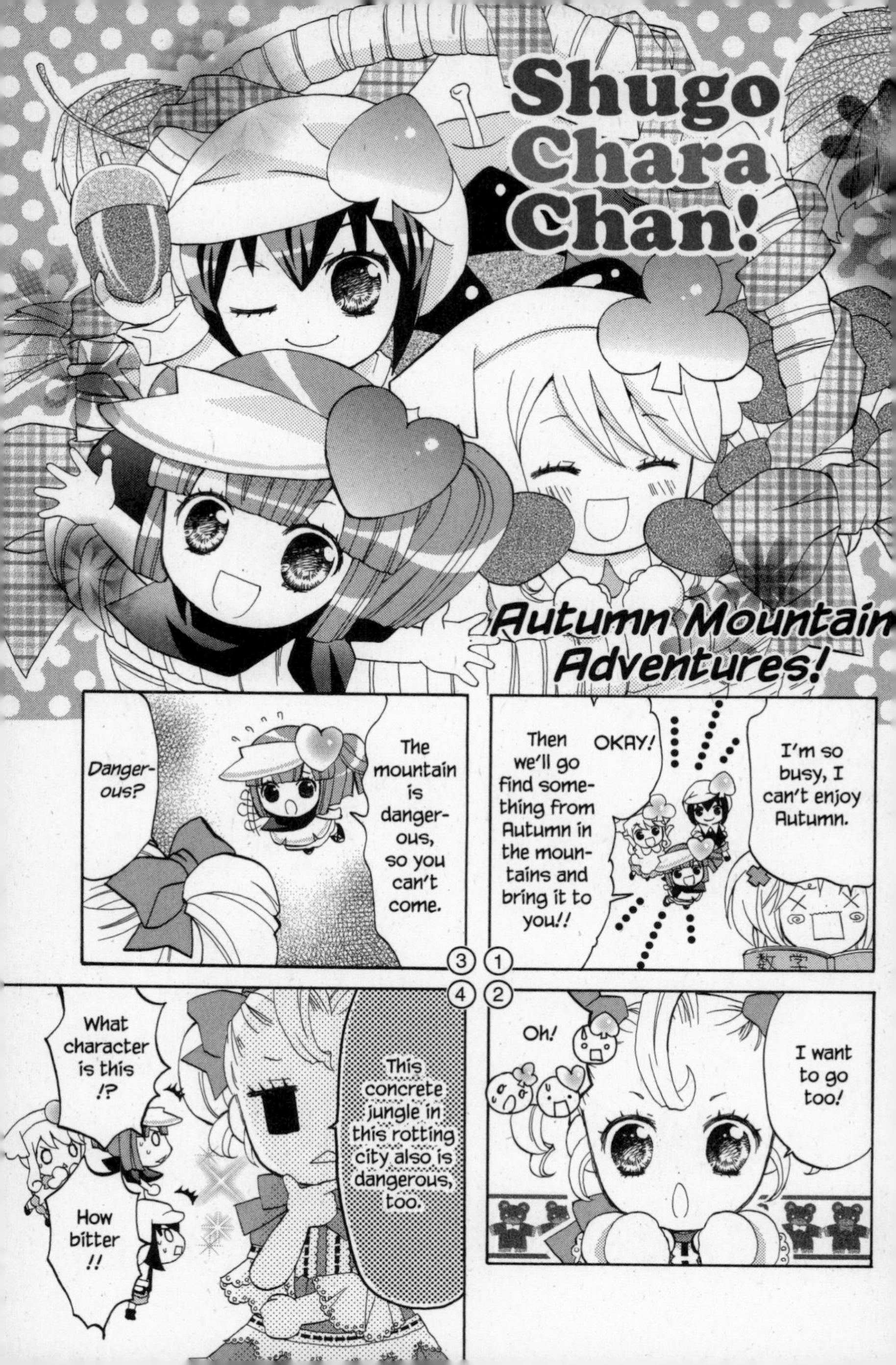
Shugo Chara Chan!
Autumn Mountain Adventures!
I'm so busy, I can't enjoy Autumn.
Then we'll go find something from Autumn in the mountains and bring it to you!!
OKAY!
1
I want to go too!
Oh!
2
The mountain is dangerous, so you can't come.
Dangerous?
3
This concrete jungle in this rotting city also is dangerous, too.
What character is this!?
How bitter!!
4

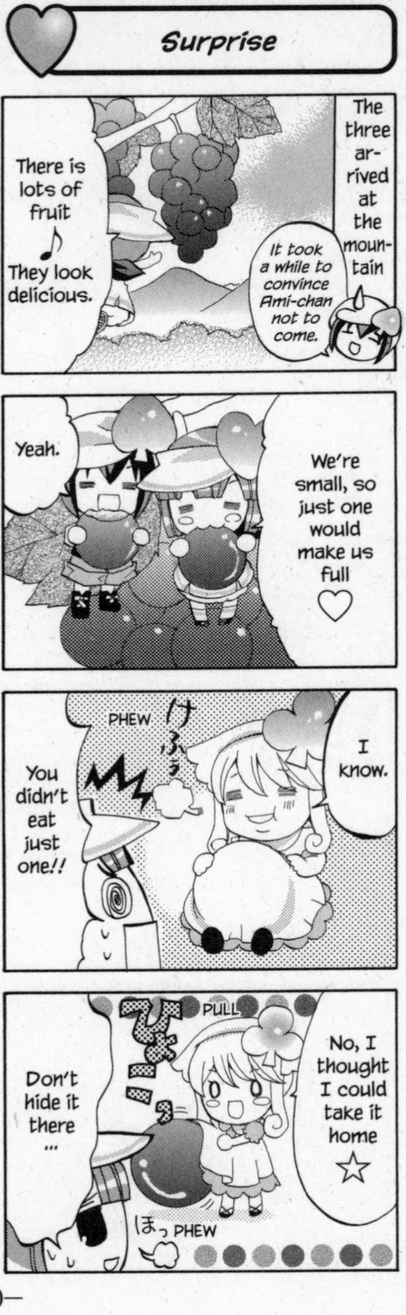
Surprise
The three ar-rived at the moun-tain
It took a while to convince Ami-chan not to come.
There is lots of fruit ♪ They look delicious.
We're small, so just one would make us full ♡
Yeah.
I know.
PHEW
You didn't eat just one!!
No, I thought I could take it home ☆
PULL
Don't hide it there ...
ほっ PHEW

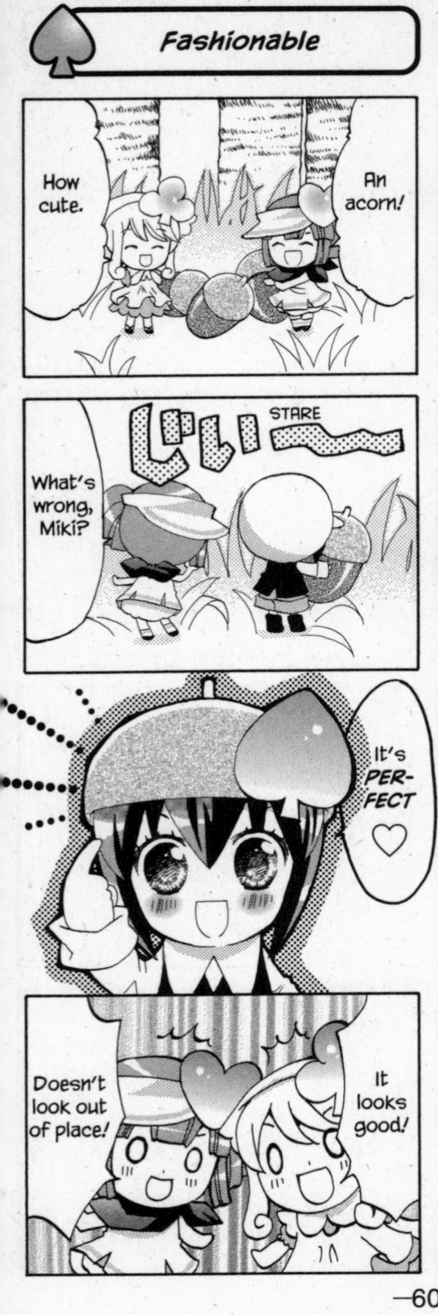
Fashionable
An acorn!
How cute.
STARE
What's wrong, Miki?
It's PERFECT ♡
It looks good!
Doesn't look out of place!

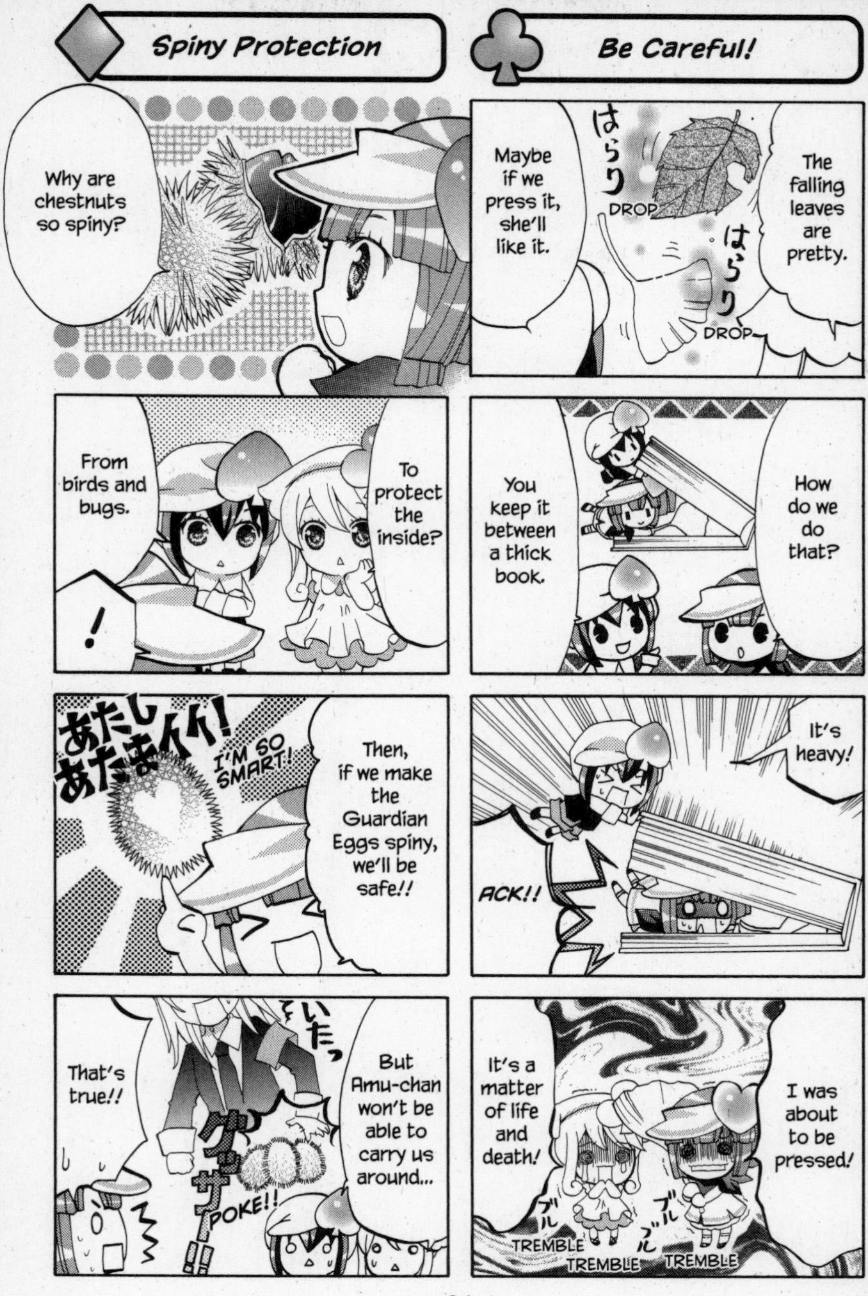
Be Careful!
The falling leaves are pretty.
はらり
DROP
はらり
DROP
Maybe if we press it, she'll like it.
How do we do that?
You keep it between a thick book.
It's heavy!
ACK!!
I was about to be pressed!
ブル ブル
TREMBLE
TREMBLE
TREMBLE
It's a matter of life and death!
Spiny Protection
Why are chestnuts so spiny?
To protect the inside?
From birds and bugs.
!
Then, if we make the Guardian Eggs spiny, we'll be safe!!
あたしあたまいい~!!
I'M SO SMART!
But Amu-chan won't be able to carry us around...
いたっ
グサ
POKE!!
That's true!!

Such a Sin ♡

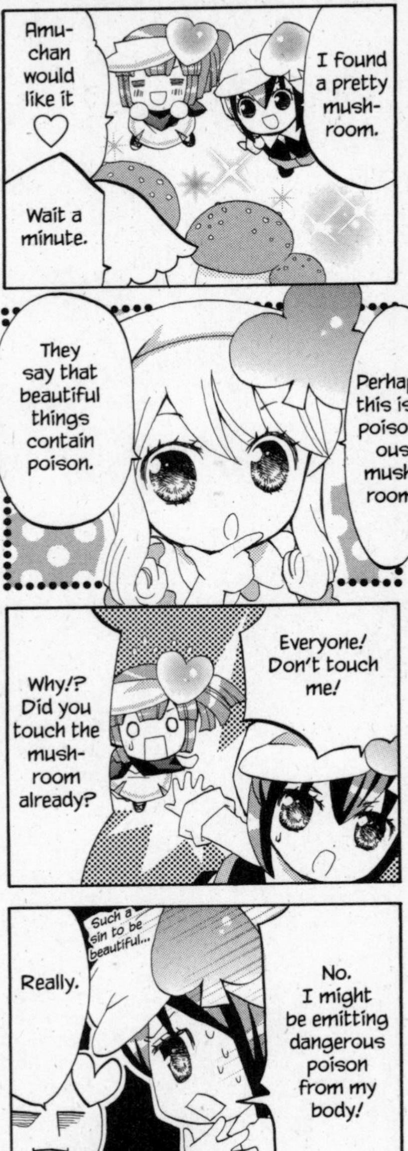
I found a pretty mush-room.
Amu-chan would like it ♡
Wait a minute.
Perhaps this is a poison-ous mush-room.
They say that beautiful things contain poison.
Everyone! Don't touch me!
Why!? Did you touch the mush-room already?
No. I might be emitting dangerous poison from my body!
Such a sin to be beautiful...
Really.

Mushroom Power

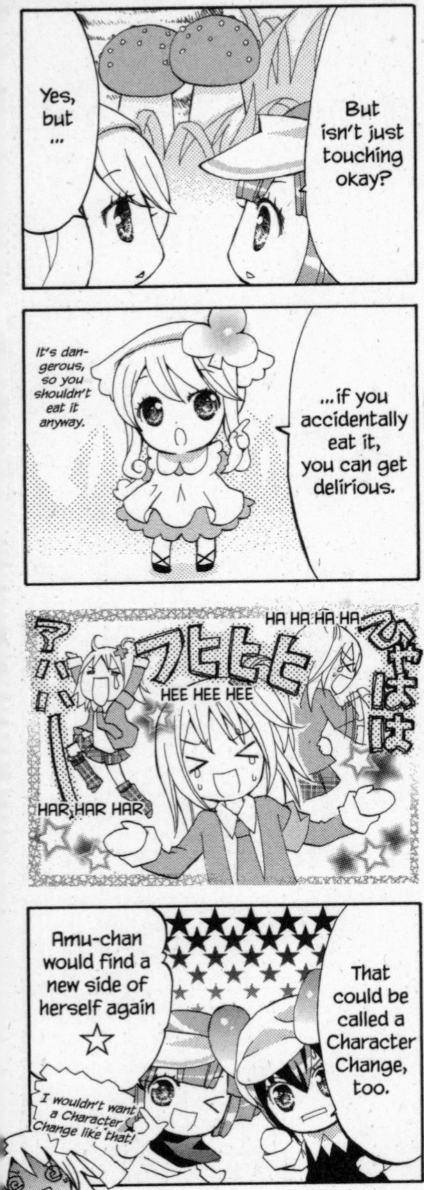
But isn't just touching okay?
Yes, but ...
...if you accidentally eat it, you can get delirious.
It's dangerous, so you shouldn't eat it anyway.
ひゃはは
HA HA HA HA
フヒヒヒ
HEE HEE HEE
アハハー
HAR HAR HAR
That could be called a Character Change, too.
Amu-chan would find a new side of herself again ☆
I wouldn't want a Character Change like that!

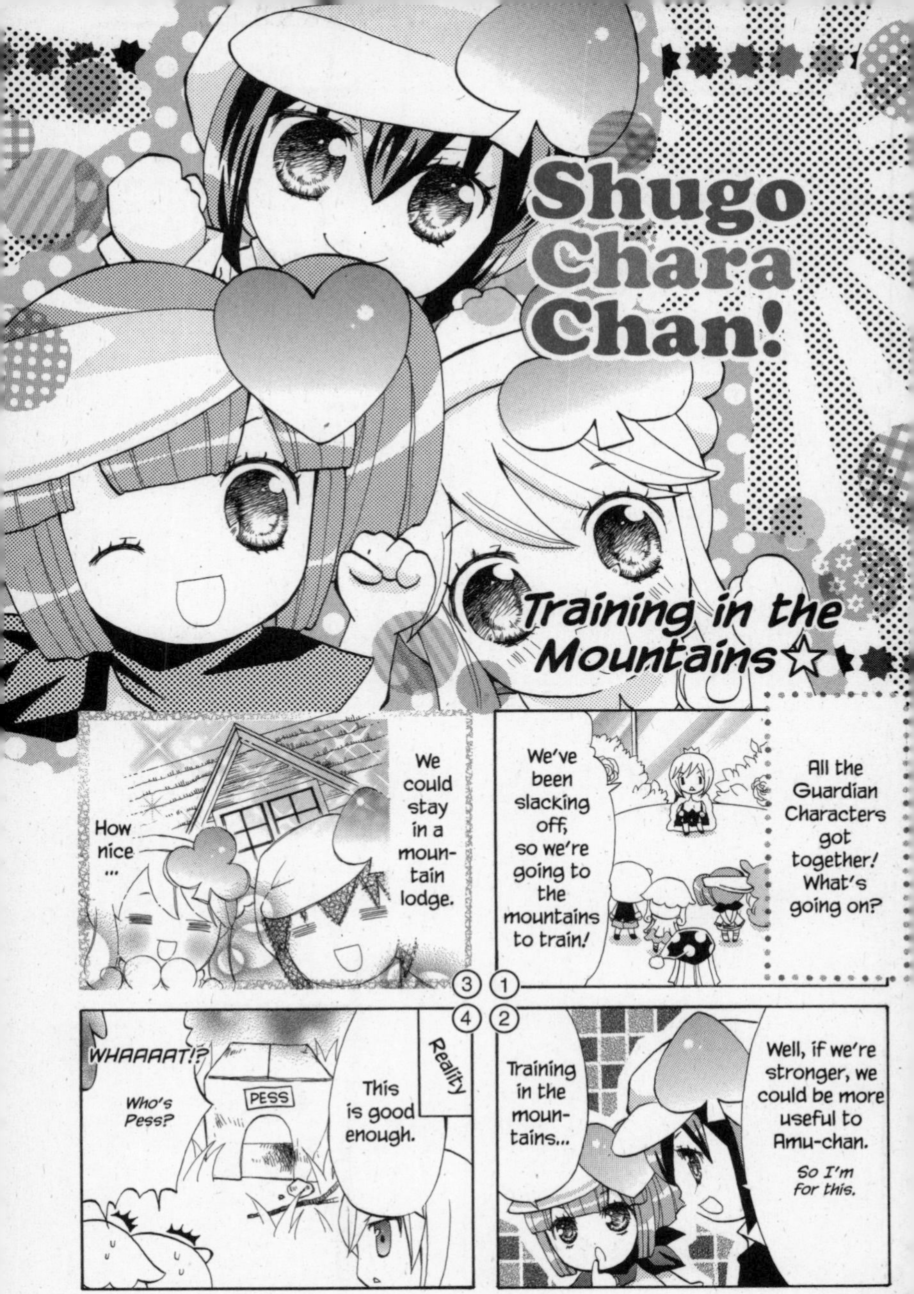
Shugo Chara Chan!
Training in the Mountains☆
All the Guardian Characters got together! What's going on?
We've been slacking off, so we're going to the mountains to train!
Well, if we're stronger, we could be more useful to Amu-chan.
So I'm for this.
Training in the mountains...
We could stay in a mountain lodge.
How nice ...
Reality
This is good enough.
PESS
WHAAAAT!?
Who's Pess?

Perhaps it's Comfortable

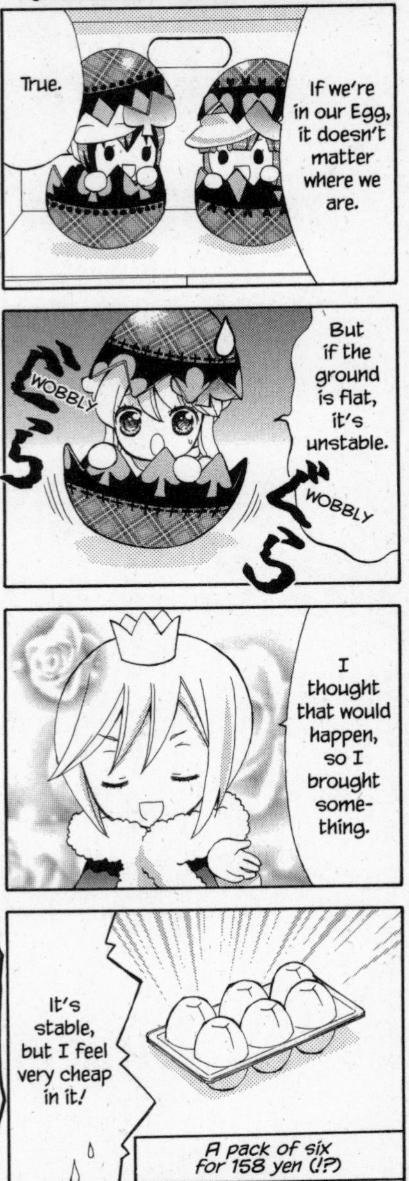
If we're in our Egg, it doesn't matter where we are.
True.
But if the ground is flat, it's unstable.
WOBBLY
WOBBLY
I thought that would happen, so I brought something.
It's stable, but I feel very cheap in it!
A pack of six for 158 yen (!?)

It Happens!

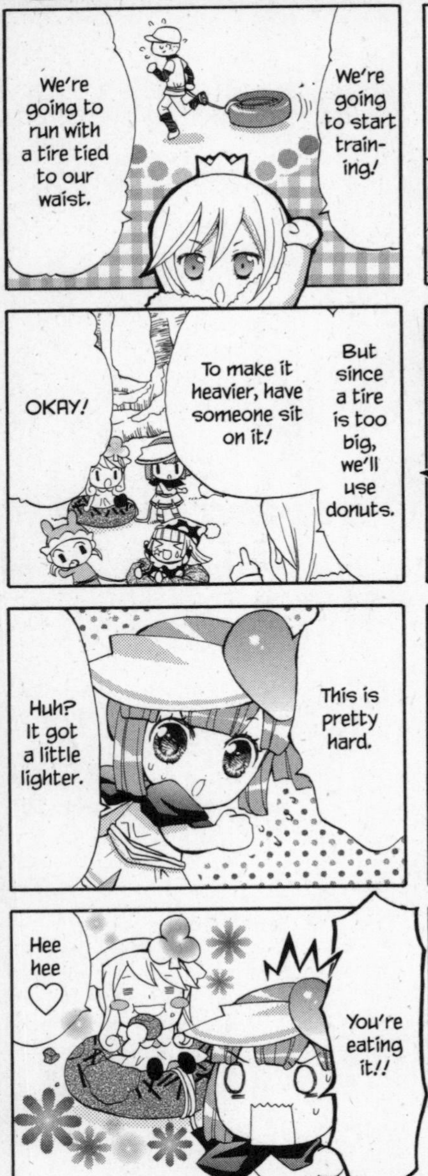
We're going to start training!
We're going to run with a tire tied to our waist.
But since a tire is too big, we'll use donuts.
To make it heavier, have someone sit on it!
OKAY!
This is pretty hard.
Huh? It got a little lighter.
You're eating it!!
Hee hee ♡

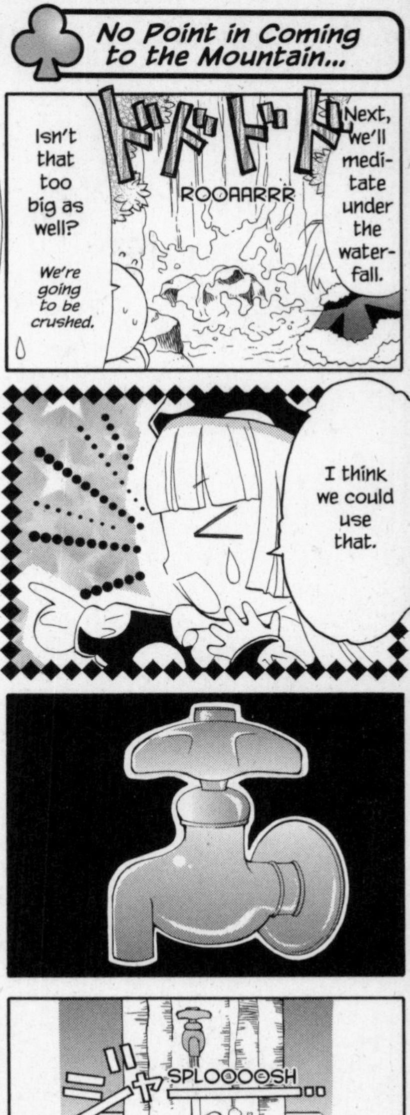
No Point in Coming to the Mountain...
Next, we'll meditate under the waterfall.
ドドドドド
ROOAARRR
Isn't that too big as well?
We're going to be crushed.
I think we could use that.
ジャー
SPLOOOOSH
We could do this at home.

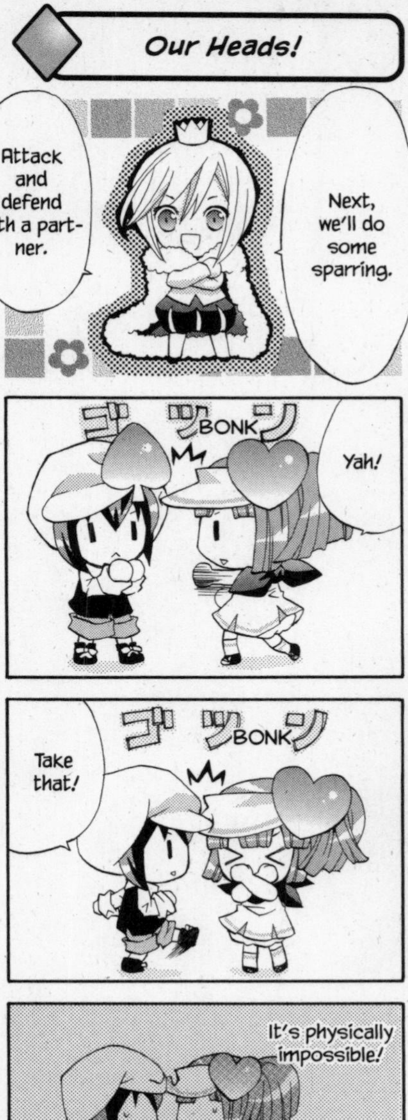
Our Heads!
Next, we'll do some sparring.
Attack and defend with a partner.
ゴツン
BONK
Yah!
ゴツン
BONK
Take that!
It's physically impossible!
スカ
MISS
スカ
MISS
スカ
MISS
スカ
MISS

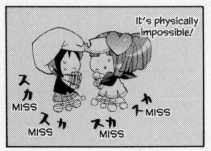

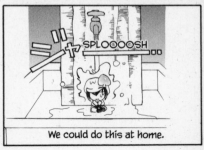

Special Move!?

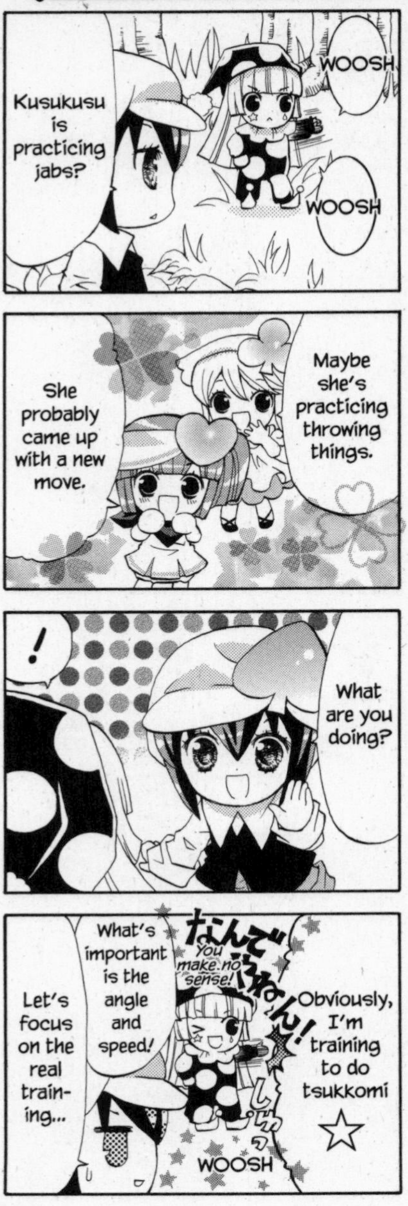
WOOSH
WOOSH
Kusukusu is practicing jabs?
Maybe she's practicing throwing things.
She probably came up with a new move.
What are you doing?
!
Obviously, I'm training to do tsukkomi ☆
なんでやねん!
You make no sense!
WOOSH
What's important is the angle and speed!
Let's focus on the real training...

Full Power

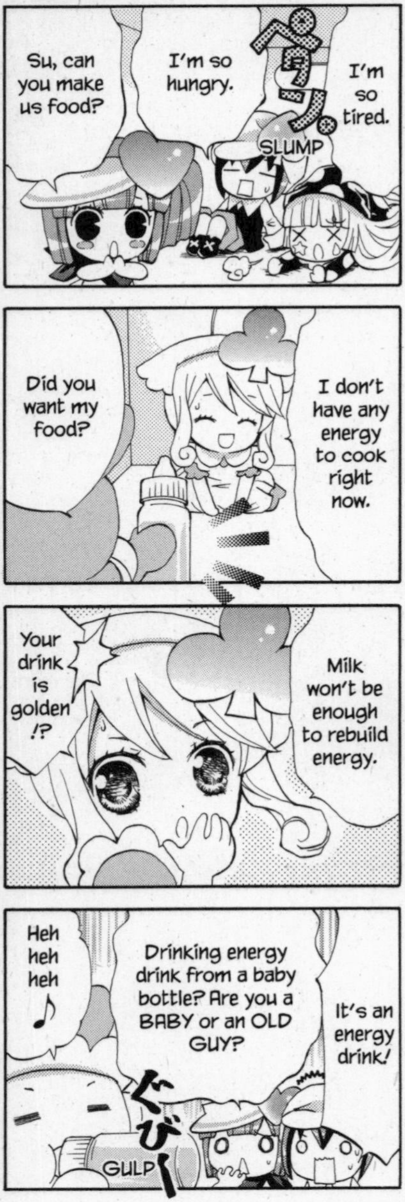
I'm so tired.
SLUMP
I'm so hungry.
Su, can you make us food?
I don't have any energy to cook right now.
Did you want my food?
Milk won't be enough to rebuild energy.
Your drink is golden !?
It's an energy drink!
Drinking energy drink from a baby bottle? Are you a BABY or an OLD GUY?
Heh heh heh ♪
GULP

Murmuring in Sleep

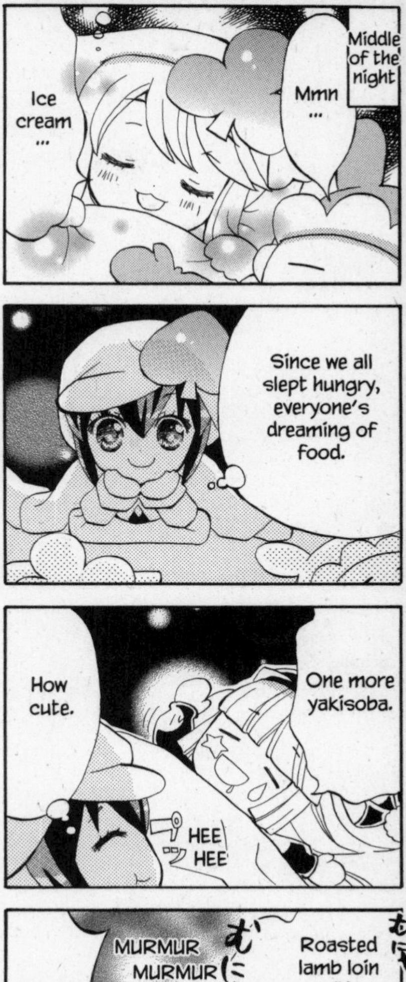
Middle of the night
Mmn ...
Ice cream ...
Since we all slept hungry, everyone's dreaming of food.
One more yakisoba.
How cute.
HEE HEE
Roasted lamb loin with truffles...
むにゃ
Chef, it's not as good today.
むにゃ
MURMUR MURMUR
むにゃ
How cheeky!
MURMUR

Weaksauce!

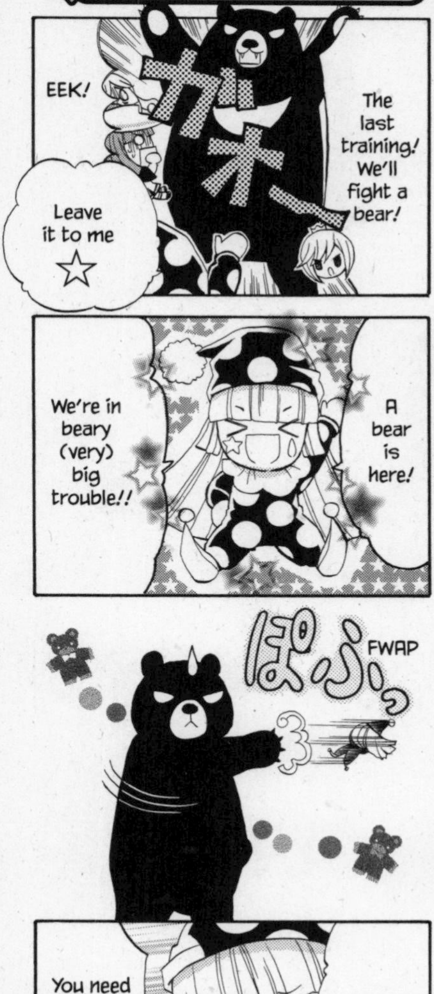
The last training! We'll fight a bear!
EEK!
Leave it to me ☆
A bear is here!
We're in beary (very) big trouble!!
ぽふっ
FWAP
He was supposed to laugh to death!
You need more pun skills!

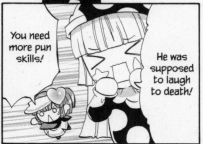

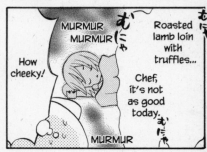

Changing Perspective ☆

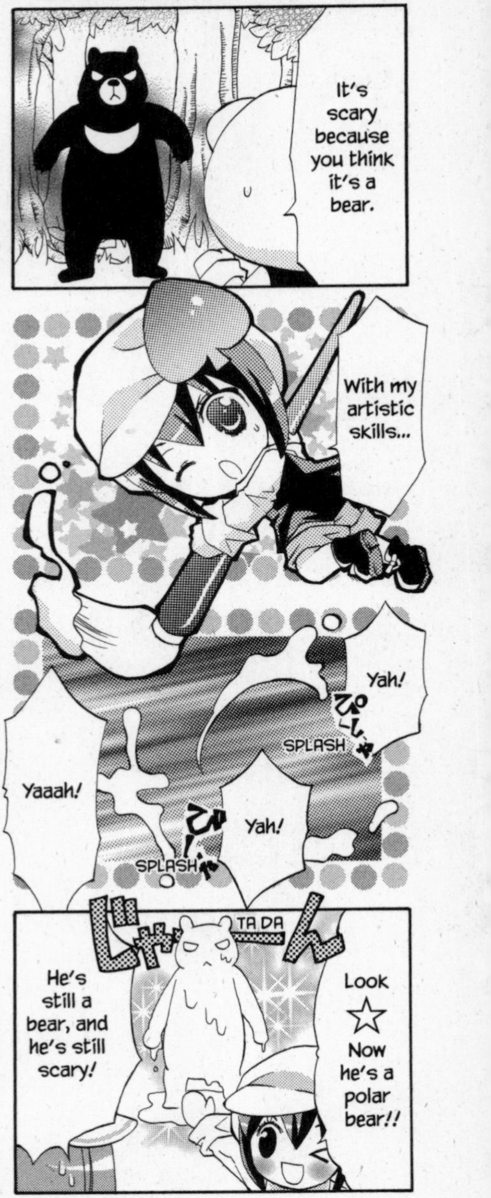
It's scary because you think it's a bear.
With my artistic skills...
Yah!
SPLASH
Yah!
SPLASH
Yaaah!
TA DA
Look ☆ Now he's a polar bear!!
He's still a bear, and he's still scary!

We Worked Hard

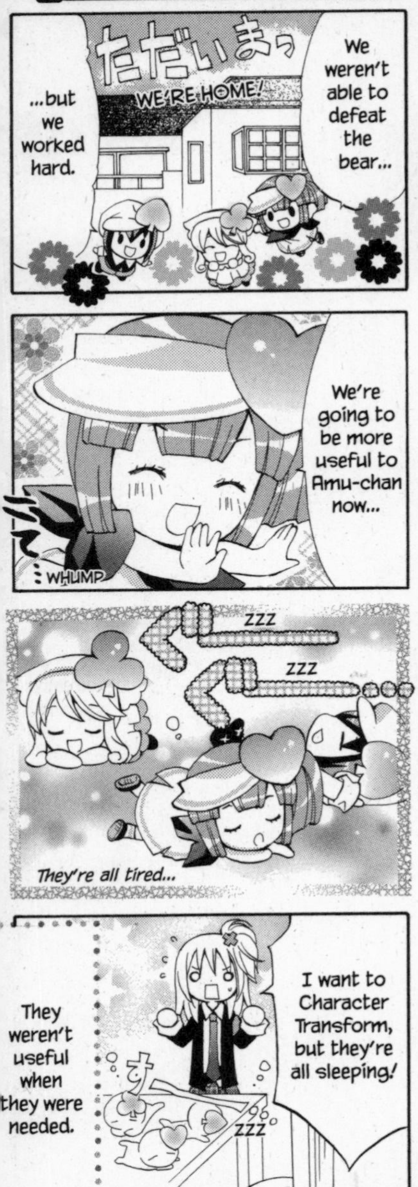
We weren't able to defeat the bear...
ただいまっ
WE'RE HOME!
...but we worked hard.
We're going to be more useful to Amu-chan now...
WHUMP
ZZZ
ZZZ
They're all tired...
I want to Character Transform, but they're all sleeping!
ZZZ
They weren't useful when they were needed.

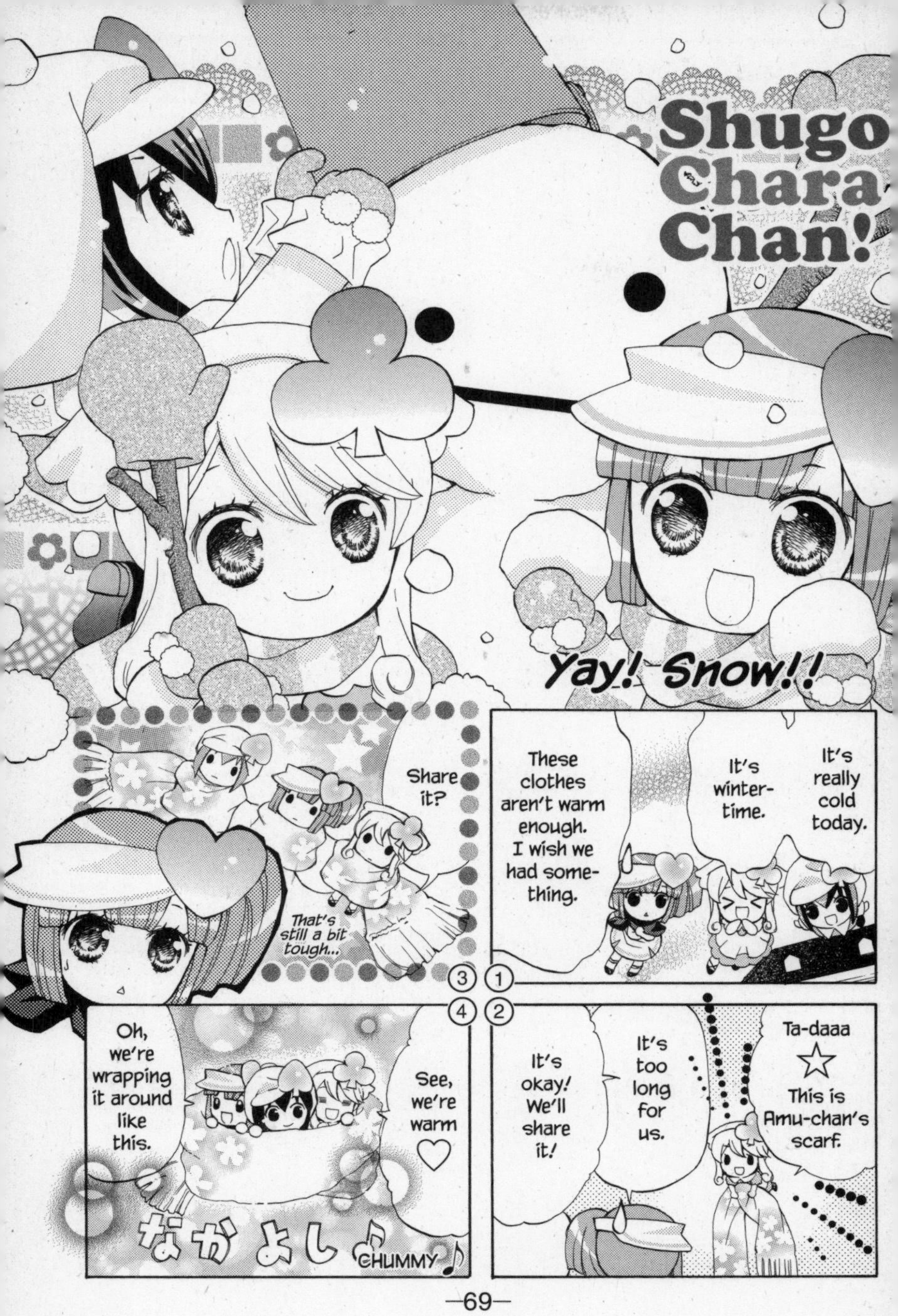
Shugo Chara Chan!
Yay! Snow!!
It's really cold today.
It's wintertime.
These clothes aren't warm enough. I wish we had something.
Ta-daaa ☆ This is Amu-chan's scarf.
It's too long for us.
It's okay! We'll share it!
Share it?
That's still a bit tough...
See, we're warm ♡
Oh, we're wrapping it around like this.
なかよし♪
CHUMMY♪

Fashionable Gloves

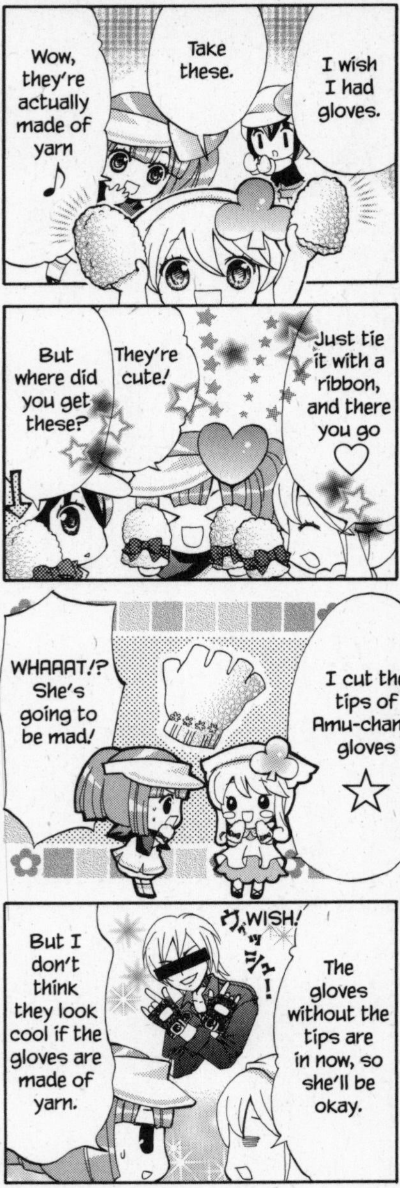

I wish I had gloves.
Take these.
Wow, they're actually made of yarn ♪
Just tie it with a ribbon, and there you go ♡
They're cute!
But where did you get these?
I cut the tips of Amu-chan's gloves ☆
WHAAAT!? She's going to be mad!
The gloves without the tips are in now, so she'll be okay.
WISH!
ウィッシュー!
But I don't think they look cool if the gloves are made of yarn.

Destroying Evidence

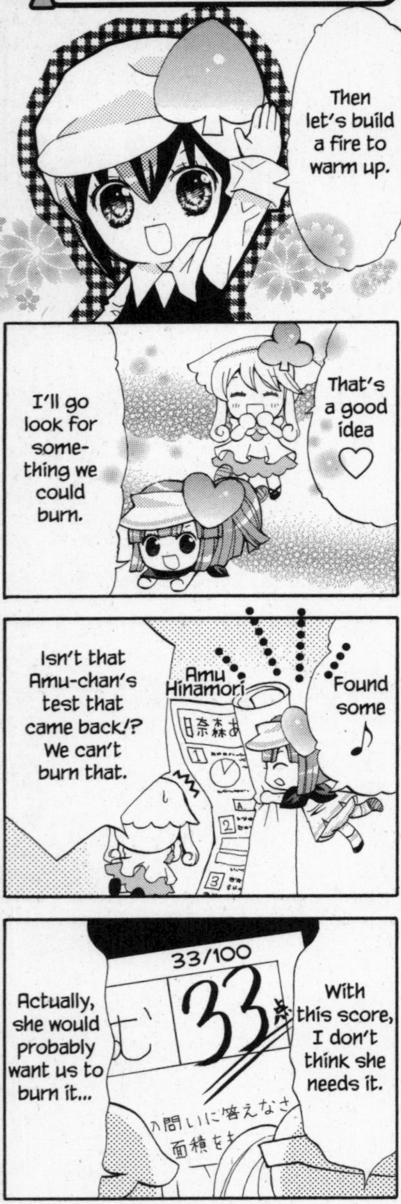

Then let's build a fire to warm up.
That's a good idea ♡
I'll go look for some-thing we could burn.
Found some ♪
Amu Hinamori
日奈森あ
Isn't that Amu-chan's test that came back!? We can't burn that.
With this score, I don't think she needs it.
33/100
33点
Actually, she would probably want us to burn it...

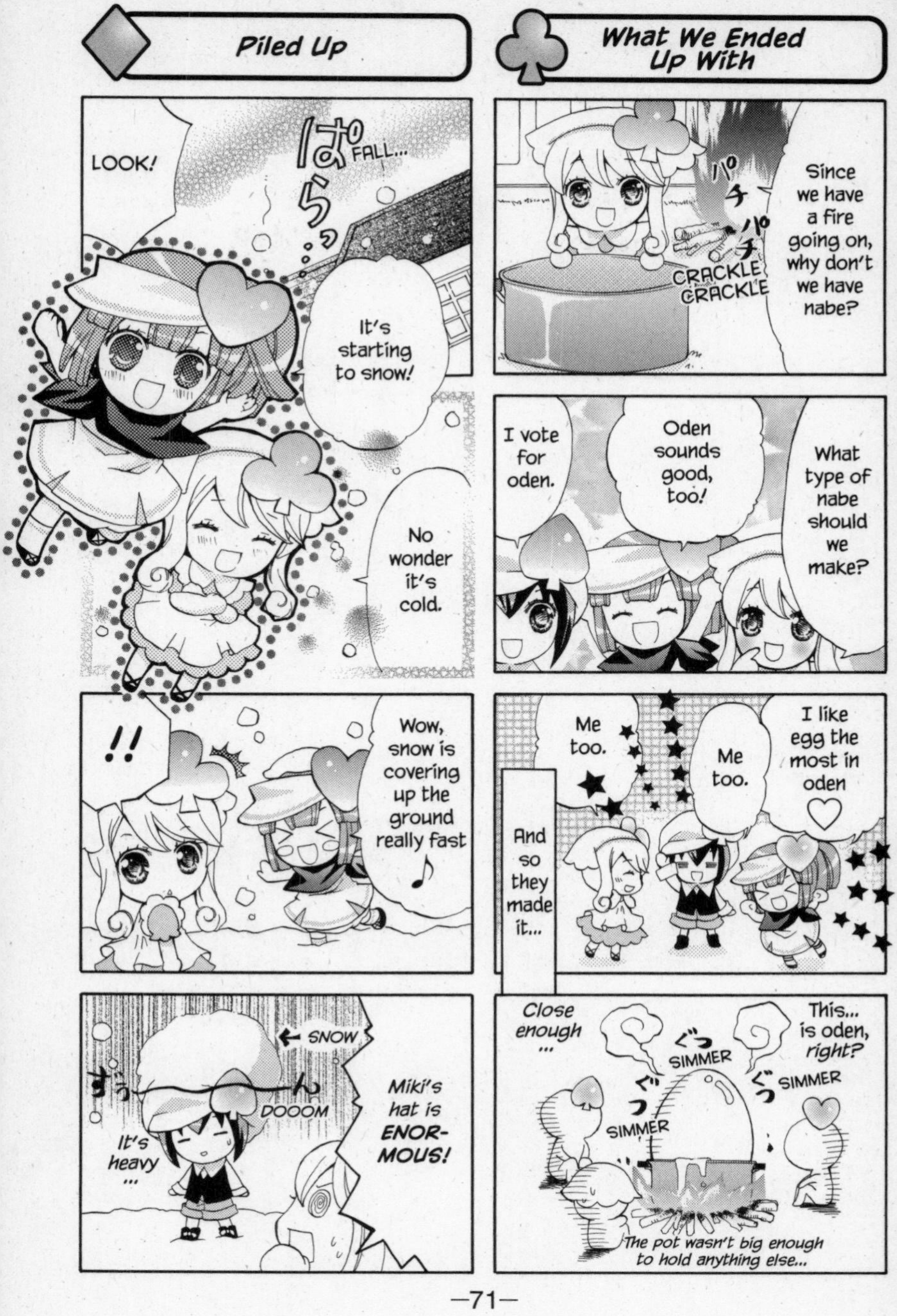
What We Ended Up With
Since we have a fire going on, why don't we have nabe?
パチ パチ
CRACKLE CRACKLE
What type of nabe should we make?
Oden sounds good, too!
I vote for oden.
I like egg the most in oden ♡
Me too.
Me too.
And so they made it...
This... is oden, right?
ぐつ SIMMER
ぐつ SIMMER
ぐつ SIMMER
Close enough ...
The pot wasn't big enough to hold anything else...
Piled Up
ぱらっ FALL...
LOOK!
It's starting to snow!
No wonder it's cold.
Wow, snow is covering up the ground really fast ♪
!!
Miki's hat is ENORMOUS!
← SNOW
すぅ ん DOOOM
It's heavy ...

Appetite is Greater Than Aesthetics

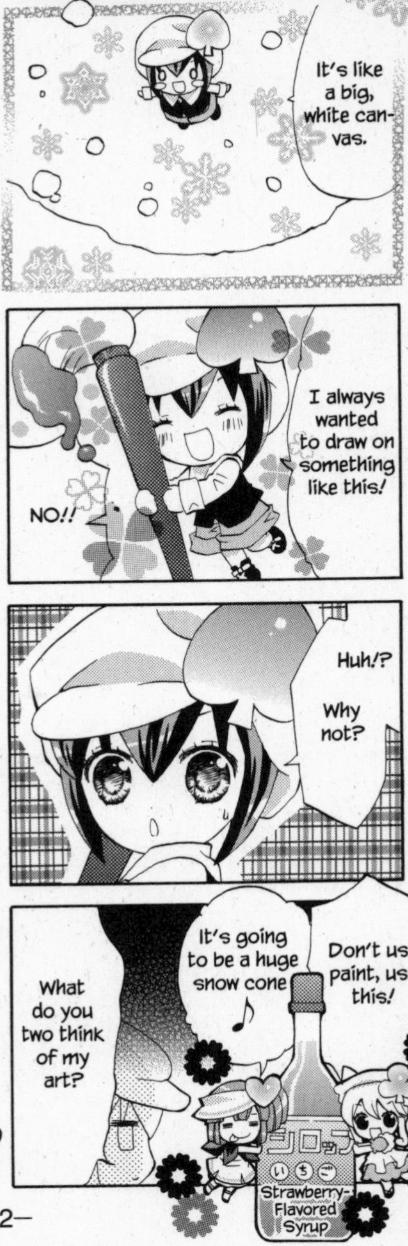
It's like a big, white can-vas.
I always wanted to draw on something like this!
NO!!
Huh!?
Why not?
Don't use paint, use this!
It's going to be a huge snow cone ♪
What do you two think of my art?
Strawberry-Flavored Syrup

Perfect Size

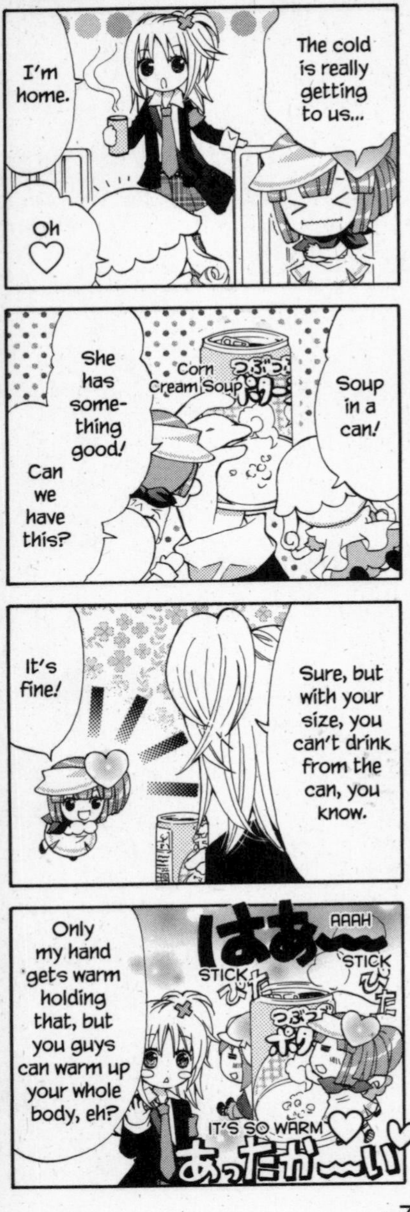
The cold is really getting to us...
I'm home.
Oh ♡
Soup in a can!
Corn Cream Soup
She has something good!
Can we have this?
Sure, but with your size, you can't drink from the can, you know.
It's fine!
はあ〜〜
AAAH
STICK
STICK
Only my hand gets warm holding that, but you guys can warm up your whole body, eh?
IT'S SO WARM ♡
あったか〜い ♡

Shugo Chara Chan! Kids☆ is going to start!

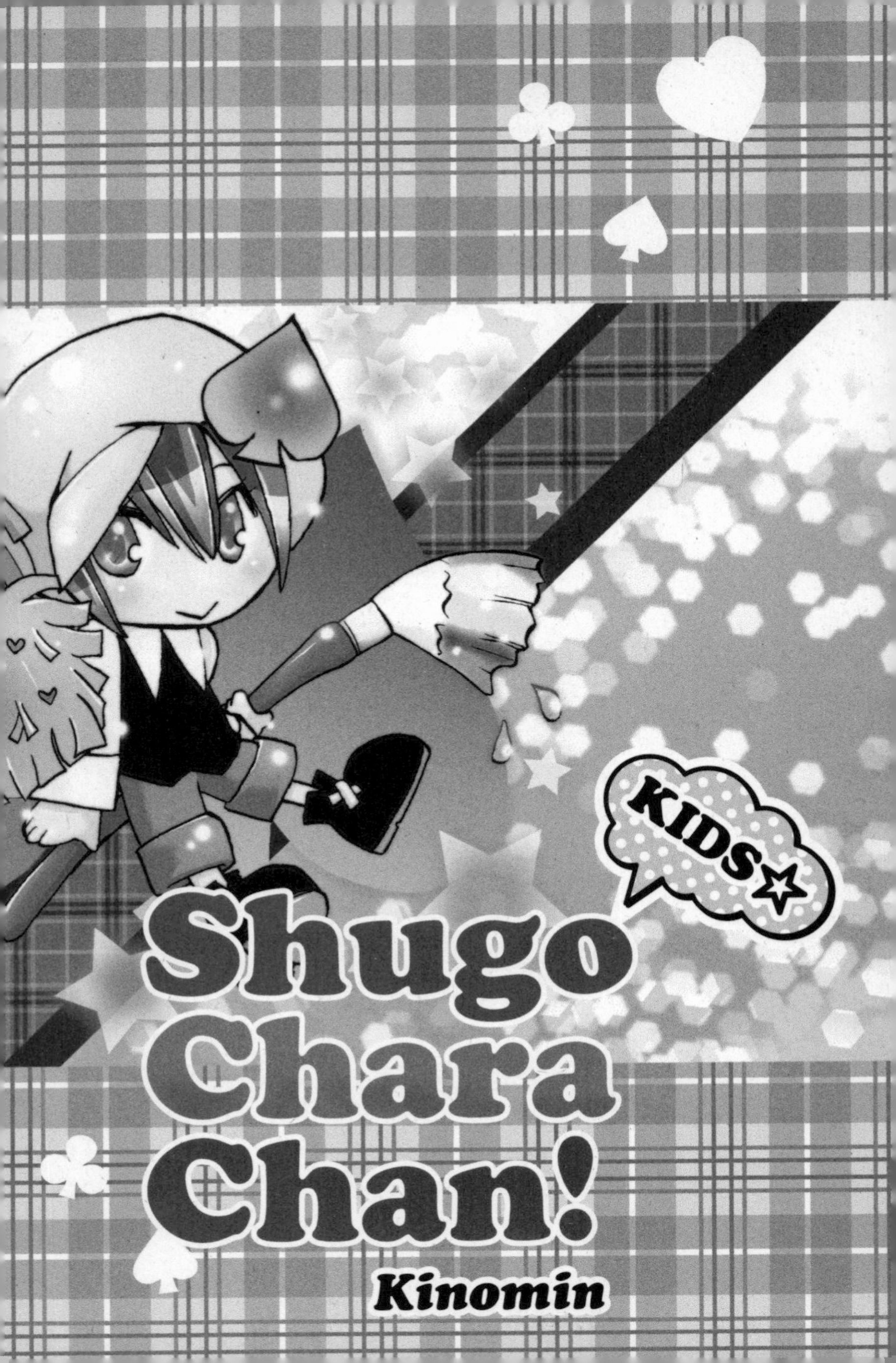
KIDS☆
Shugo Chara Chan!
Kinomin

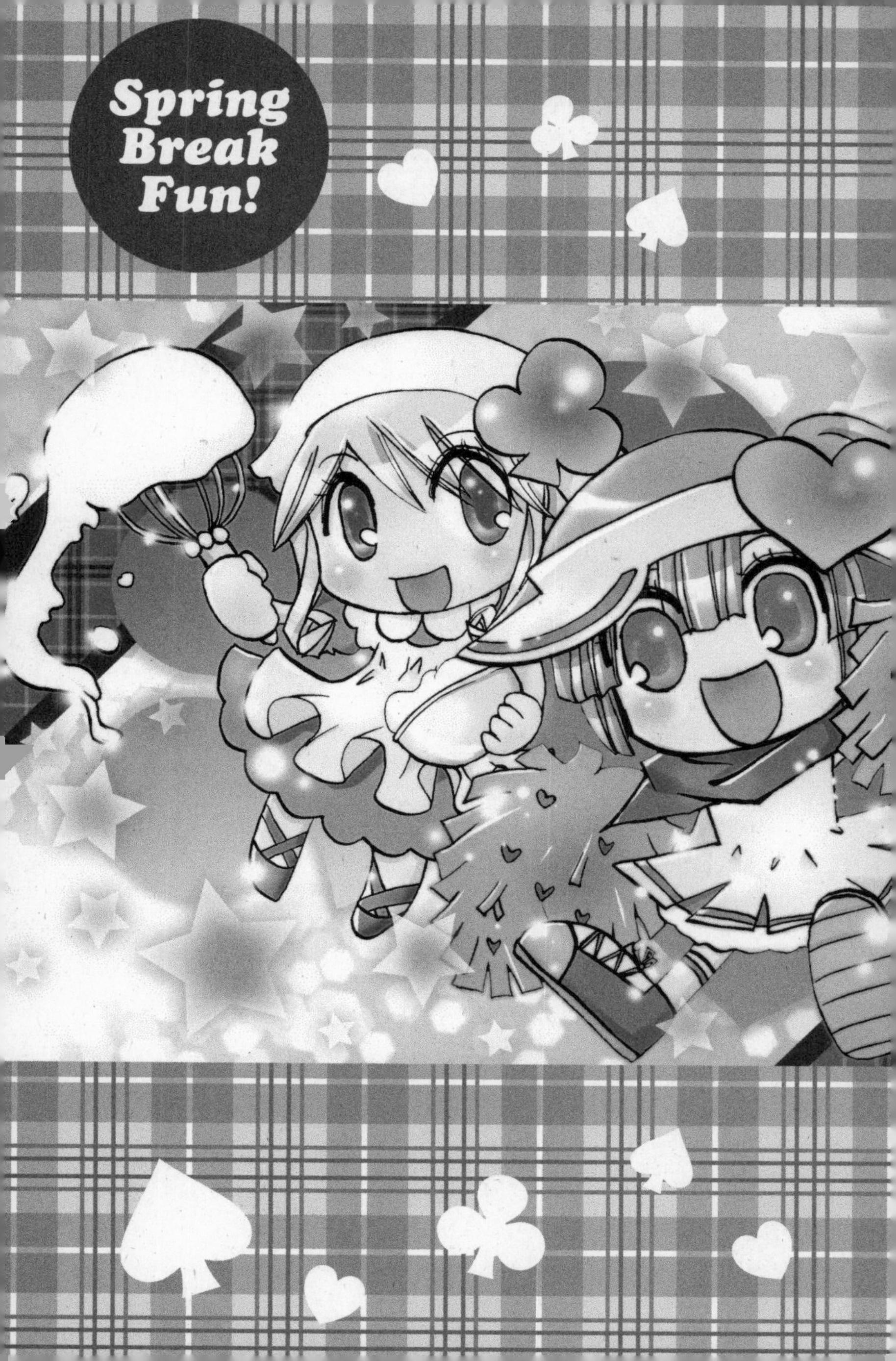
Spring Break Fun!

We are "Guardian Characters!"

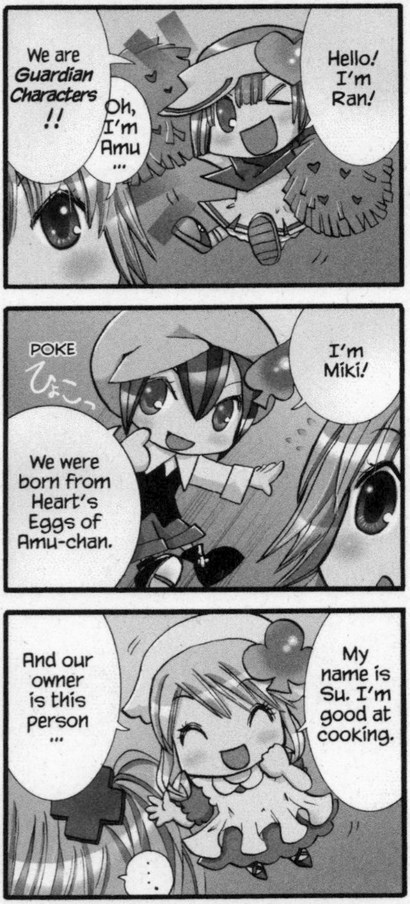

Hello! I'm Ran!
Oh, I'm Amu ...
We are Guardian Characters !!
I'm Miki!
POKE
ひょこっ
We were born from Heart's Eggs of Amu-chan.
My name is Su. I'm good at cooking.
And our owner is this person ...
...
I've been here since the beginning.
GLOOM
It's fine. I'm not the main character in this manga, so...
Oh no! Amu-chan!!
Believe in yourself, Amu-chan!
Or an X is going to be placed on your Egg!
GLOOM

Ran is Good at Sports!

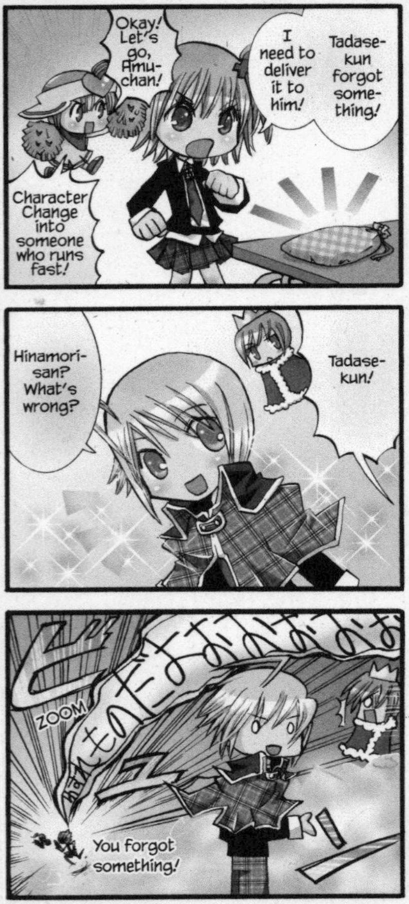

Tadase-kun forgot something!
I need to deliver it to him!
Okay! Let's go, Amu-chan!
Character Change into someone who runs fast!
Tadase-kun!
Hinamori-san? What's wrong?
ZOOM
You forgot something!
You ran right past him!!
I'm running too fast!
DASH
Someone stop me! Actually, Ran, it's your job to stop me!!

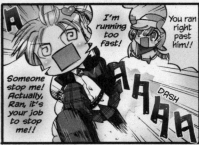

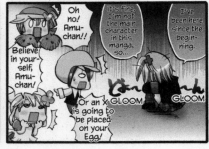

Miki is Good at Art!

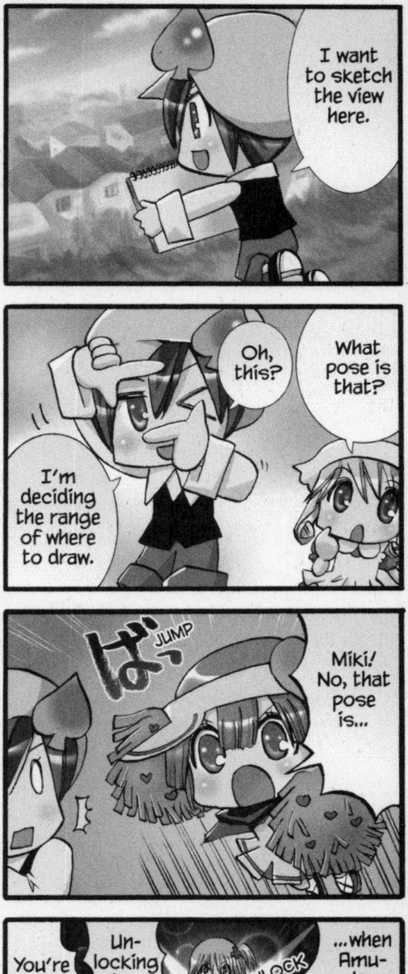
I want to sketch the view here.
What pose is that?
Oh, this?
I'm deciding the range of where to draw.
Miki! No, that pose is...
ぱっ JUMP
...when Amu-chan Character Transforms!
UNLOCK
解錠
Un-locking her heart!!
You're right!!

Su is Good at Cleaning!

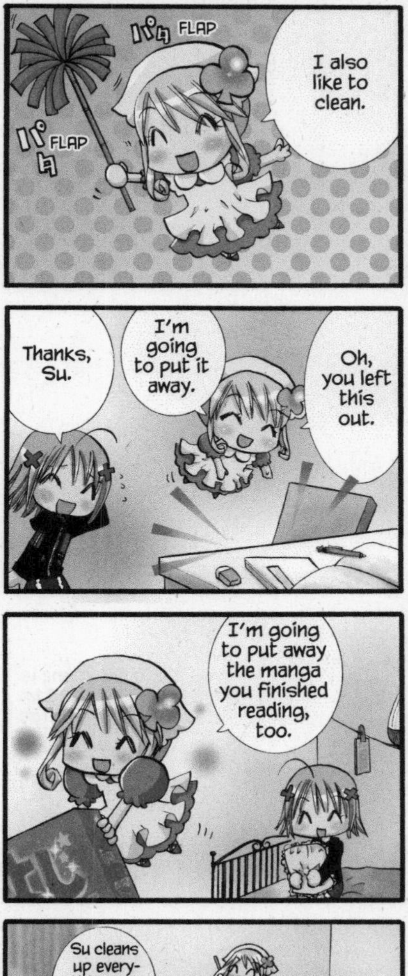
I also like to clean.
FLAP
FLAP
Oh, you left this out.
I'm going to put it away.
Thanks, Su.
I'm going to put away the manga you finished reading, too.
LAZY LAZY
Su cleans up every-thing, so Amu-chan's become lazy.
Are you sure that's how you want to be, Amu-chan!?

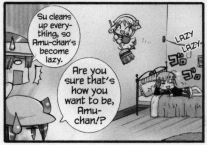

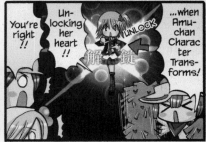

Change of Seasons

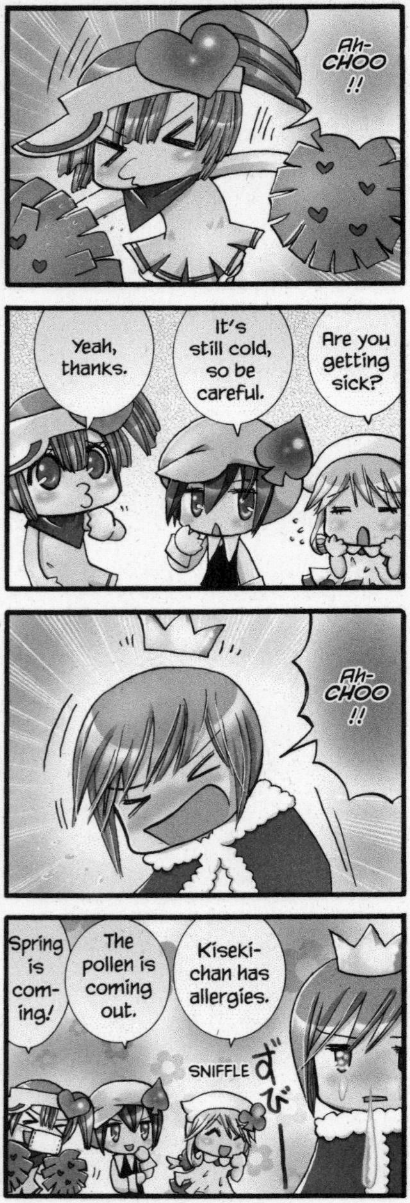
Ah-CHOO!!
Are you getting sick?
It's still cold, so be careful.
Yeah, thanks.
Ah-CHOO!!
Kiseki-chan has allergies.
ずび SNIFFLE
The pollen is coming out.
Spring is com-ing!

Inside the Bag

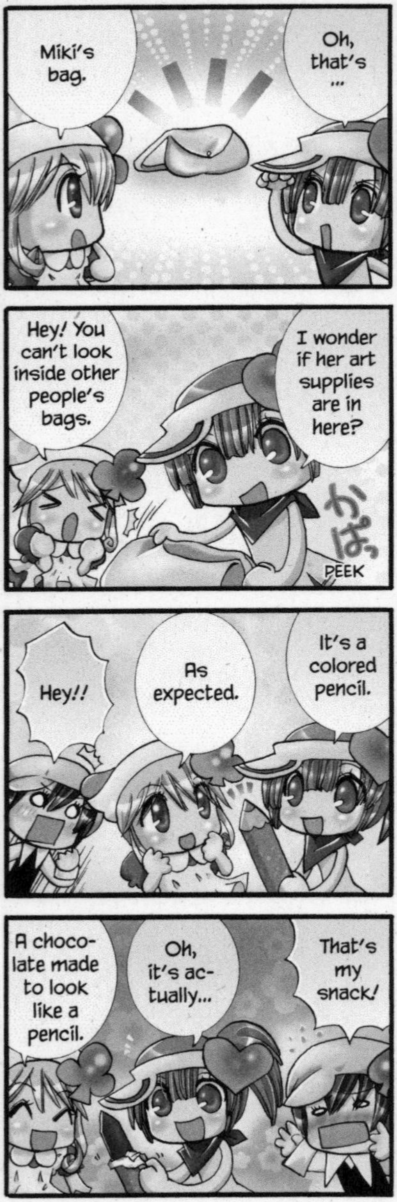
Oh, that's ...
Miki's bag.
I wonder if her art supplies are in here?
かぱっ PEEK
Hey! You can't look inside other people's bags.
It's a colored pencil.
As expected.
Hey!!
That's my snack!
Oh, it's ac-tually...
A choco-late made to look like a pencil.

Beginning of a Cold

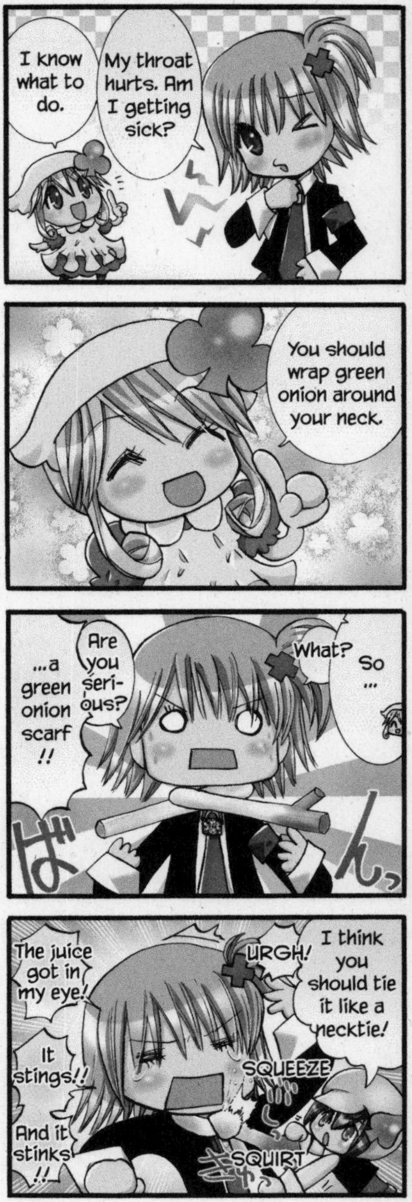
My throat hurts. Am I getting sick?
I know what to do.
You should wrap green onion around your neck.
So ...
What?
Are you seri-ous?
...a green onion scarf !!
ばんっ
I think you should tie it like a necktie!
URGH!
The juice got in my eye!
SQUEEZE
It stings!!
SQUIRT
And it stinks!!

More Inside the Bag!

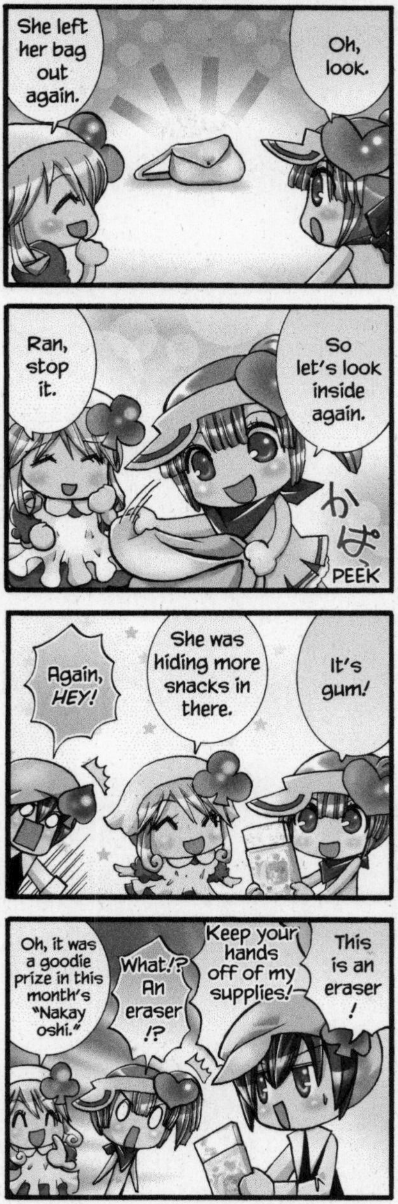
Oh, look.
She left her bag out again.
So let's look inside again.
Ran, stop it.
かぱ
PEEK
It's gum!
She was hiding more snacks in there.
Again, HEY!
This is an eraser!
Keep your hands off of my supplies!
What!? An eraser!?
Oh, it was a goodie prize in this month's "Nakay oshi."

Cheerleading

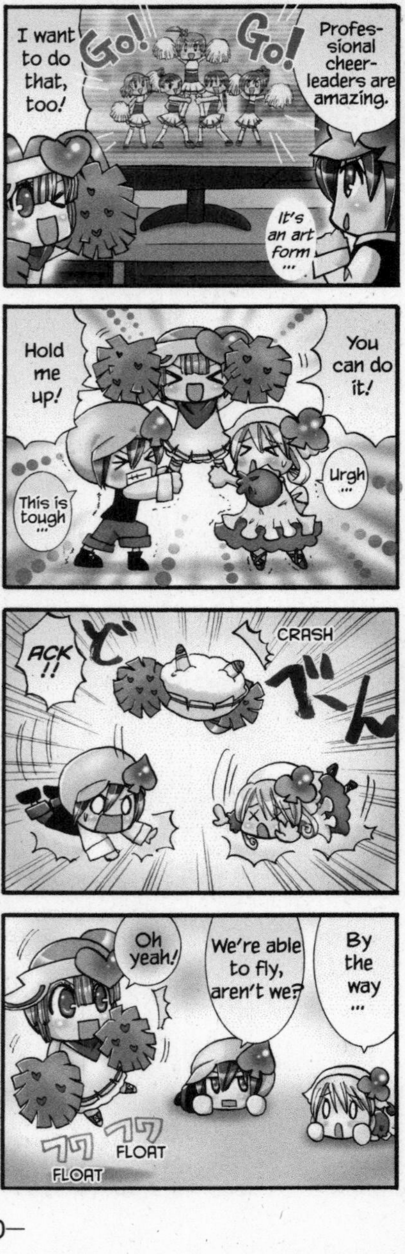

Professional cheerleaders are amazing.
Go!
Go!
I want to do that, too!
It's an art form...
You can do it!
Hold me up!
Urgh...
This is tough...
CRASH
ACK!!
By the way...
We're able to fly, aren't we?
Oh yeah!
FLOAT
FLOAT

Cheer!!

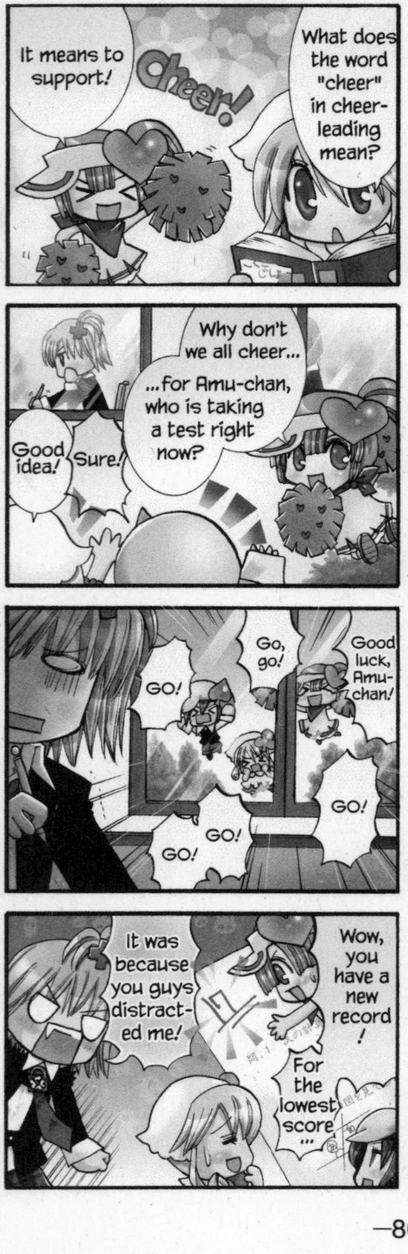

What does the word "cheer" in cheerleading mean?
Cheer!
It means to support!
Why don't we all cheer...
...for Amu-chan, who is taking a test right now?
Sure!
Good idea!
Good luck, Amu-chan!
Go, go!
GO!
GO!
GO!
GO!
Wow, you have a new record!
For the lowest score...
It was because you guys distracted me!

Wolf

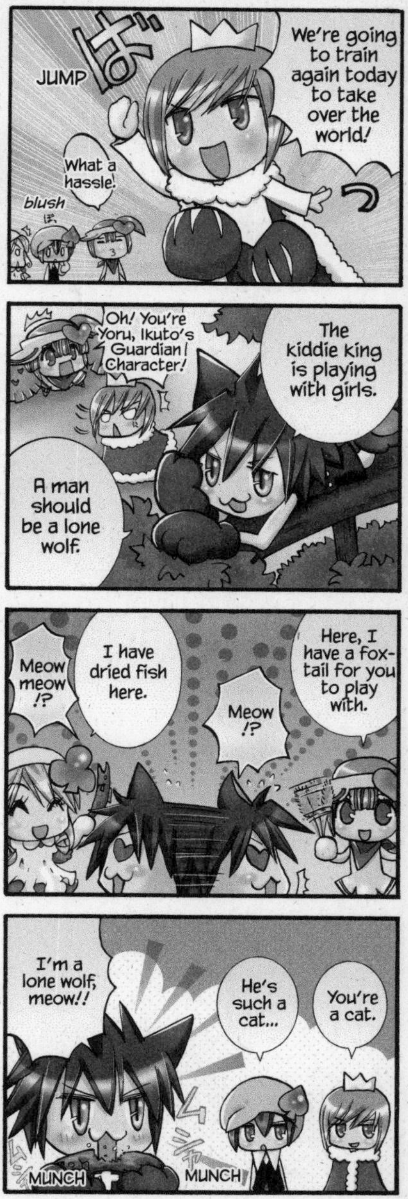
We're going to train again today to take over the world!
JUMP
What a hassle!
blush
The kiddie king is playing with girls.
Oh! You're Yoru, Ikuto's Guardian Character!
A man should be a lone wolf.
Here, I have a fox-tail for you to play with.
Meow !?
I have dried fish here.
Meow meow !?
You're a cat.
He's such a cat...
I'm a lone wolf, meow!!
MUNCH
MUNCH

Bed Hair

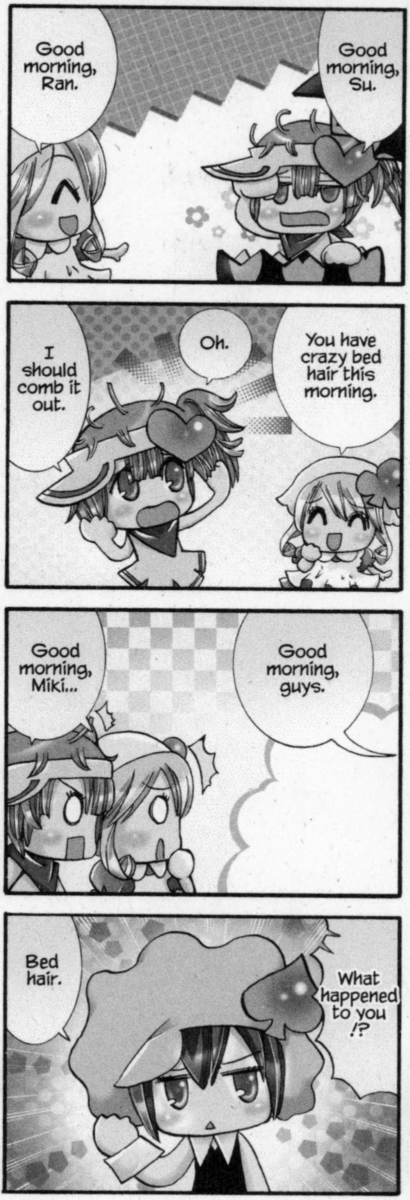
Good morning, Su.
Good morning, Ran.
You have crazy bed hair this morning.
Oh.
I should comb it out.
Good morning, guys.
Good morning, Miki...
What happened to you !?
Bed hair.

Peak

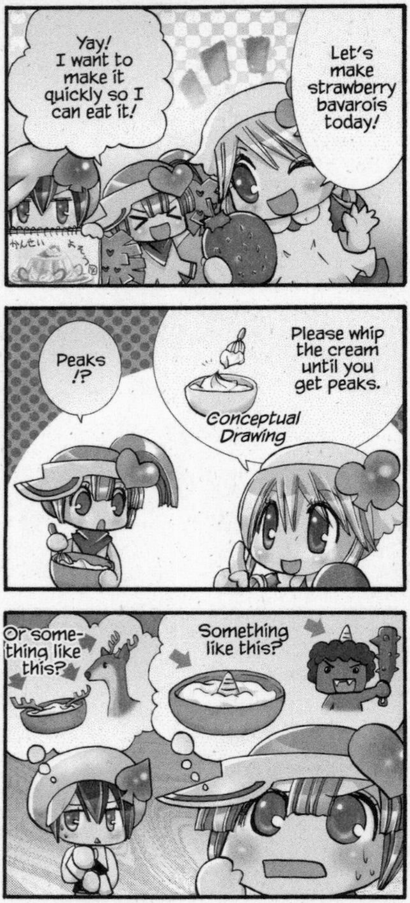

Let's make strawberry bavarois today!
Yay! I want to make it quickly so I can eat it!
Please whip the cream until you get peaks.
Conceptual Drawing
Peaks !?
Something like this?
Or something like this?
I can't get what I want!
Yes, but because you spend time on it, it comes out delicious.

Can't Wait

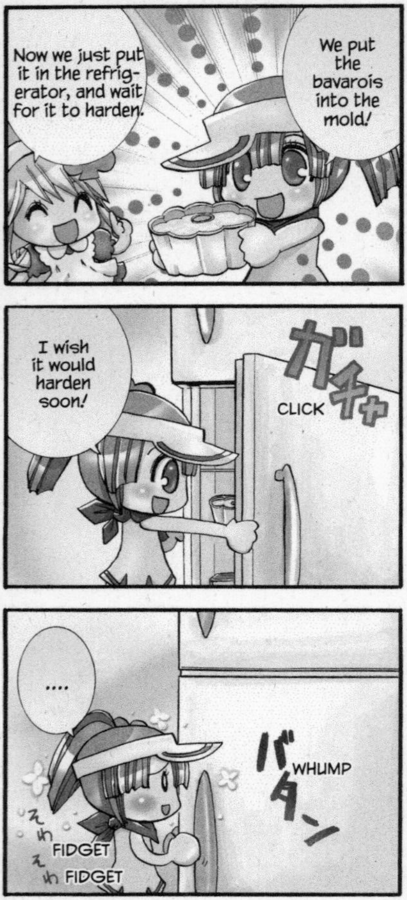

We put the bavarois into the mold!
Now we just put it in the refrigerator, and wait for it to harden.
ガチャ
CLICK
I wish it would harden soon!
バタン
WHUMP
....
FIDGET
FIDGET
CLICK
ガチャ
Is it ready yet?
If you keep opening the refrigerator, it won't harden!

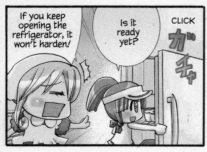

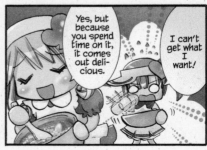

Weather Forecast

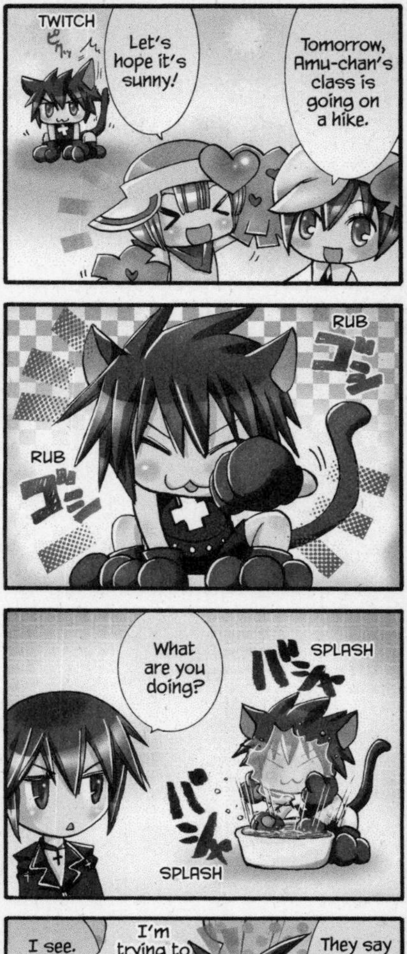
Tomorrow, Amu-chan's class is going on a hike.
Let's hope it's sunny!
TWITCH
RUB
RUB
SPLASH
What are you doing?
SPLASH
They say when a cat washes behind its ear, it's going to rain.
I'm trying to make it rain to spite them!!
I see. Good luck with that.
SCRUB
SCRUB
SHINE
SHINE

Blanket

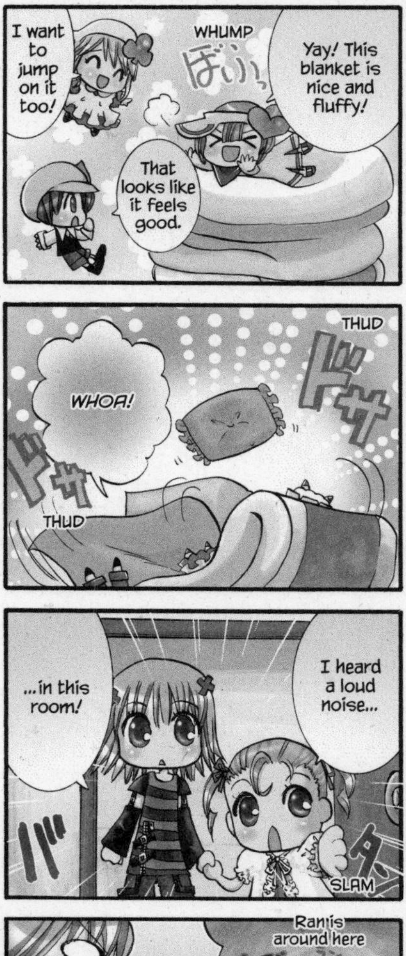
Yay! This blanket is nice and fluffy!
WHUMP
I want to jump on it too!
That looks like it feels good.
THUD
WHOA!
THUD
I heard a loud noise...
...in this room!
SLAM
WANDER
Ran is around here
Miki
Su
WANDER
AAAGHH! A GHOST!!

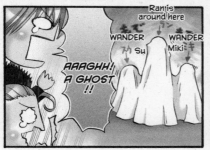

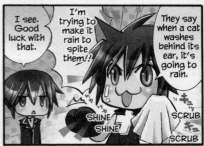

Kotatsu

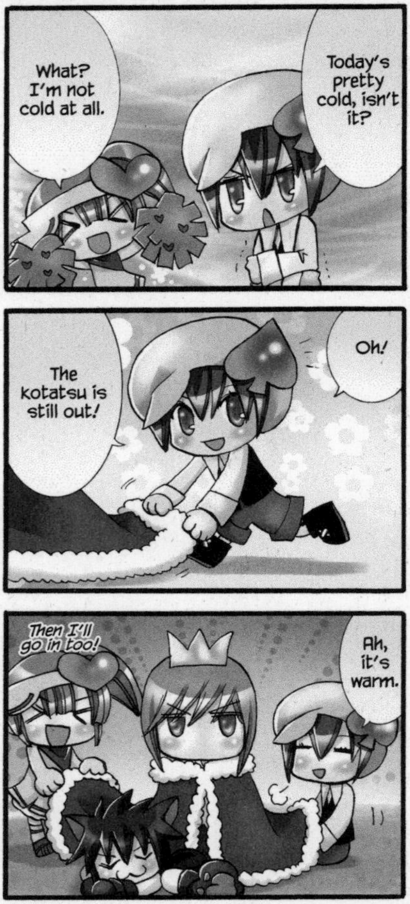
Today's pretty cold, isn't it?
What? I'm not cold at all.
Oh!
The kotatsu is still out!
Ah, it's warm.
Then I'll go in too!
ARGH!
ALL OF YOU, GET OUT!!

Duster

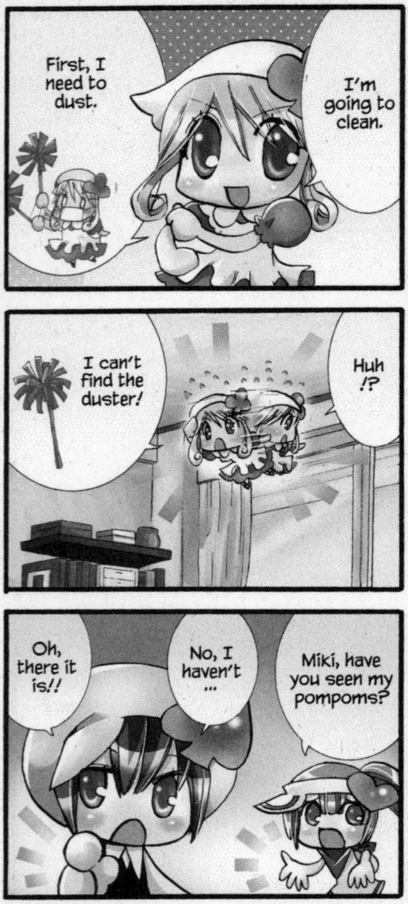
I'm going to clean.
First, I need to dust.
Huh !?
I can't find the duster!
Miki, have you seen my pompoms?
No, I haven't ...
Oh, there it is!!
These work just as well.
DUST
フキ
AAAAGH!!
フキ
DUST

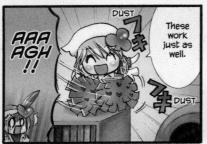

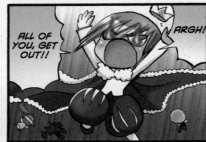

Guess Who?

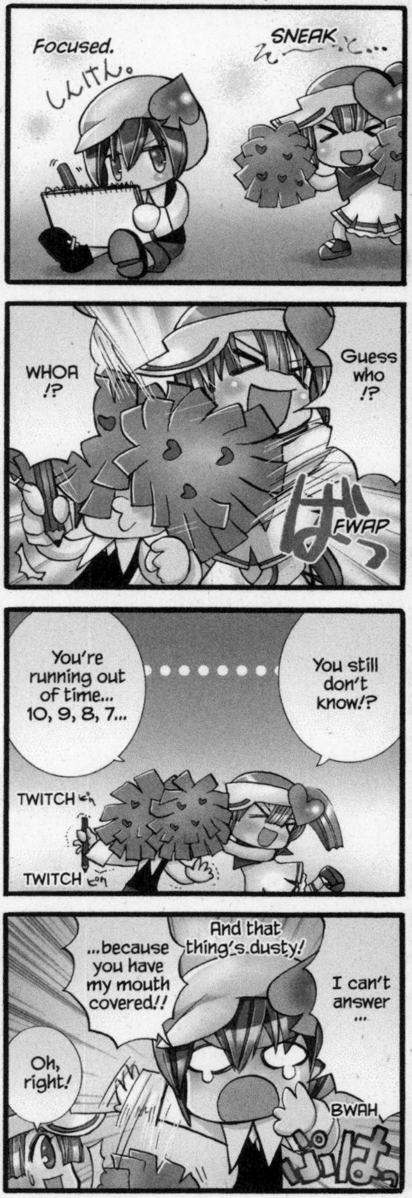
SNEAK
Focused.
しんけん。
Guess who !?
WHOA !?
FWAP
ばっ
You still don't know!?
You're running out of time... 10, 9, 8, 7...
TWITCH
TWITCH
I can't answer ...
And that thing's dusty!
...because you have my mouth covered!!
Oh, right!
BWAH

Portrait

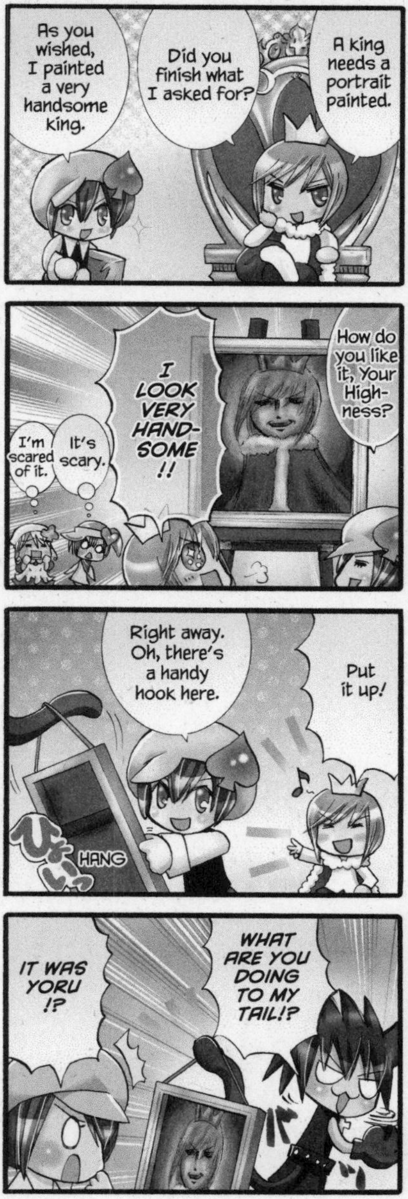
A king needs a portrait painted.
Did you finish what I asked for?
As you wished, I painted a very handsome king.
How do you like it, Your Highness?
I LOOK VERY HANDSOME!!
It's scary.
I'm scared of it.
Put it up!
Right away. Oh, there's a handy hook here.
HANG
WHAT ARE YOU DOING TO MY TAIL!?
IT WAS YORU!?

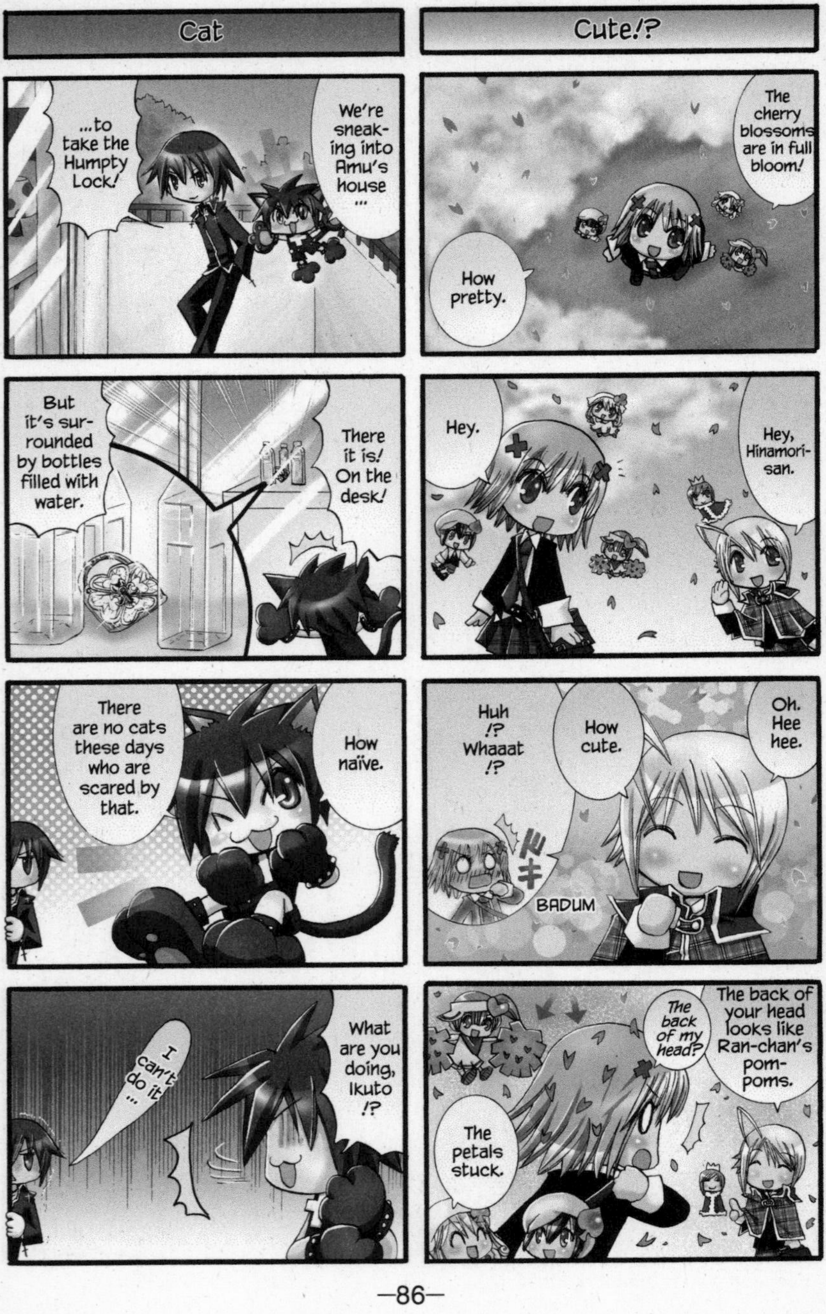
Cute!?
The cherry blossoms are in full bloom!
How pretty.
Hey, Hinamori-san.
Hey.
Oh. Hee hee.
How cute.
Huh!? Whaaat!?
BADUM
The back of your head looks like Ran-chan's pom-poms.
The back of my head?
The petals stuck.
Cat
We're sneak-ing into Amu's house ...
...to take the Humpty Lock!
There it is! On the desk!
But it's sur-rounded by bottles filled with water.
How naïve.
There are no cats these days who are scared by that.
What are you doing, Ikuto!?
I can't do it ...

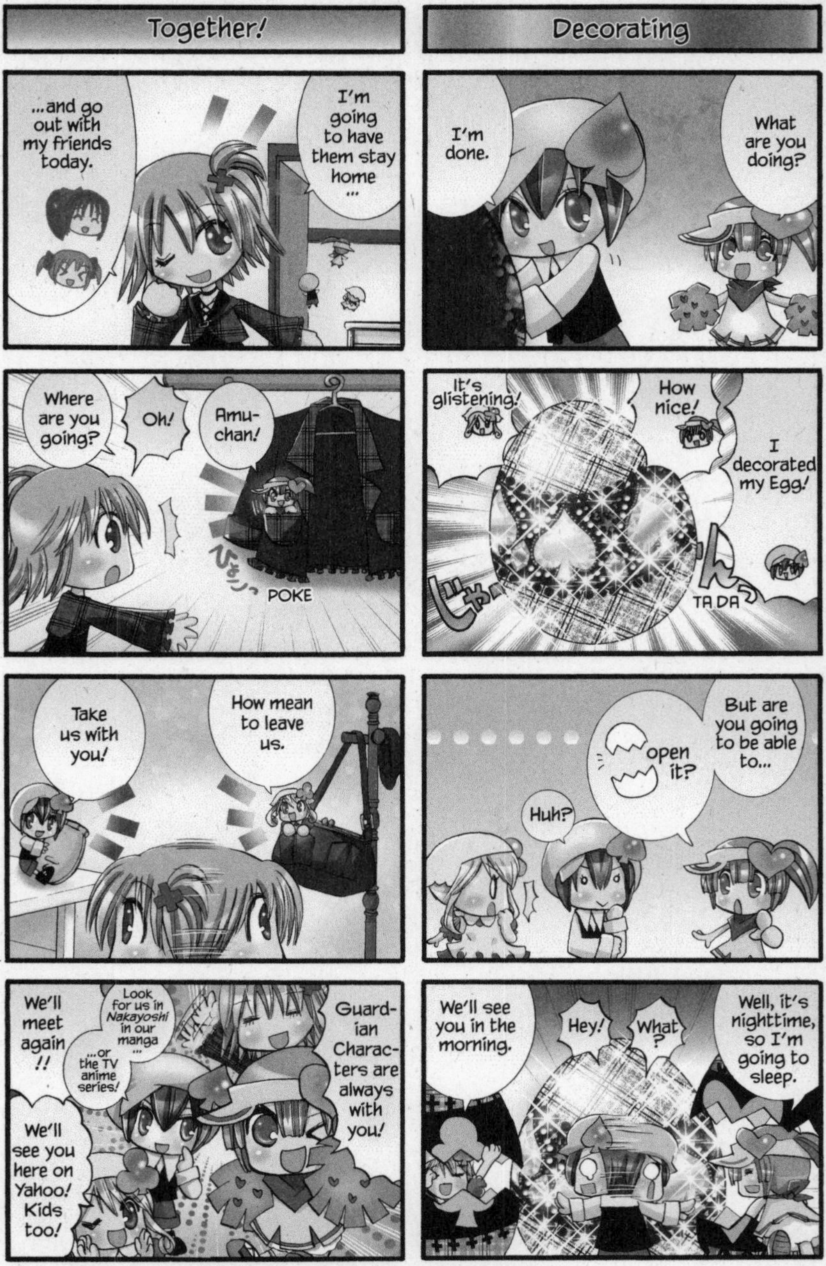
Decorating
What are you doing?
I'm done.
I decorated my Egg!
How nice!
It's glistening!
TA DA
But are you going to be able to...
open it?
Huh?
Well, it's nighttime, so I'm going to sleep.
What?
Hey!
We'll see you in the morning.
Together!
I'm going to have them stay home ...
...and go out with my friends today.
Amu-chan!
Oh!
Where are you going?
POKE
How mean to leave us.
Take us with you!
Guardian Characters are always with you!
Look for us in *Nakayoshi* in our manga ...
...or the TV anime series!
We'll meet again !!
We'll see you here on Yahoo! Kids too!

(Featured on the web on Yahoo! Kids Spring Special 2008)

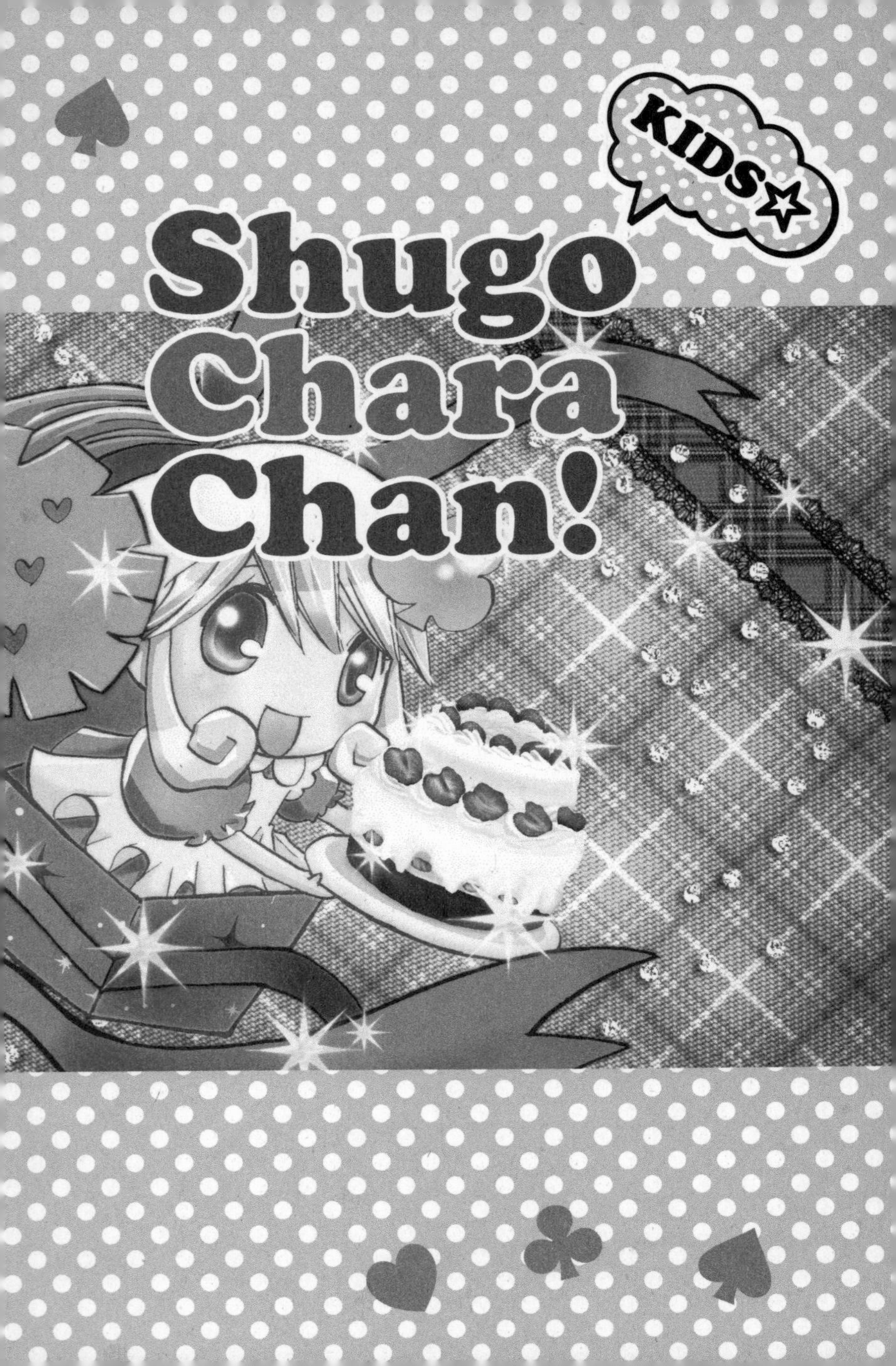
KIDS☆
Shugo Chara Chan!

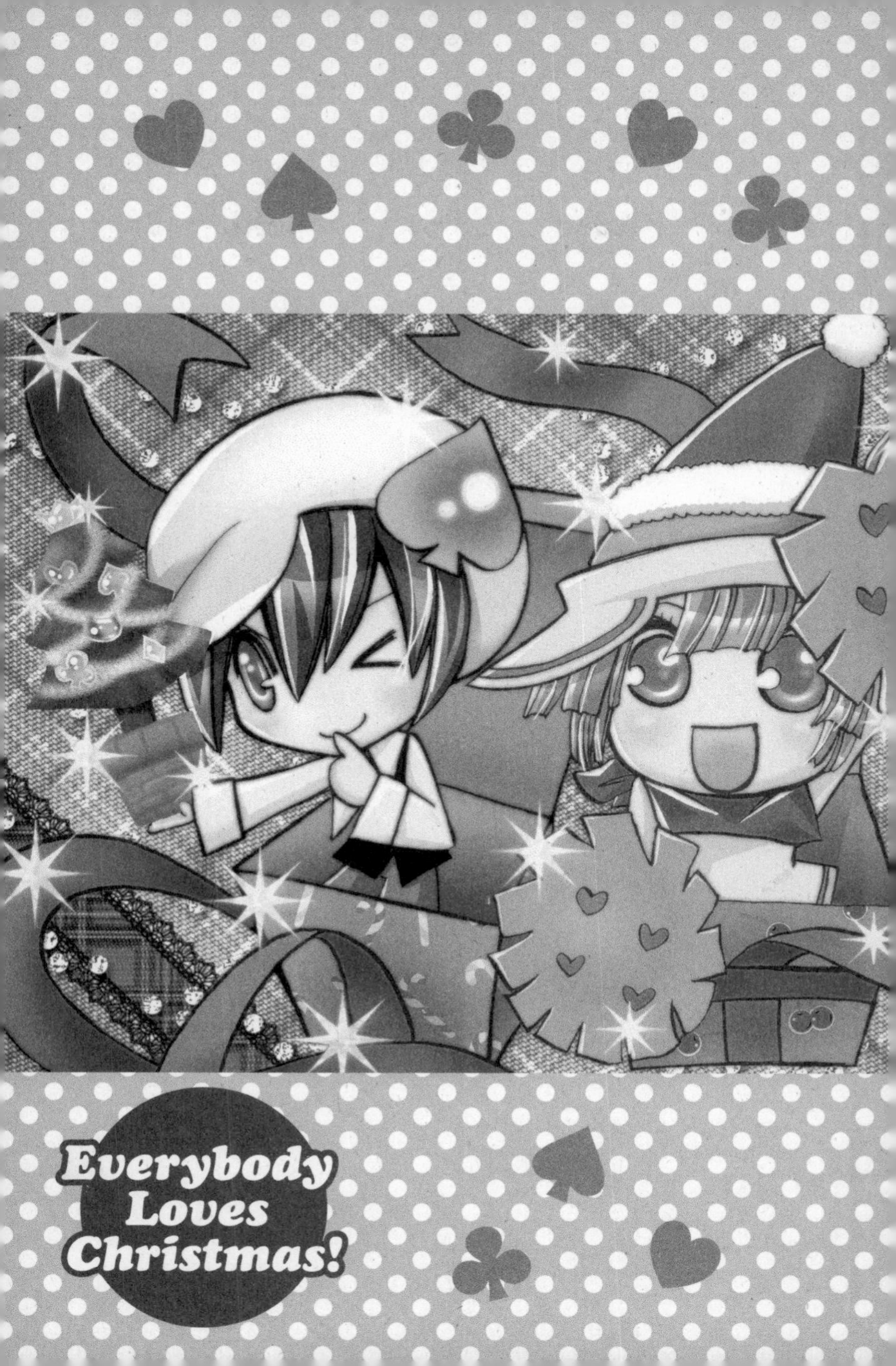
Everybody Loves Christmas!

Christmas ★ Personality Test

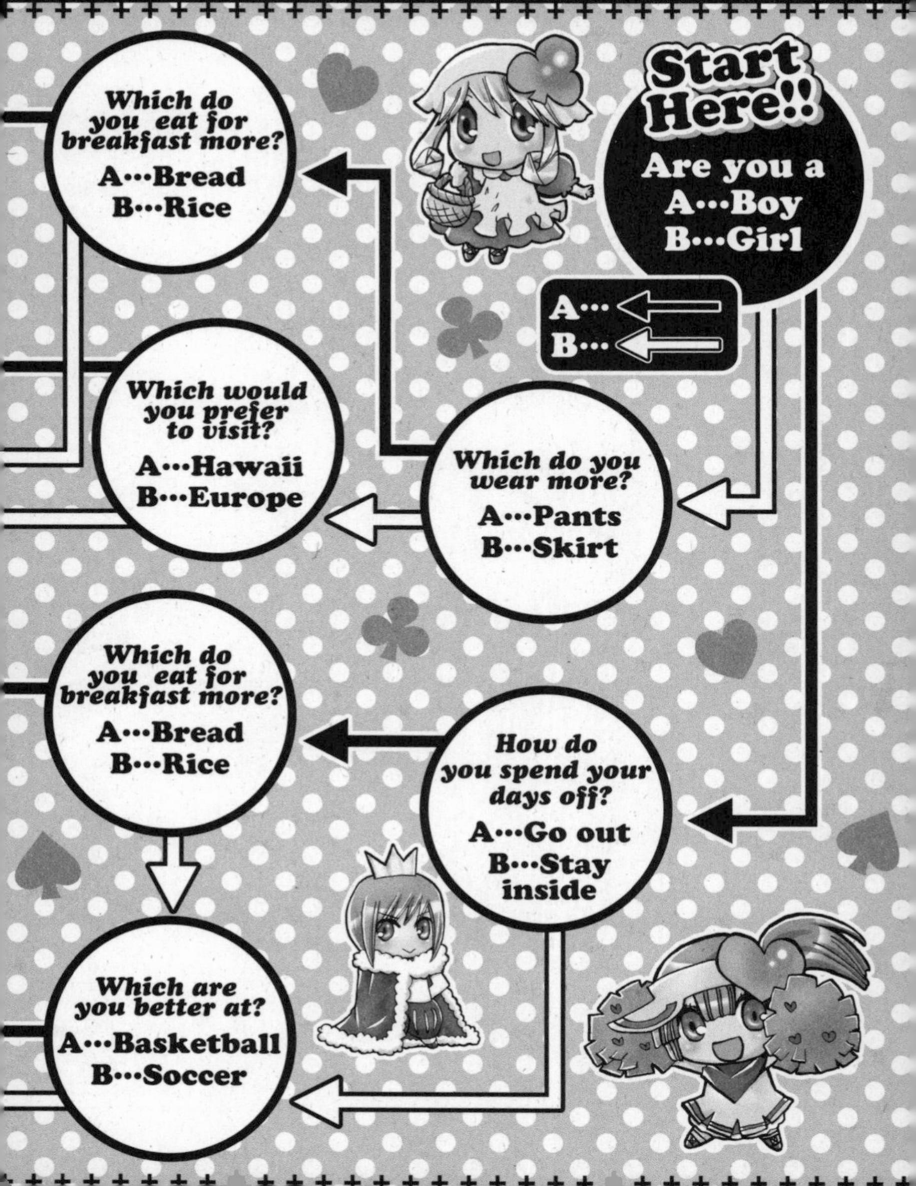

Start Here!!
Are you a
A···Boy
B···Girl
A···
B···
Which do you wear more?
A···Pants
B···Skirt
Which do you eat for breakfast more?
A···Bread
B···Rice
Which would you prefer to visit?
A···Hawaii
B···Europe
How do you spend your days off?
A···Go out
B···Stay inside
Which do you eat for breakfast more?
A···Bread
B···Rice
Which are you better at?
A···Basketball
B···Soccer

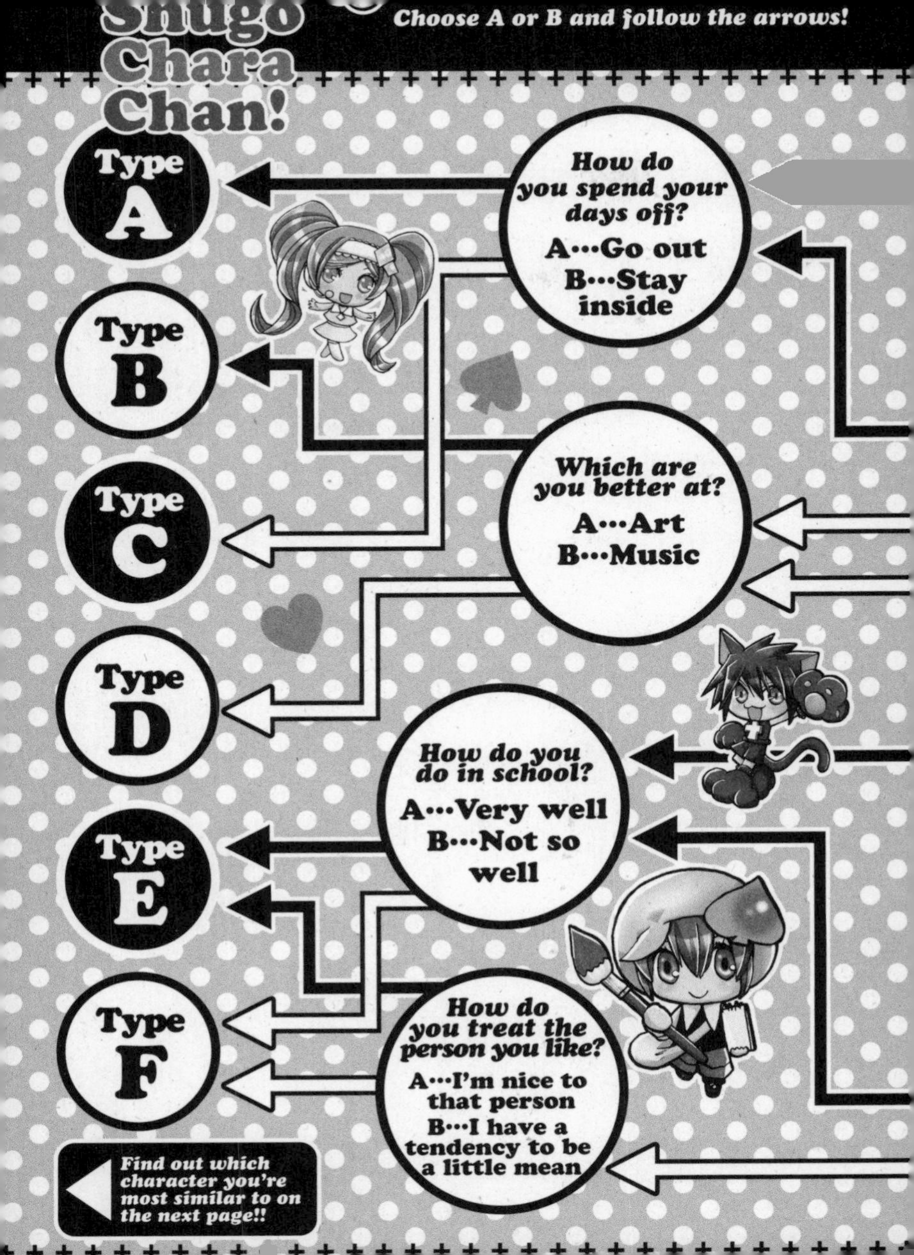

Shugo Chara Chan!
Choose A or B and follow the arrows!
How do you spend your days off?
A…Go out
B…Stay inside
Which are you better at?
A…Art
B…Music
How do you do in school?
A…Very well
B…Not so well
How do you treat the person you like?
A…I'm nice to that person
B…I have a tendency to be a little mean
Type A
Type B
Type C
Type D
Type E
Type F
Find out which character you're most similar to on the next page!!

Character Personality Result

Type A

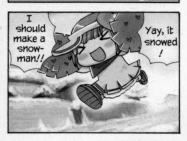

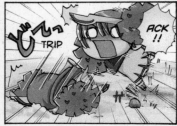

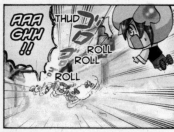

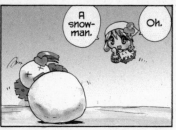

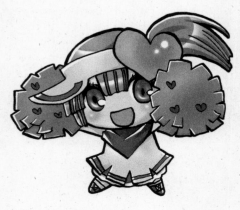

Ran

You are a straightforward girl who's full of energy, like Ran. In order to enjoy your Christmas, we recommend that you should invite a lot of friends for a Christmas party!!

Ran is Full of Energy

Yay, it snowed!
I should make a snow-man!!
ACK!!
TRIP
THUD
AAAGHH!!
ROLL
ROLL
ROLL
Oh.
A snow-man.

Character Personality Result

Type B

Miki is Artistic

Oh!
THUD
Whoa!
Sorry! I ran into you!!
SPLATTER
Don't worry about this.
Oh no, did I ruin your painting?
If I add this here, and here...
BRUSH
BRUSH
...it becomes a wreath made of poinset-tia!!
TA DA
WOW!
You're so artistic!!

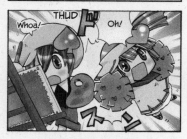

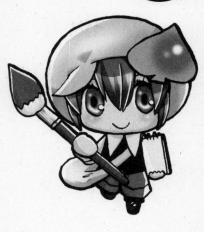

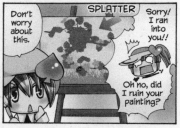

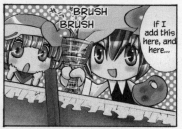

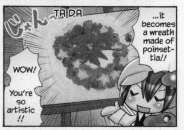

Miki

You are a girl with a lot of artistic taste, like Miki. We recommend that you give a gift using your perception for Christmas.

Character Personality Result Type C

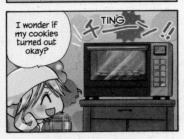

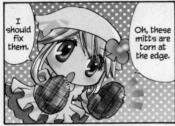

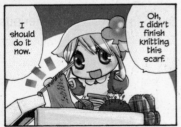

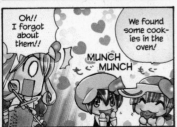

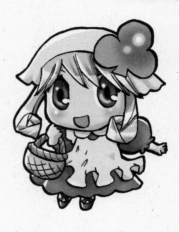

Su

You are girly and kind, like Su. We recommend using your cooking skills to make a cake for Christmas! A delicious cake would be a delightful surprise for everyone!!

Su Operates on her Own Time

TING
I wonder if my cookies turned out okay?
Oh, these mitts are torn at the edge.
I should fix them.
Oh, I didn't finish knitting this scarf.
I should do it now.
We found some cookies in the oven!
Oh!! I forgot about them!!
MUNCH MUNCH

Character Personality Result

Type D

Diamond

You are a girl with a mysterious aura, like Diamond. Maybe you can decorate a Christmas tree? Everyone is going to praise it!

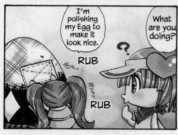

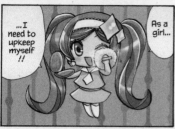

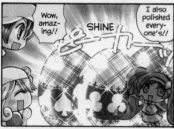

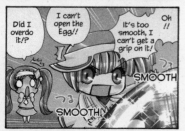

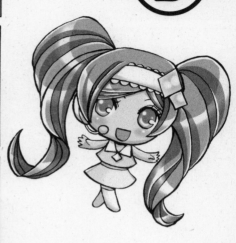

Diamond Works Hard

As a girl...
...I need to upkeep myself !!
What are you doing?
I'm polishing my Egg to make it look nice.
RUB
RUB
I also polished every-one's!!
SHINE
Wow, amaz-ing!!
Oh !!
It's too smooth, I can't get a grip on it!
I can't open the Egg!!
Did I overdo it!?
SMOOTH
SMOOTH

Character Personality Result Type E

Kiseki Gives Orders

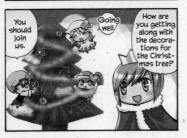

How are you getting along with the decorations for the Christmas tree?
Going well.
You should join us.
I can't do a peasant's job!
HMPH
What?
If you're acting high and mighty...
...I'm taking this!!
YOINK
SHOCK
Let's put it here.
Looks nice.
He's crying...

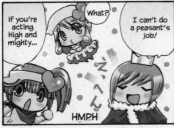

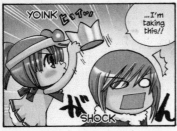

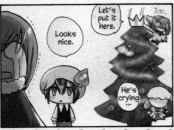

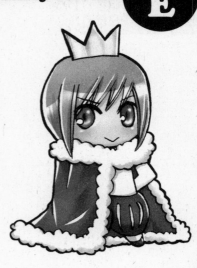

Kiseki

You are a defender of justice, like Kiseki. We recommend you to come up with a game to play at the Christmas party, to make it into a fun event for everyone ☆

Character Personality Result

Type F

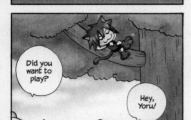

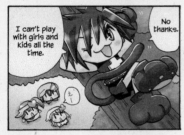

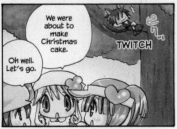

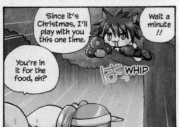

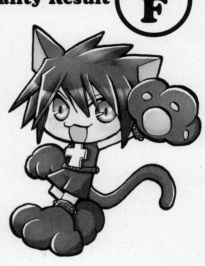

Yoru

You're a prank-loving boy, like Yoru. If you prepare a surprise party or a present for Christmas, everyone would be surprised and happy!!

Frivolous Yoru

Hey, Yoru!
Did you want to play?
No thanks.
I can't play with girls and kids all the time.
TWITCH
We were about to make Christmas cake.
Oh well. Let's go.
Wait a minute!!
Since it's Christmas, I'll play with you this one time.
WHIP
You're in it for the food, eh?

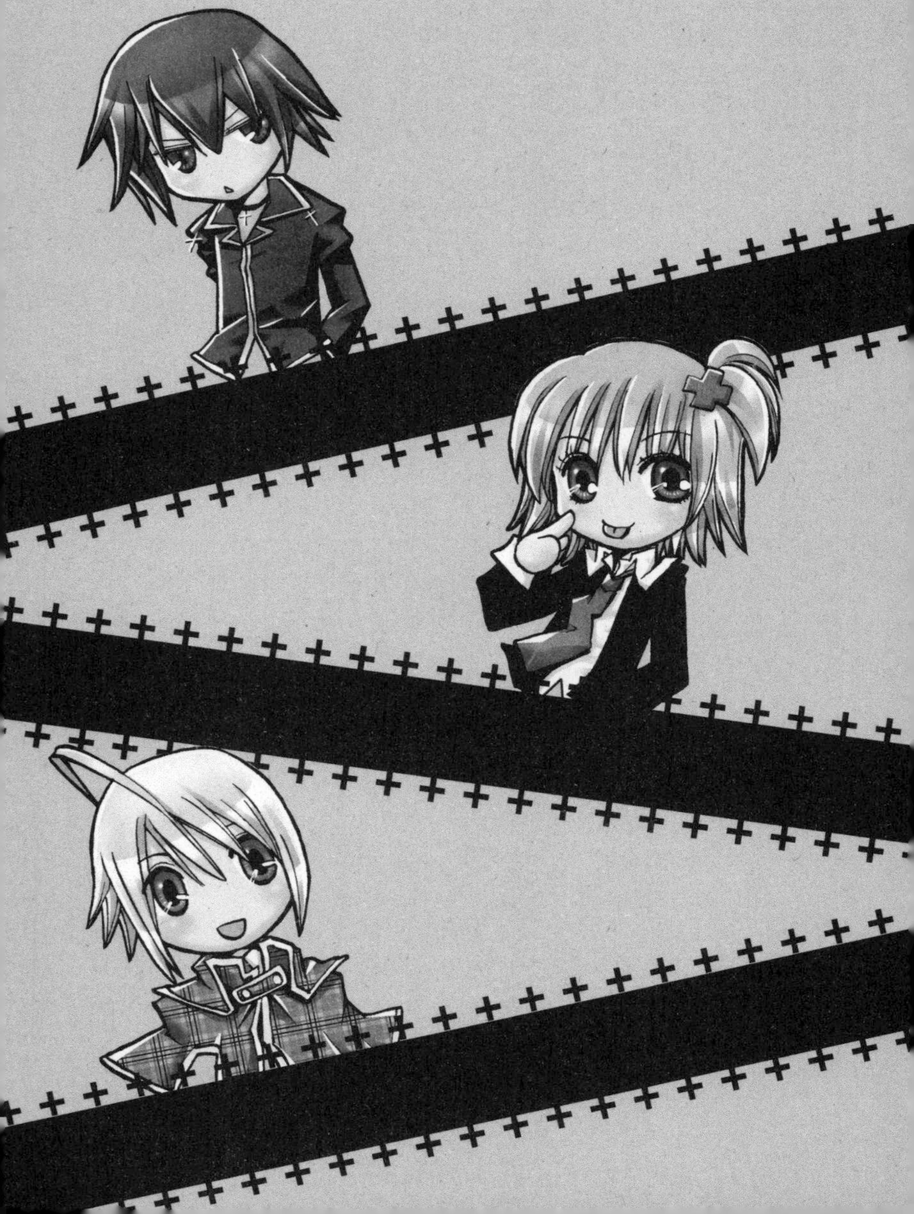

Ran's New Tree

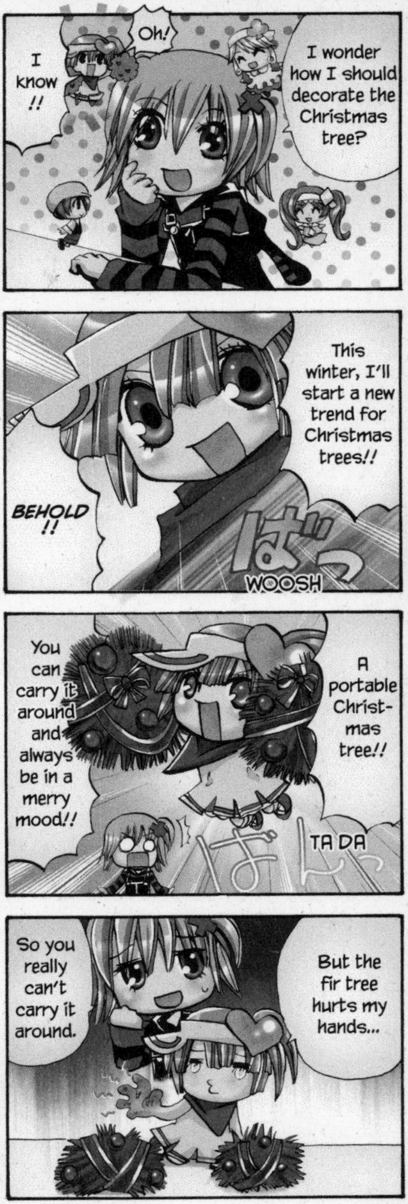
I wonder how I should decorate the Christmas tree?
Oh!
I know!!
This winter, I'll start a new trend for Christmas trees!!
BEHOLD!!
WOOSH
A portable Christmas tree!!
You can carry it around and always be in a merry mood!!
TA DA
But the fir tree hurts my hands...
So you really can't carry it around.

Miki's Tree Plan

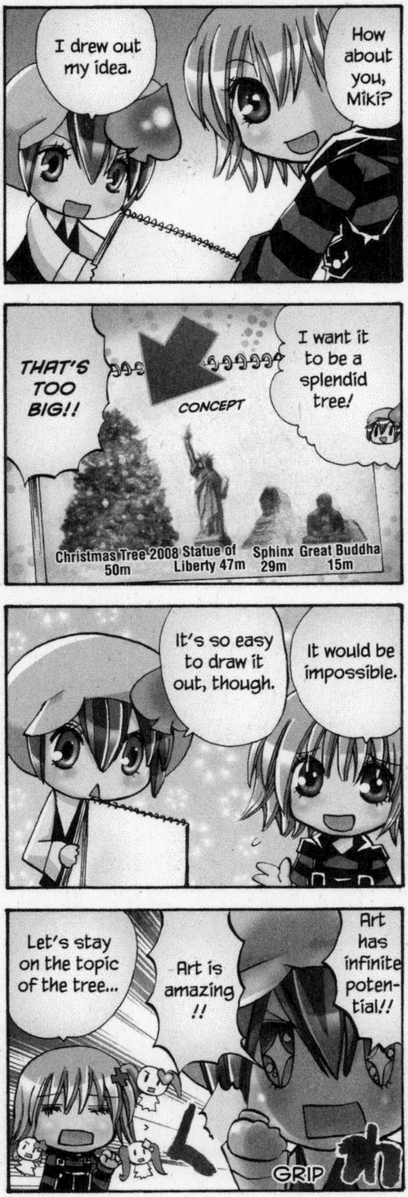
How about you, Miki?
I drew out my idea.
I want it to be a splendid tree!
CONCEPT
THAT'S TOO BIG!!
Christmas Tree 2008 50m
Statue of Liberty 47m
Sphinx 29m
Great Buddha 15m
It would be impossible.
It's so easy to draw it out, though.
Art has infinite poten-tial!!
Art is amazing!!
Let's stay on the topic of the tree...
GRIP

Su's Sweet Tree

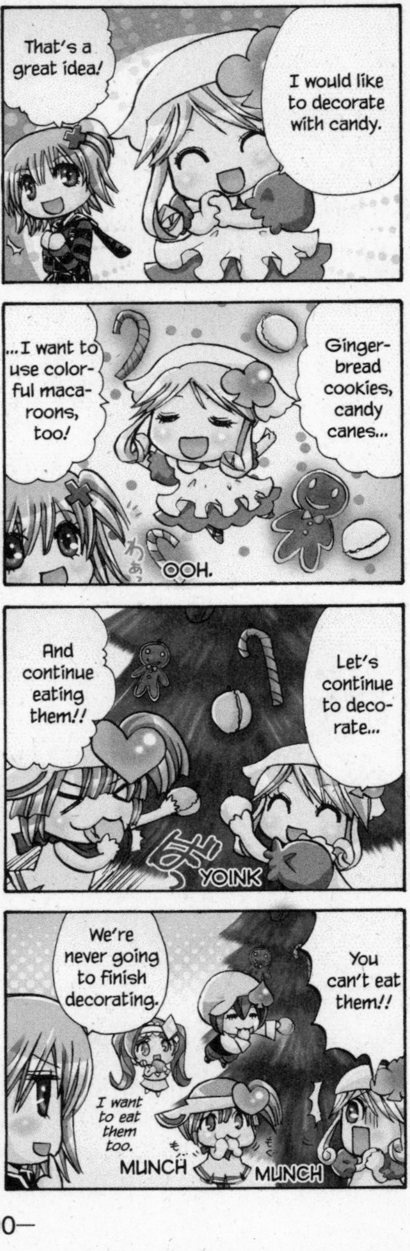

I would like to decorate with candy.
That's a great idea!
Ginger-bread cookies, candy canes...
...I want to use color-ful maca-roons, too!
OOH.
Let's continue to deco-rate...
And continue eating them!!
YOINK
You can't eat them!!
We're never going to finish decorating.
I want to eat them too.
MUNCH
MUNCH

Diamond's Glimmering Tree

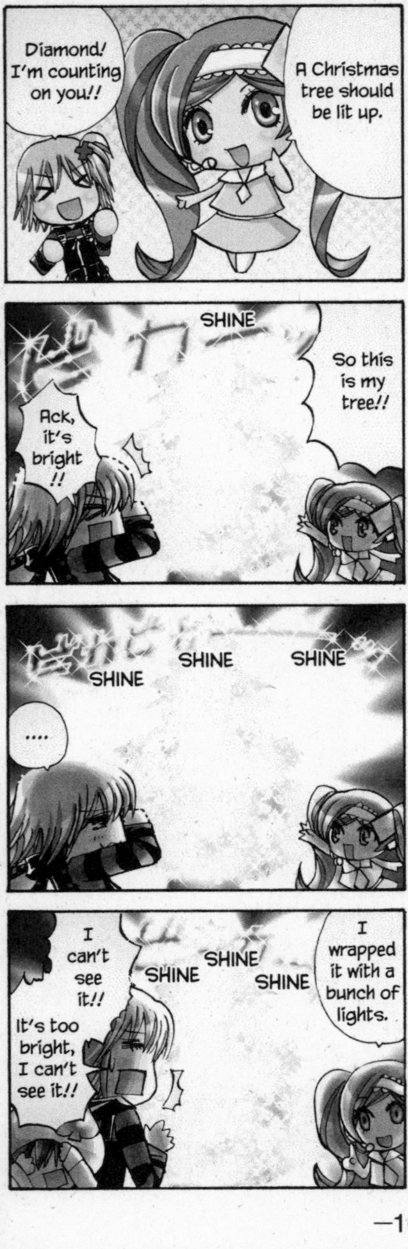

A Christmas tree should be lit up.
Diamond! I'm counting on you!!
SHINE
So this is my tree!!
Ack, it's bright!!
SHINE
SHINE
SHINE
....
I wrapped it with a bunch of lights.
SHINE
SHINE
SHINE
SHINE
I can't see it!!
It's too bright, I can't see it!!

Let's Tell Santa

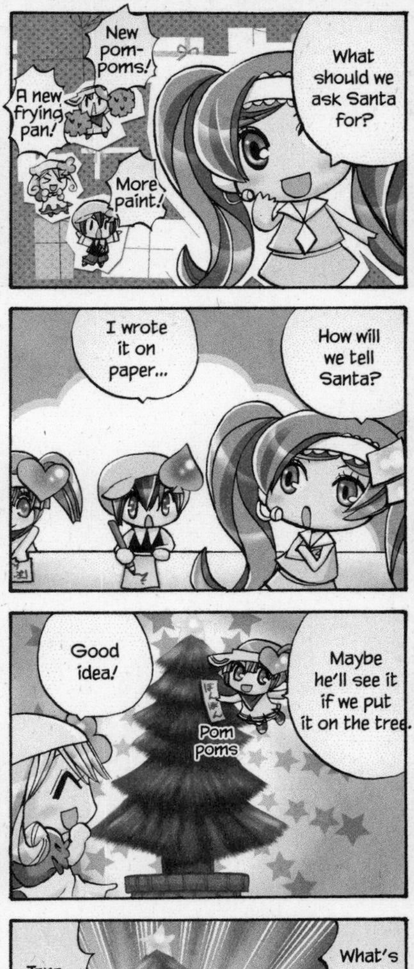
What should we ask Santa for?
New pom-poms!
A new frying pan!
More paint!
How will we tell Santa?
I wrote it on paper...
Maybe he'll see it if we put it on the tree.
Pom poms
Good idea!
What's this !?
Tanabata !?

Stockings

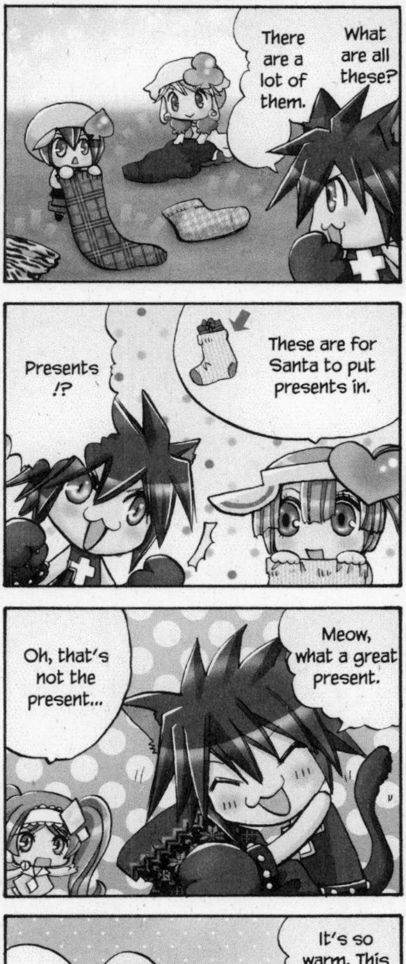
What are all these?
There are a lot of them.
These are for Santa to put presents in.
Presents !?
Meow, what a great present.
Oh, that's not the present...
It's so warm. This is my new bed.
Oh well.
At least he's enjoying it.

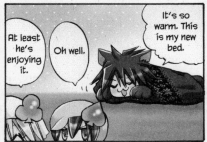

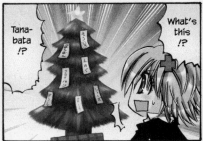

Like Santa

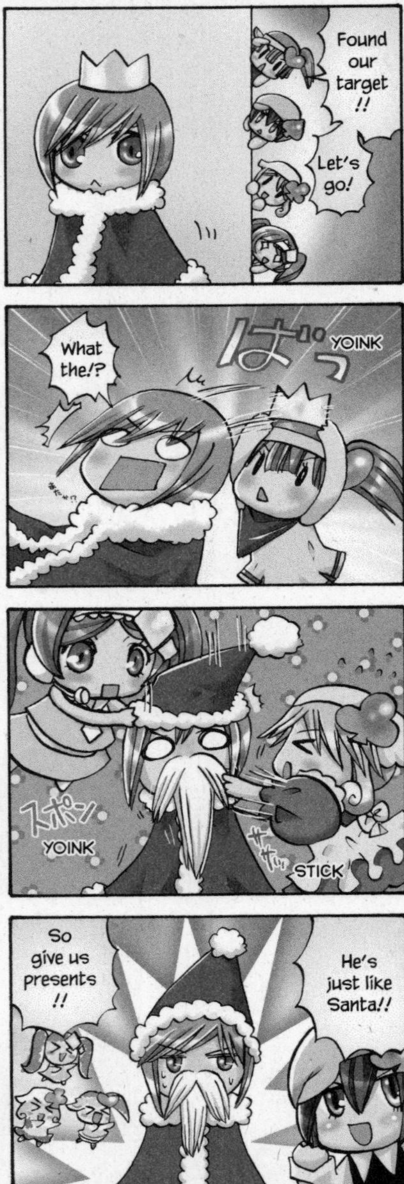
Found our target!!
Let's go!
ぱっ
YOINK
What the!?
スポーン
YOINK
STICK
He's just like Santa!!
So give us presents!!

Buche de Noel

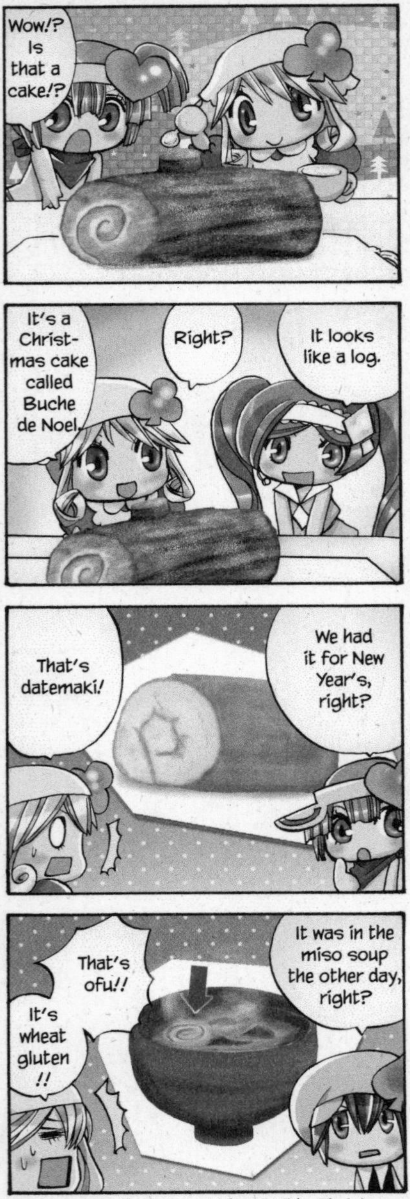
Wow!? Is that a cake!?
It looks like a log.
Right?
It's a Christmas cake called Buche de Noel.
We had it for New Year's, right?
That's datemaki!
It was in the miso soup the other day, right?
That's ofu!!
It's wheat gluten!!

(Featured on the web on Yahoo! Kids Christmas Special 2008)

**You can
read the rest of
SHUGO CHARA
CHAN! KIDS☆
here on the web!**
http://special.kids.yahoo.co.jp/xmas2008
(Available from November 20, 2008
to December 25, 2008)

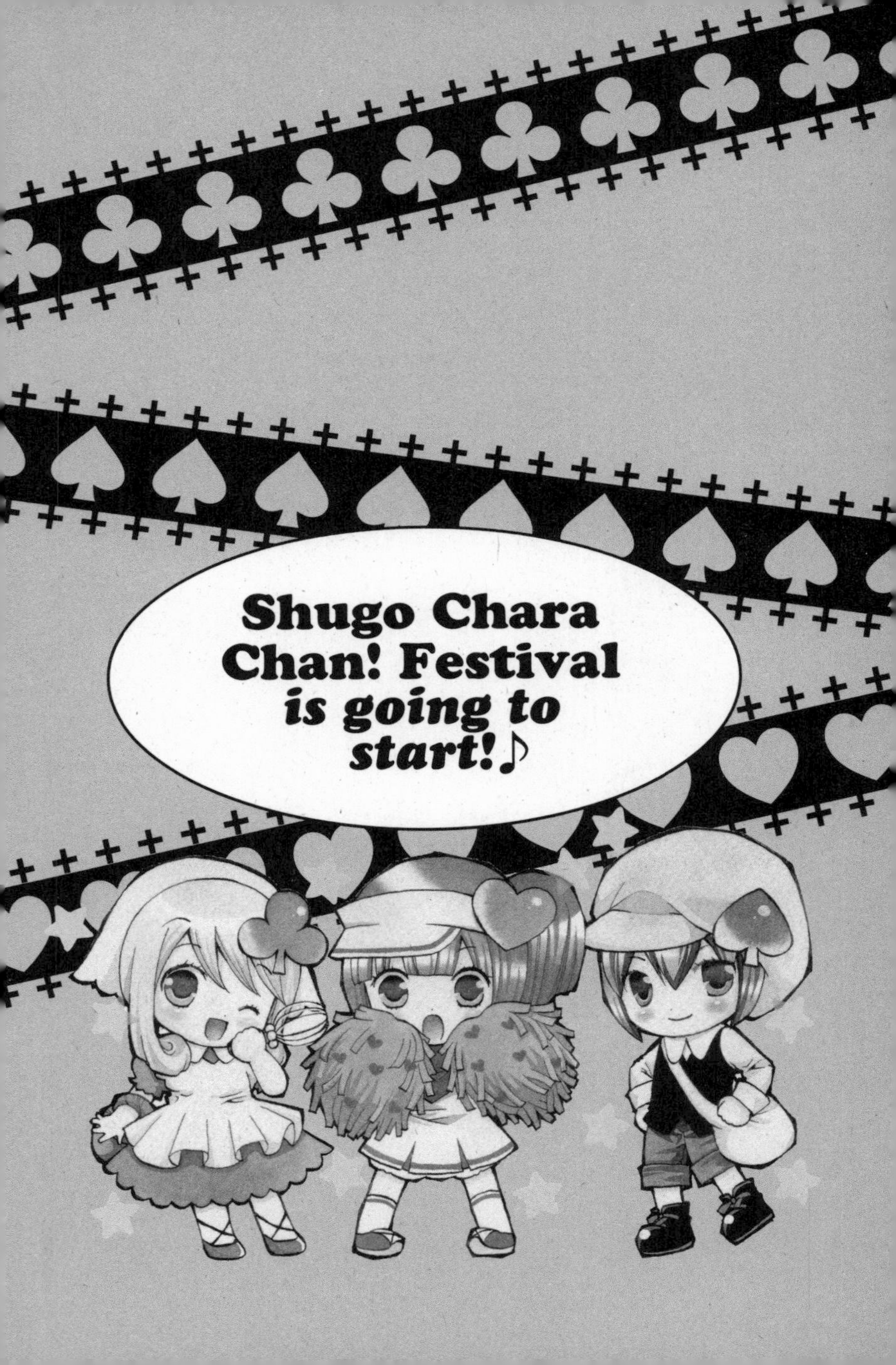
Shugo Chara Chan! Festival is going to start!♪

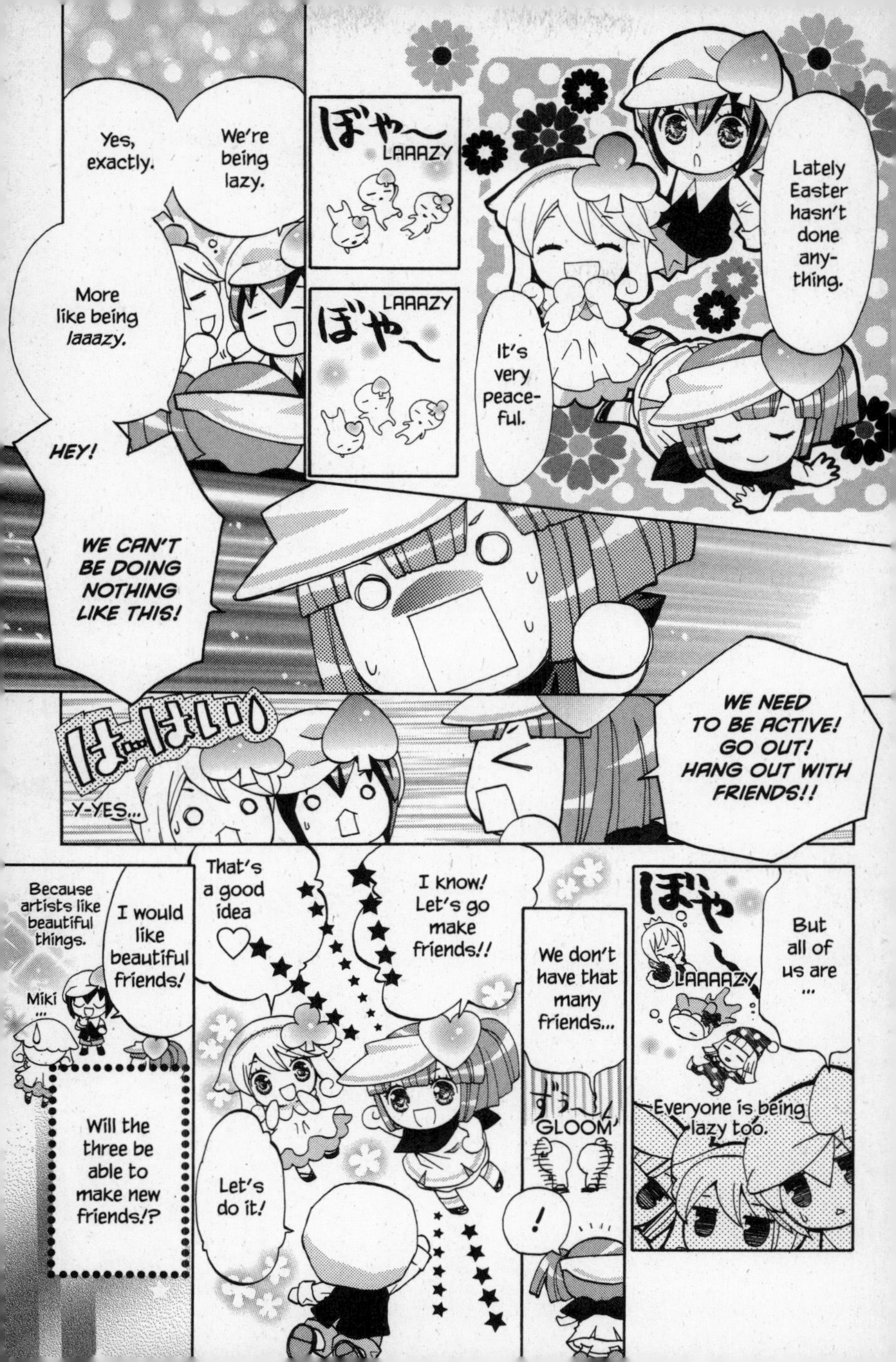

Lately Easter hasn't done anything.
It's very peaceful.
ぼや～
LAAAZY
LAAAZY
ぼや～
We're being lazy.
Yes, exactly.
More like being *laaazy.*
HEY!
WE CAN'T BE DOING NOTHING LIKE THIS!
WE NEED TO BE ACTIVE! GO OUT! HANG OUT WITH FRIENDS!!
は…はい
Y-YES...
But all of us are ...
ぼや～
LAAAAZY
Everyone is being lazy too.
We don't have that many friends...
ずう～ん
GLOOM
!
I know! Let's go make friends!!
That's a good idea ♡
Let's do it!
I would like beautiful friends!
Because artists like beautiful things.
Miki ...
Will the three be able to make new friends!?

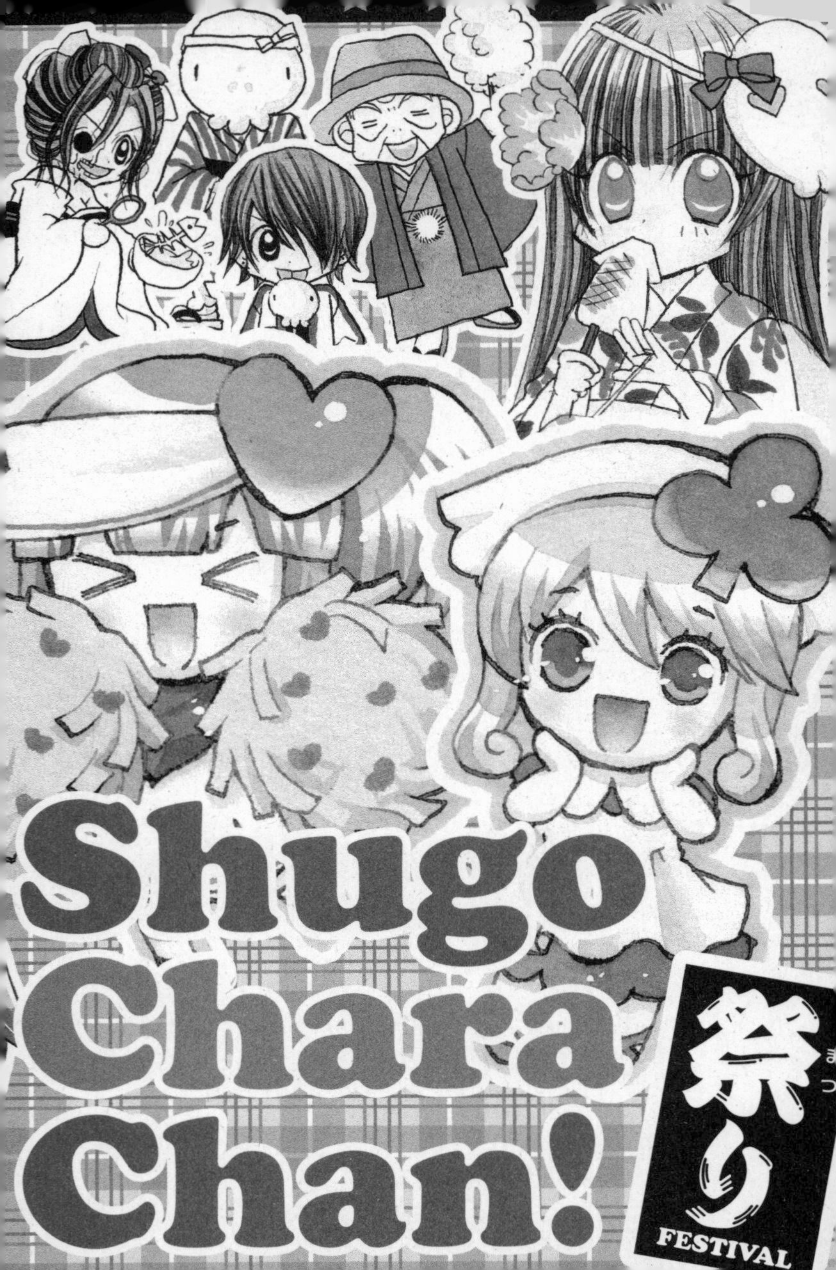
Shugo Chara Chan!
祭り
FESTIVAL

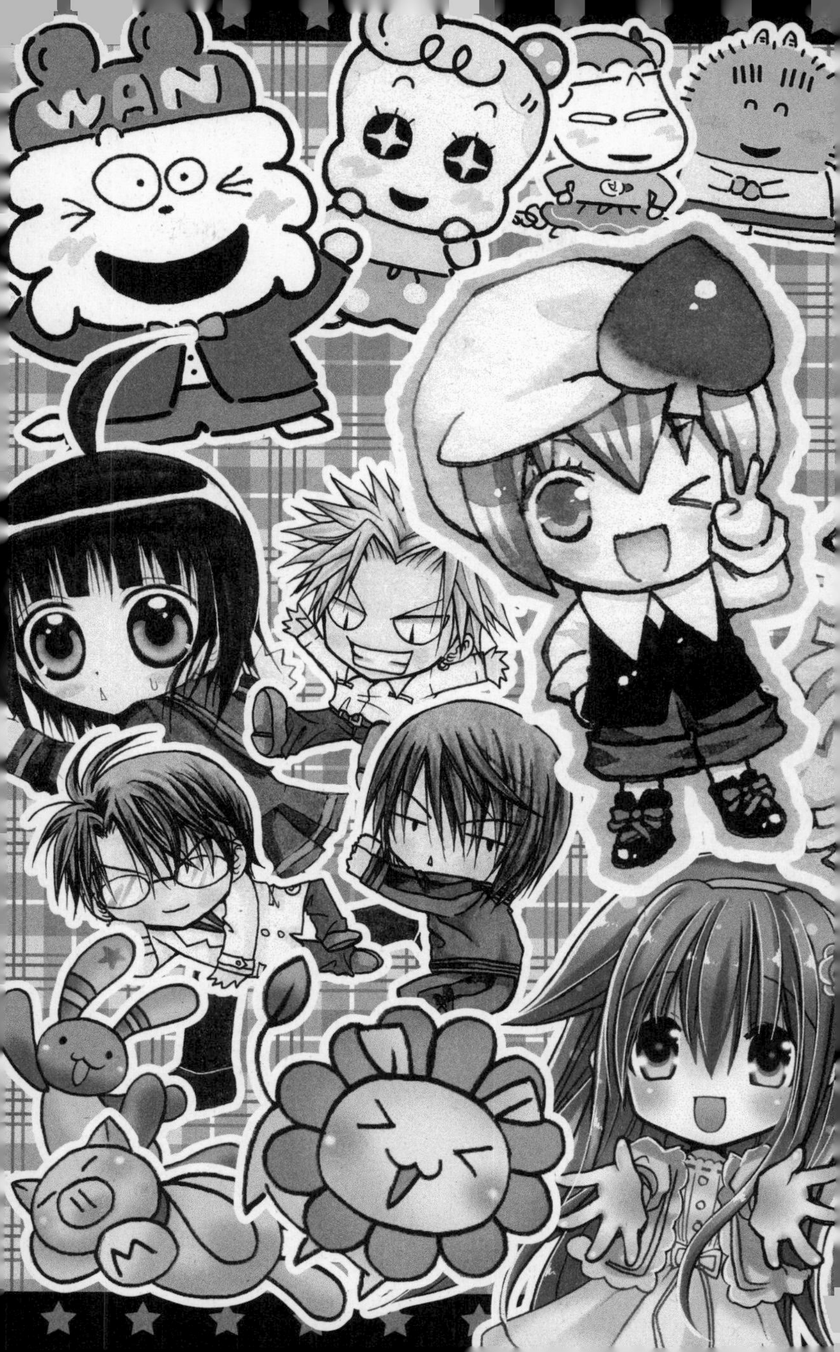
WAN

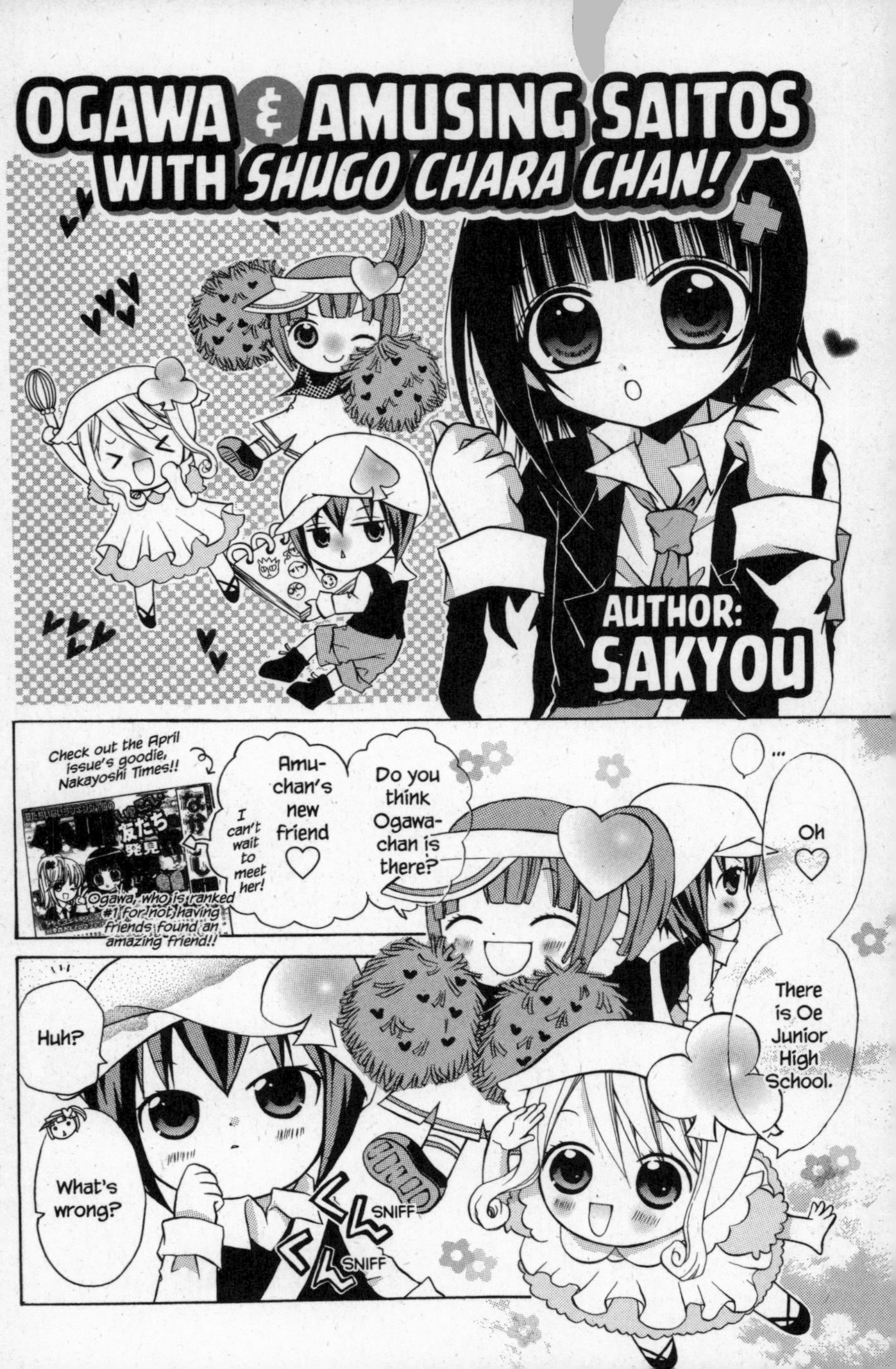
OGAWA & AMUSING SAITOS WITH SHUGO CHARA CHAN!
AUTHOR: SAKYOU
Amu-chan's new friend ♡
Do you think Ogawa-chan is there?
...
Oh ♡
There is Oe Junior High School.
Check out the April issue's goodie, Nakayoshi Times!!
I can't wait to meet her!
Ogawa, who is ranked #1 for not having friends found an amazing friend!!
Huh?
What's wrong?
SNIFF
SNIFF

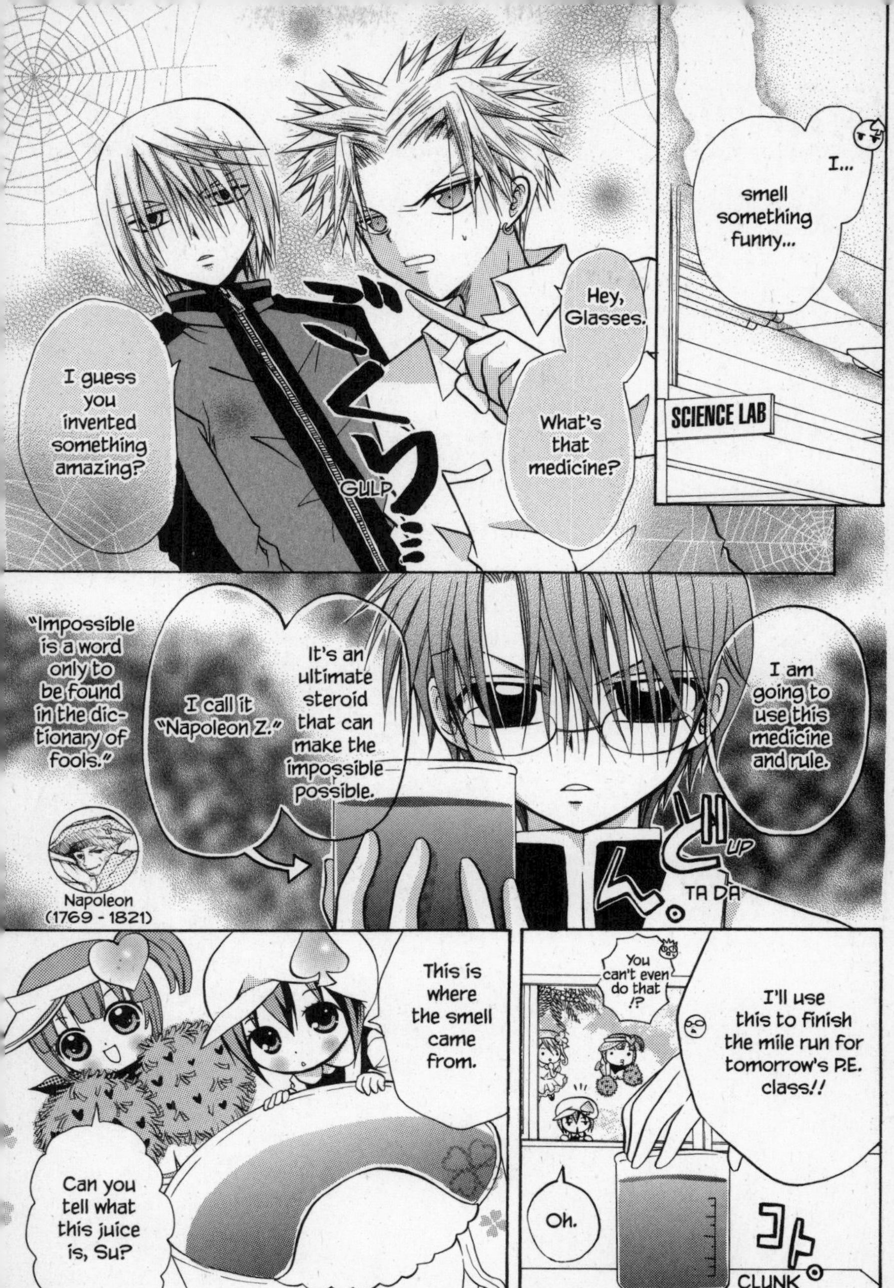
I...
smell something funny...
SCIENCE LAB
Hey, Glasses.
What's that medicine?
GULP
I guess you invented something amazing?
I am going to use this medicine and rule.
UP
TA DA
It's an ultimate steroid that can make the impossible possible.
I call it "Napoleon Z."
"Impossible is a word only to be found in the dictionary of fools."
Napoleon (1769 - 1821)
I'll use this to finish the mile run for tomorrow's P.E. class!!
You can't even do that !?
Oh.
CLUNK
This is where the smell came from.
Can you tell what this juice is, Su?

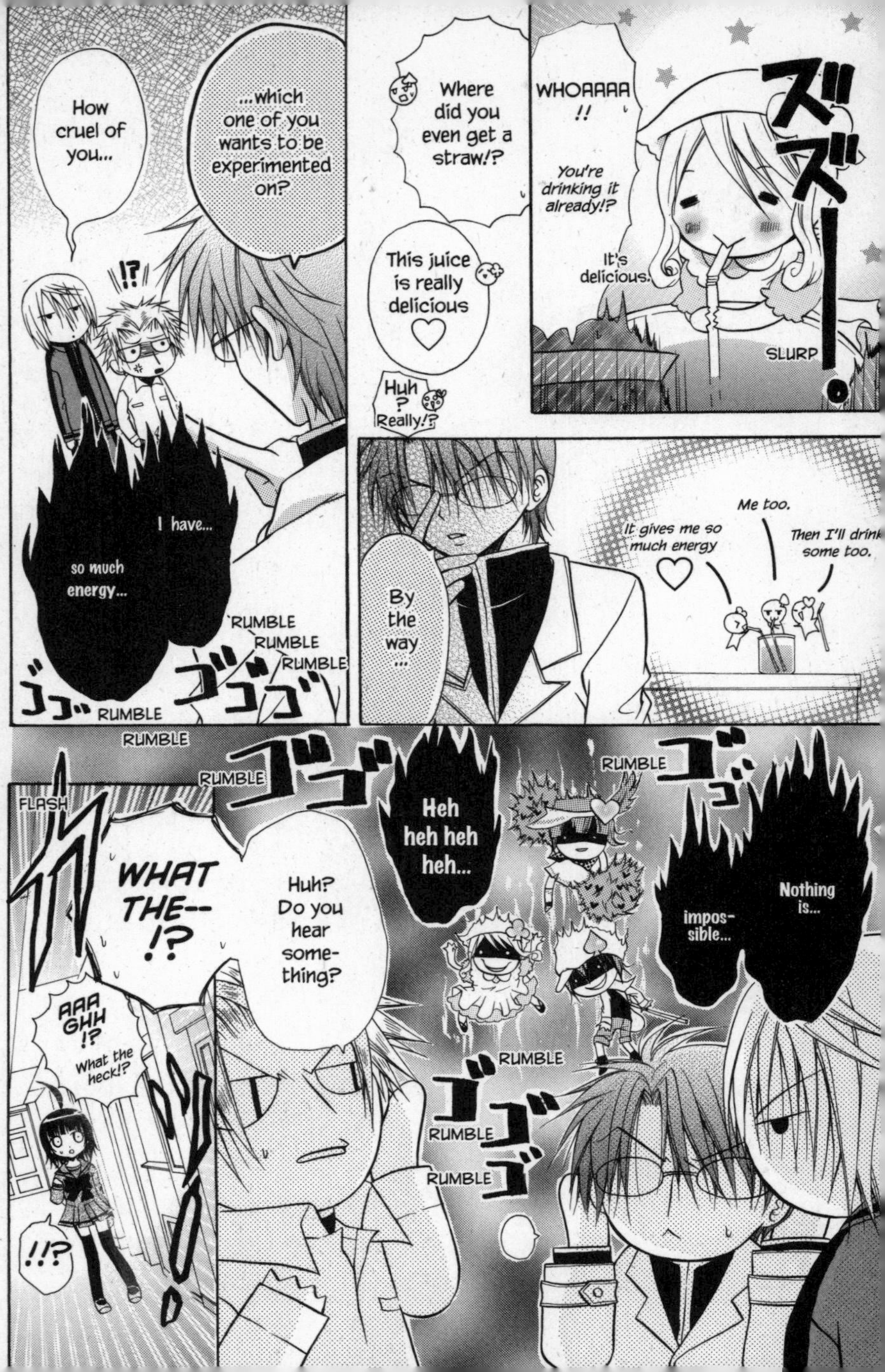
WHOAAAA !!
You're drinking it already!?
It's delicious.
ズズー
SLURP
Where did you even get a straw!?
This juice is really delicious ♥
Huh? Really!?
Then I'll drink some too.
Me too.
It gives me so much energy ♥
By the way...
...which one of you wants to be experimented on?
How cruel of you...
!?
I have...
so much energy...
RUMBLE RUMBLE RUMBLE
ゴゴゴ
ゴゴ
RUMBLE
RUMBLE
Nothing is...
impossible...
RUMBLE
ゴゴ
Heh heh heh heh...
RUMBLE
ゴゴ
RUMBLE
ゴゴゴ
RUMBLE
RUMBLE
Huh? Do you hear something?
WHAT THE--!?
FLASH
AAAGHH!?
What the heck!?
!!?

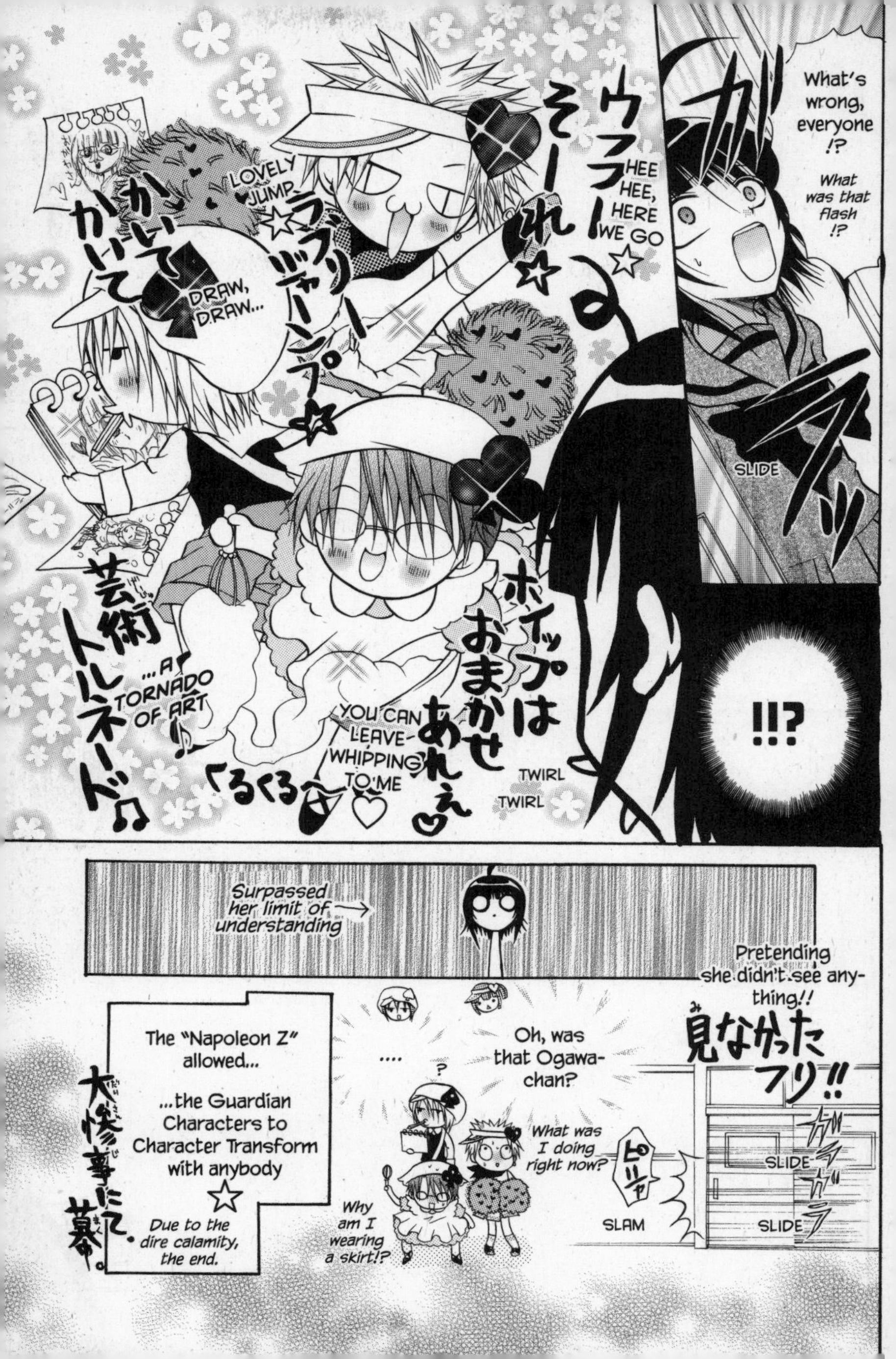

What's wrong, everyone!?
What was that flash!?
SLIDE
!!?
ウフフ そーれ☆
HEE HEE, HERE WE GO☆
ラブリージャーンプ☆
LOVELY JUMP☆
かいてかいて
DRAW, DRAW...
芸術トルネード♫
...A TORNADO OF ART♪
ホイップはおまかせあれえ
YOU CAN LEAVE WHIPPING TO ME♡
くるくる~
TWIRL TWIRL
Surpassed her limit of understanding
Pretending she didn't see anything!!
見なかったフリ!!
SLIDE
SLIDE
ピシャ
SLAM
What was I doing right now?
Oh, was that Ogawa-chan?
....
?
Why am I wearing a skirt!?
The "Napoleon Z" allowed...
...the Guardian Characters to Character Transform with anybody☆
大惨事にて幕。
Due to the dire calamity, the end.

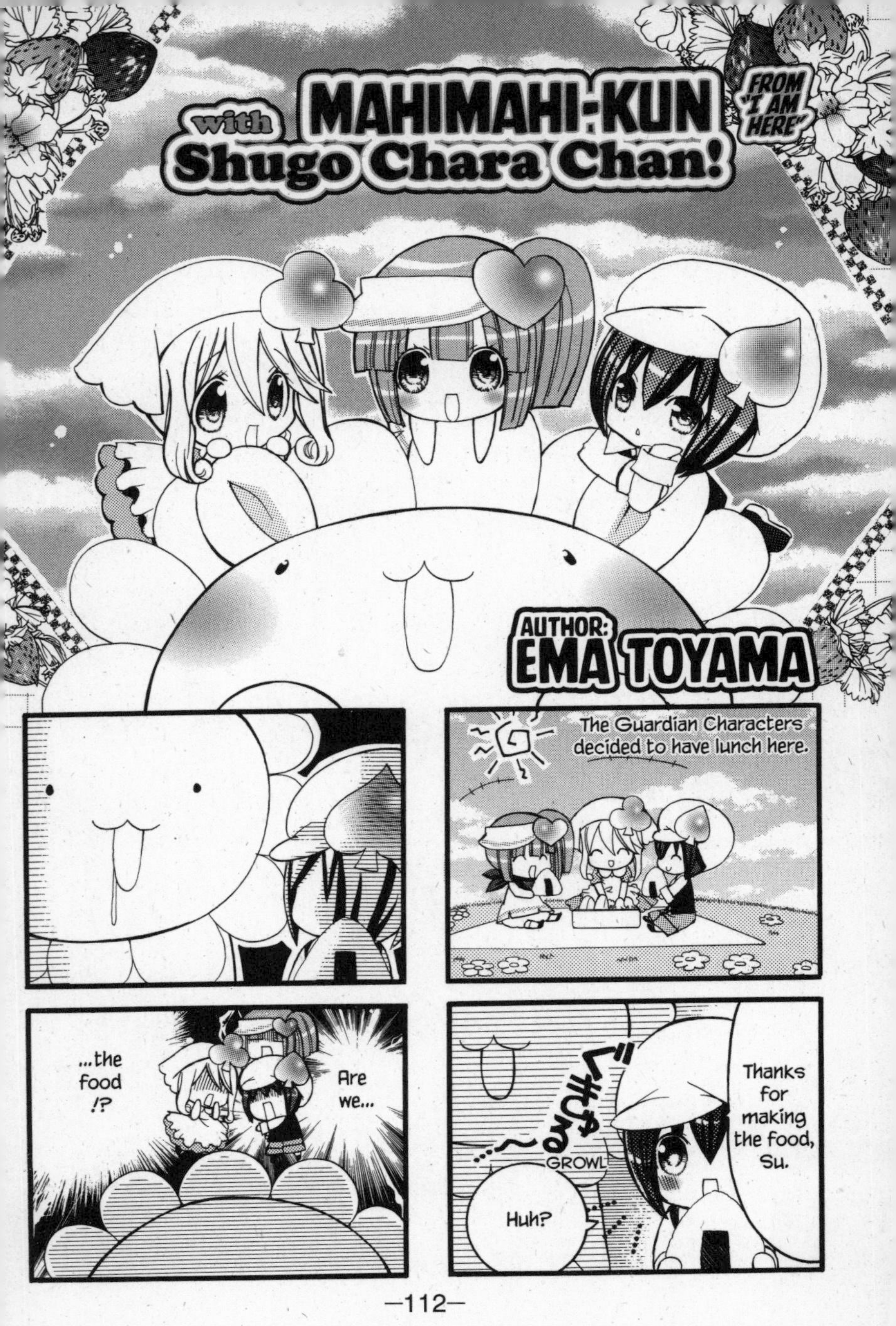
with MAHIMAHI-KUN FROM "I AM HERE"
Shugo Chara Chan!
AUTHOR: EMA TOYAMA
The Guardian Characters decided to have lunch here.
Thanks for making the food, Su.
GROWL
Huh?
Are we...
...the food !?

Mahimahi

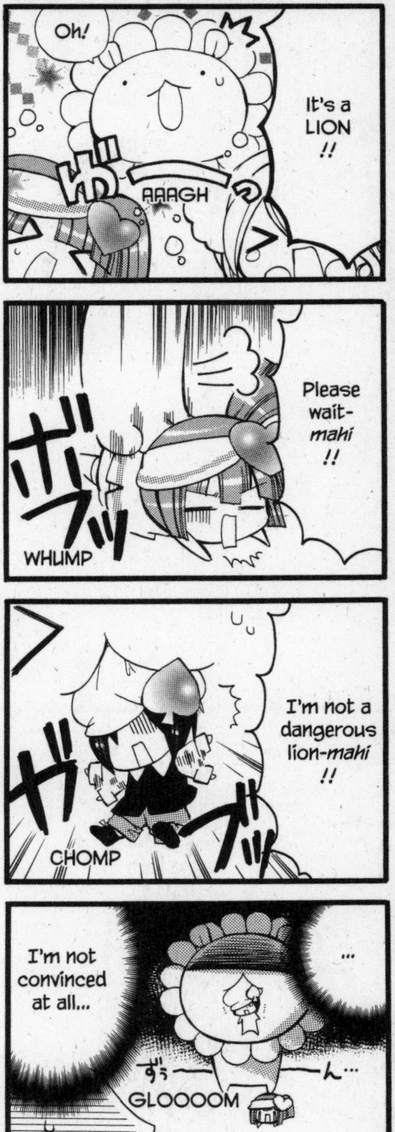

Oh!
It's a LION !!
AAAGH
Please wait-mahi !!
WHUMP
I'm not a dangerous lion-mahi !!
CHOMP
...
I'm not convinced at all...
GLOOOOM

Still Hungry

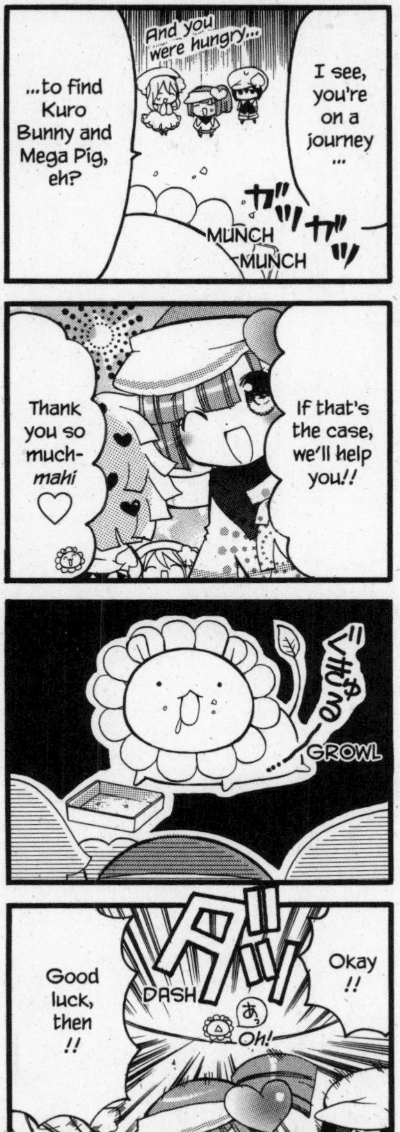

And you were hungry...
I see, you're on a journey ...
...to find Kuro Bunny and Mega Pig, eh?
MUNCH
MUNCH
If that's the case, we'll help you!!
Thank you so much-mahi ♡
GROWL
Okay !!
DASH
Oh!
Good luck, then !!

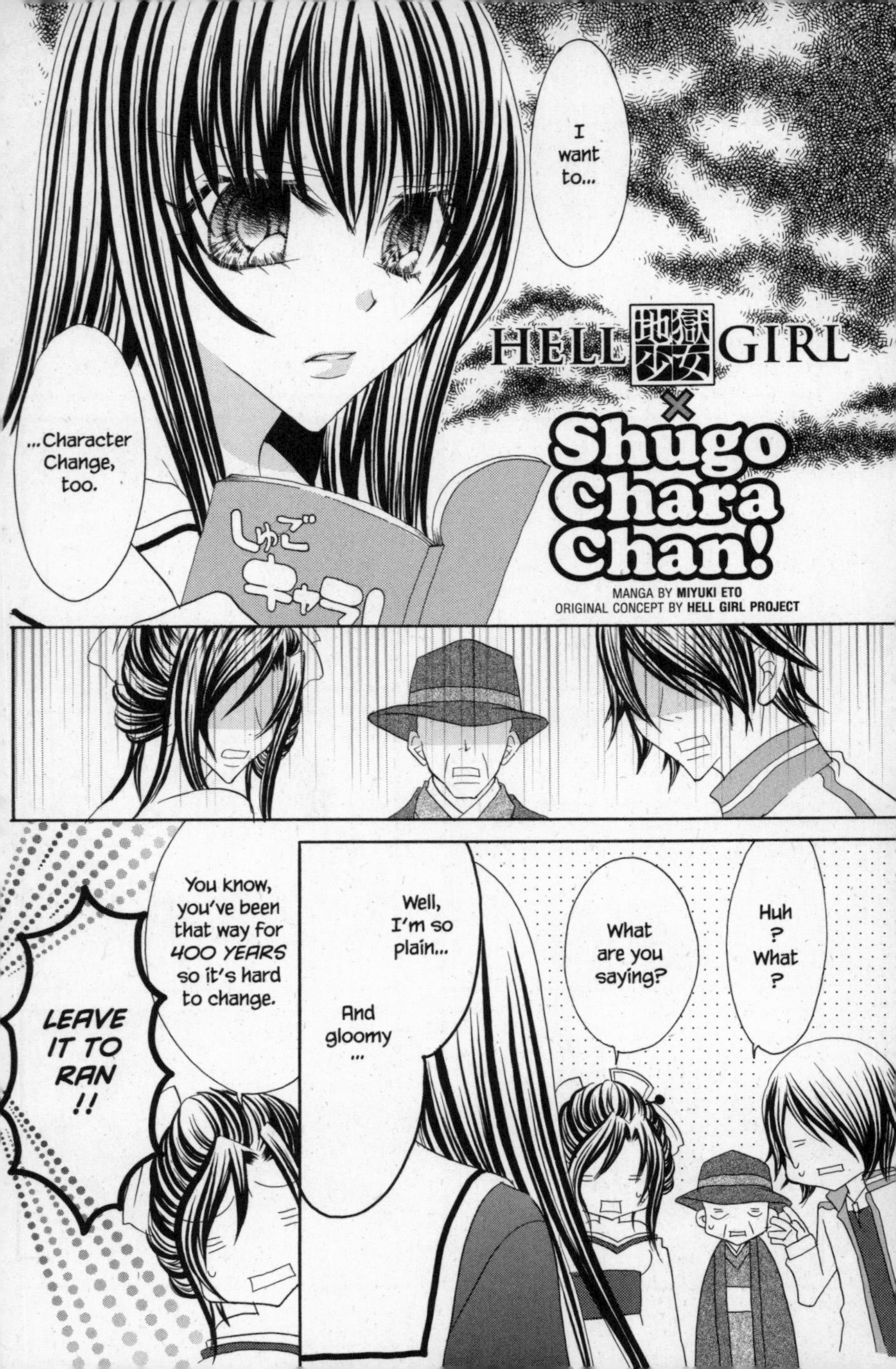
I want to...
...Character Change, too.
HELL 地獄少女 GIRL
×
Shugo Chara Chan!
MANGA BY MIYUKI ETO
ORIGINAL CONCEPT BY HELL GIRL PROJECT
しゅご キャラ
Huh? What?
What are you saying?
Well, I'm so plain...
And gloomy ...
You know, you've been that way for 400 YEARS so it's hard to change.
LEAVE IT TO RAN!!

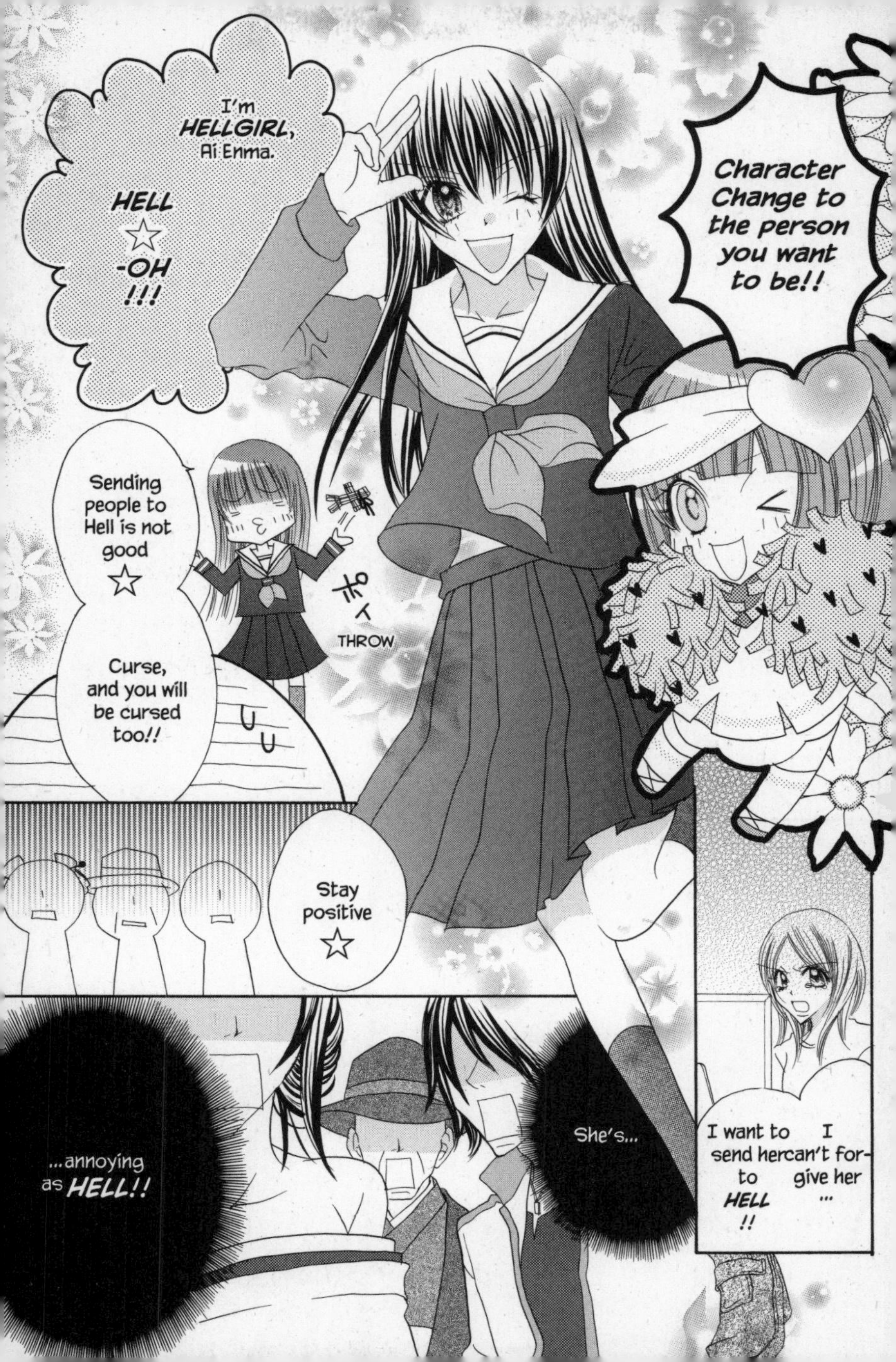
Character Change to the person you want to be!!
I'm HELLGIRL, Ai Enma.
HELL ☆ -OH !!!
Sending people to Hell is not good ☆
Curse, and you will be cursed too!!
ポイ
THROW
I can't forgive her...
I want to send her to HELL!!
Stay positive ☆
She's...
...annoying as HELL!!

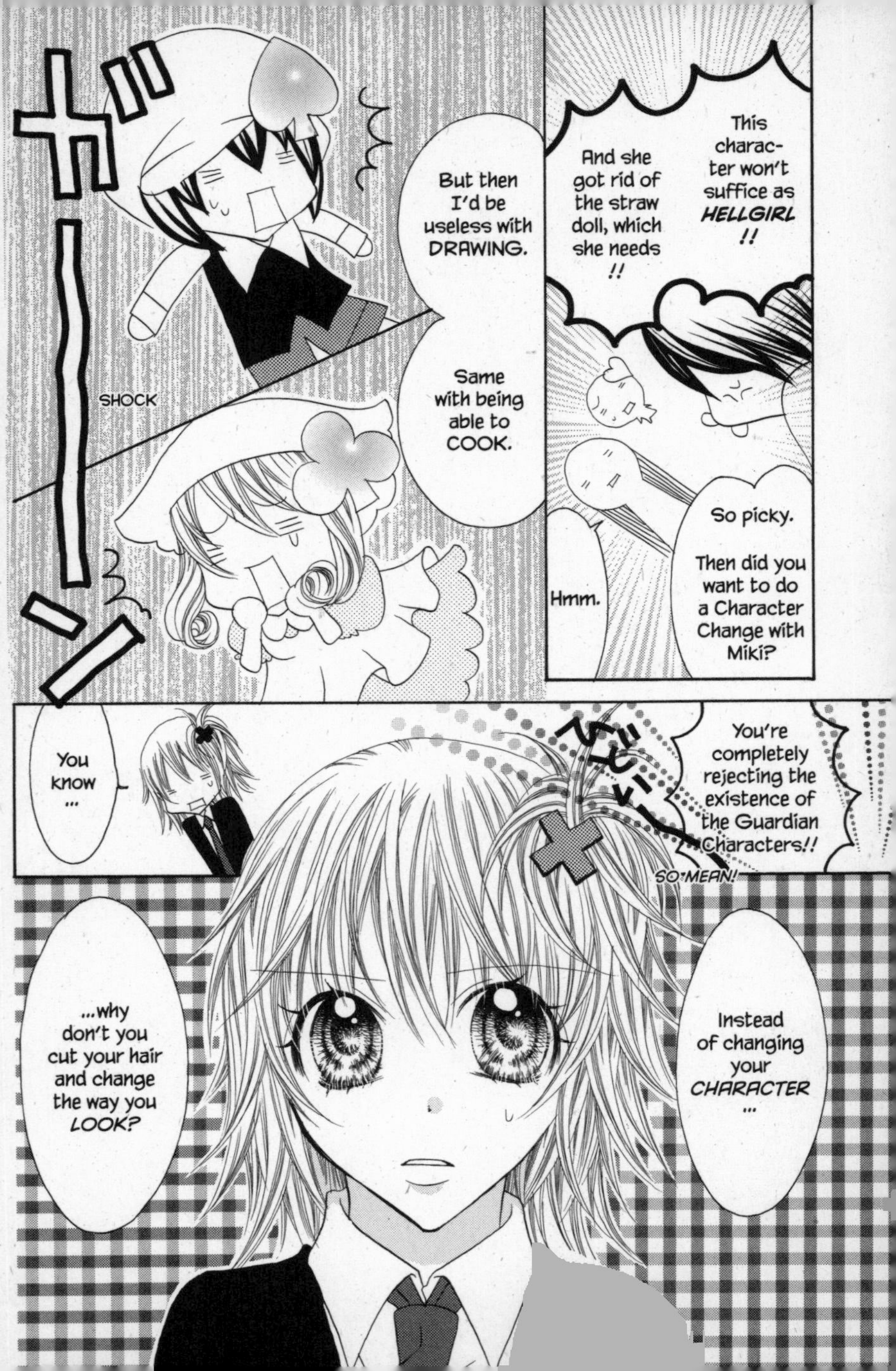
This character won't suffice as HELLGIRL!!
And she got rid of the straw doll, which she needs!!
So picky. Then did you want to do a Character Change with Miki?
Hmm.
But then I'd be useless with DRAWING.
Same with being able to COOK.
SHOCK
You're completely rejecting the existence of the Guardian Characters!!
SO MEAN!
You know...
Instead of changing your CHARACTER...
...why don't you cut your hair and change the way you LOOK?

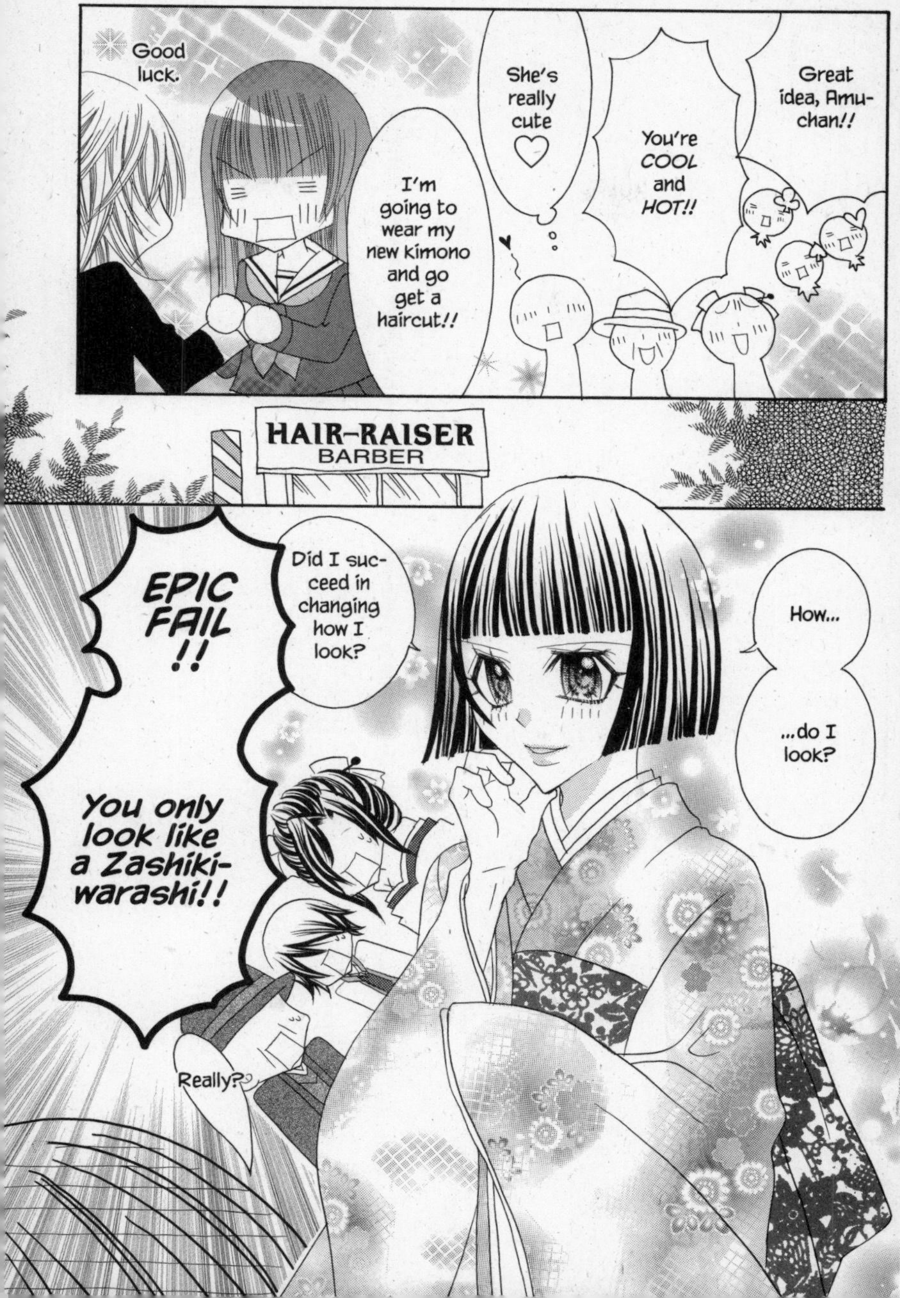
Great idea, Amu-chan!!
You're COOL and HOT!!
She's really cute ♡
I'm going to wear my new kimono and go get a haircut!!
Good luck.
HAIR-RAISER
BARBER
How... ...do I look?
Did I succeed in changing how I look?
EPIC FAIL!!
You only look like a Zashiki-warashi!!
Really?

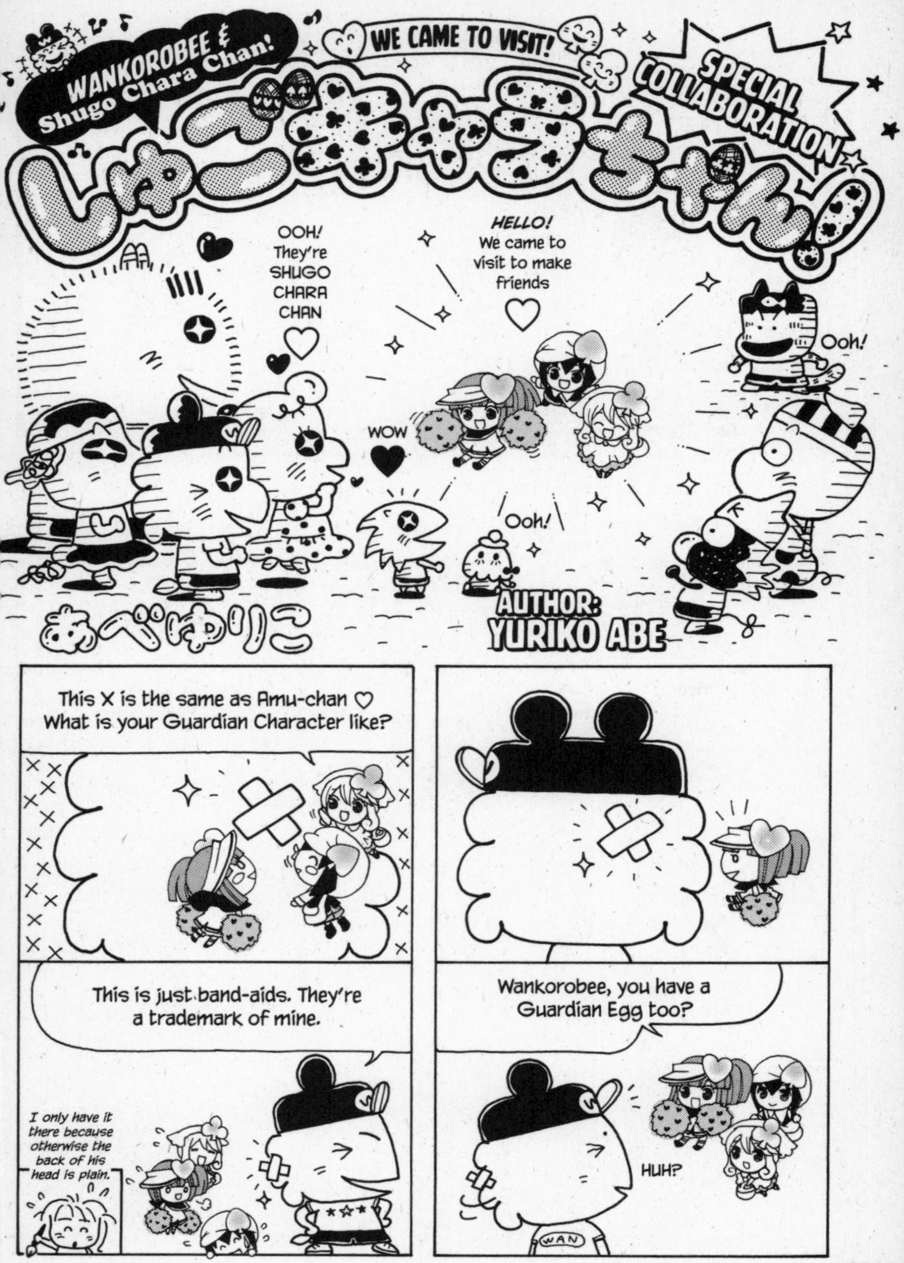
SPECIAL COLLABORATION
WE CAME TO VISIT!
WANKOROBEE & Shugo Chara Chan!
しゅごキャラちゃん!
Ooh!
HELLO! We came to visit to make friends ♡
OOH! They're SHUGO CHARA CHAN ♡
WOW
Ooh!
AUTHOR: YURIKO ABE
あべゆりこ
This X is the same as Amu-chan ♡ What is your Guardian Character like?
Wankorobee, you have a Guardian Egg too?
HUH?
This is just band-aids. They're a trademark of mine.
I only have it there because otherwise the back of his head is plain.
WAN

I Want to Be Strong!

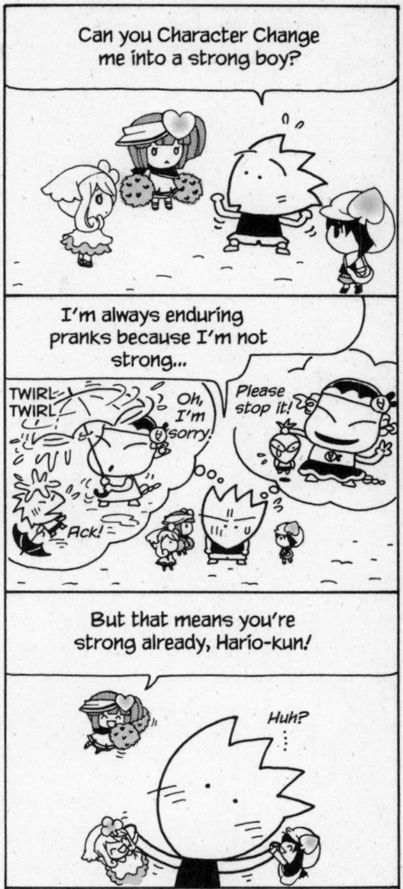
Can you Character Change me into a strong boy?
I'm always enduring pranks because I'm not strong...
TWIRL TWIRL
Please stop it!
Oh, I'm sorry!
Ack!
But that means you're strong already, Hario-kun!
Huh?
Having endurance means you're strong ♡
What!? Really!?

Guardian Characters?

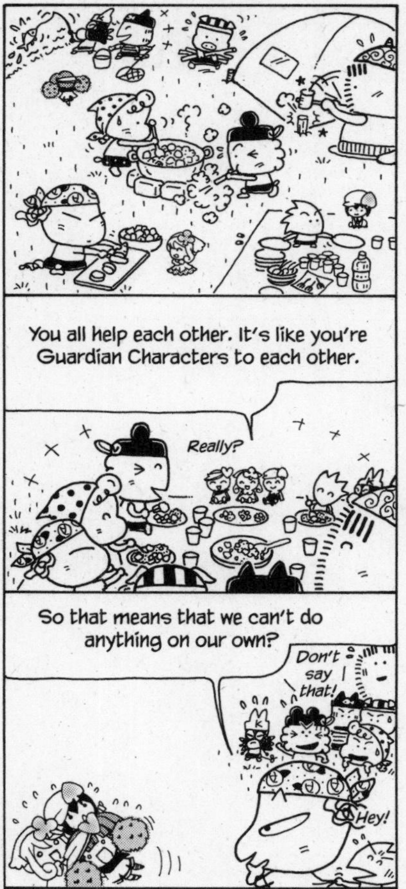
You all help each other. It's like you're Guardian Characters to each other.
Really?
So that means that we can't do anything on our own?
Don't say that!
Hey!
Oh, Amu-chan's going to start missing us, so we should go.
Come again!

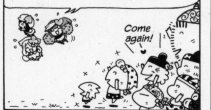

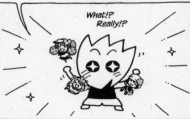

The Way You Talk

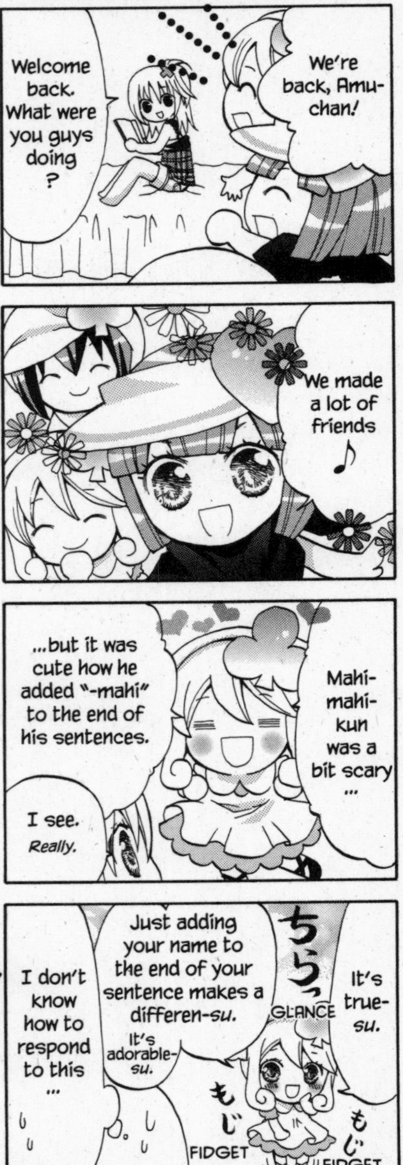
We're back, Amu-chan!
Welcome back. What were you guys doing?
We made a lot of friends ♪
Mahi-mahi-kun was a bit scary...
...but it was cute how he added "-mahi" to the end of his sentences.
I see.
Really.
It's true-su.
GLANCE
Just adding your name to the end of your sentence makes a differen-su.
It's adorable-su.
I don't know how to respond to this...
FIDGET
FIDGET

Daydream

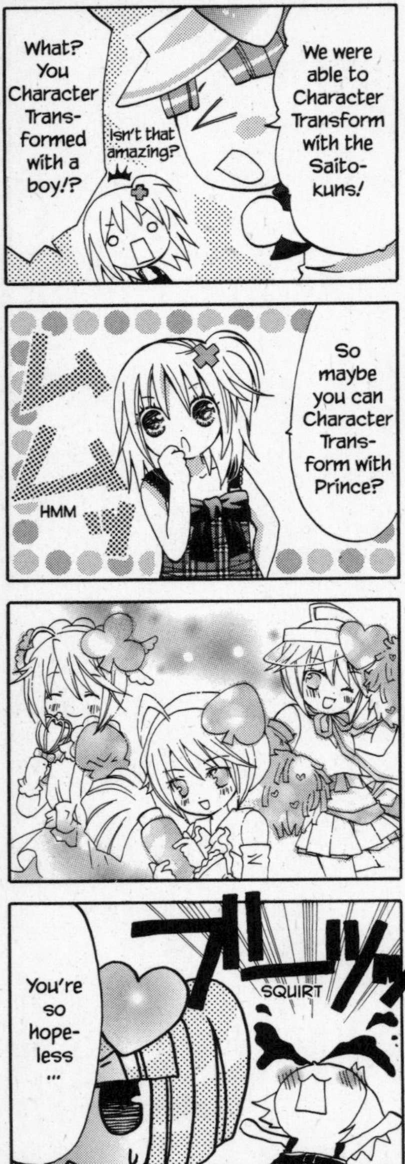
We were able to Character Transform with the Saito-kuns!
Isn't that amazing?
What? You Character Trans-formed with a boy!?
So maybe you can Character Trans-form with Prince?
HMM
SQUIRT
You're so hope-less...

Doesn't Work

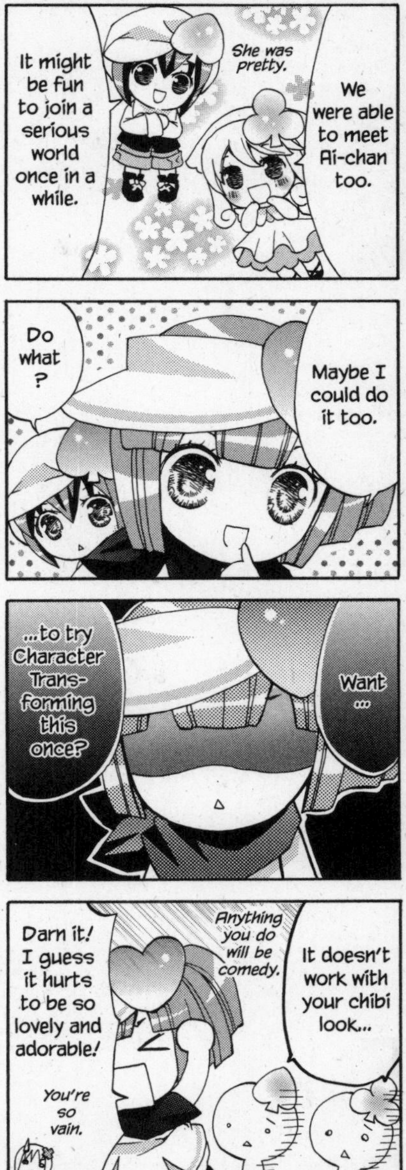
We were able to meet Ai-chan too.
She was pretty.
It might be fun to join a serious world once in a while.
Maybe I could do it too.
Do what?
Want...
...to try Character Transforming this once?
It doesn't work with your chibi look...
Anything you do will be comedy.
Darn it! I guess it hurts to be so lovely and adorable!
You're so vain.

Only One Aspect

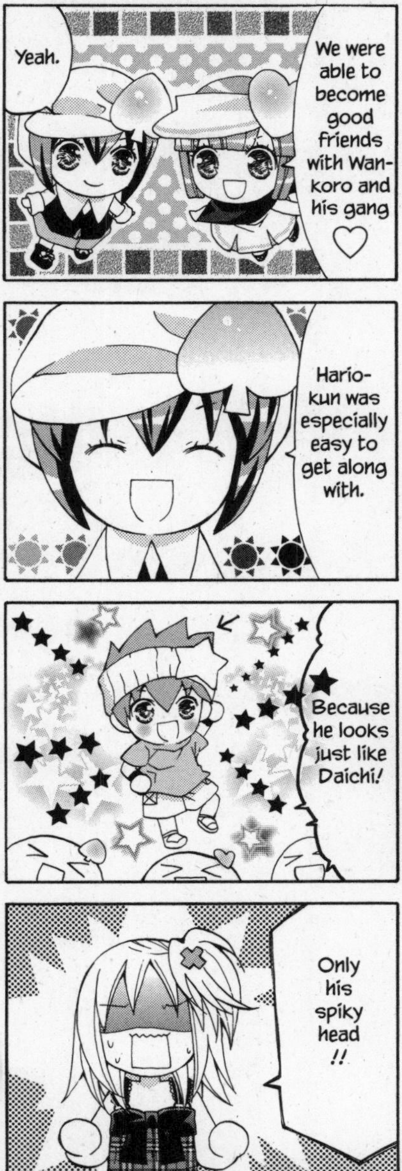
We were able to become good friends with Wan-koro and his gang ♡
Yeah.
Hario-kun was especially easy to get along with.
Because he looks just like Daichi!
Only his spiky head!!

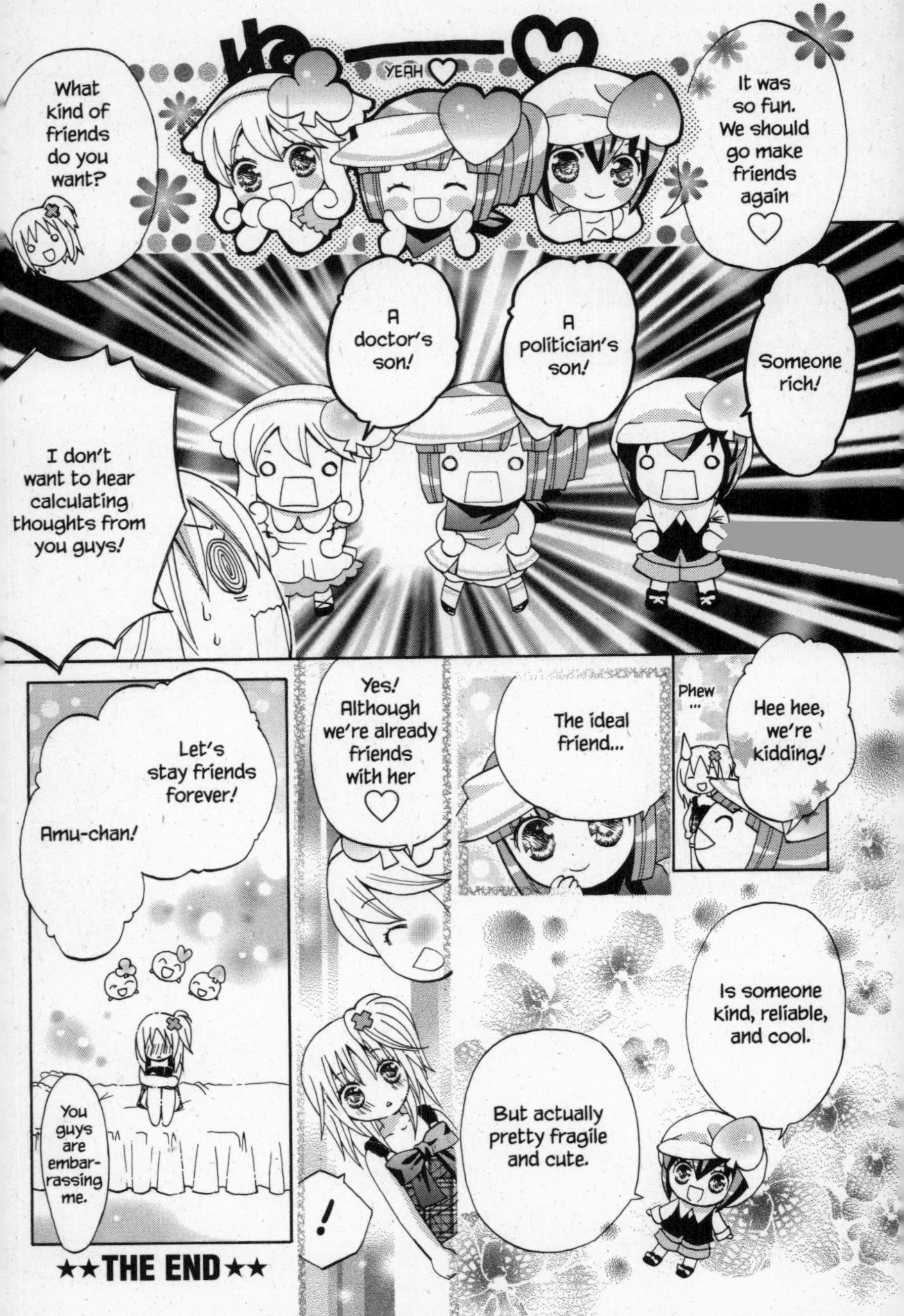
It was so fun. We should go make friends again ♡
YEAH ♡
What kind of friends do you want?
Someone rich!
A politician's son!
A doctor's son!
I don't want to hear calculating thoughts from you guys!
Hee hee, we're kidding!
Phew ...
The ideal friend...
Is someone kind, reliable, and cool.
But actually pretty fragile and cute.
Yes! Although we're already friends with her ♡
!
Let's stay friends forever!
Amu-chan!
You guys are embarrassing me.
★★THE END★★

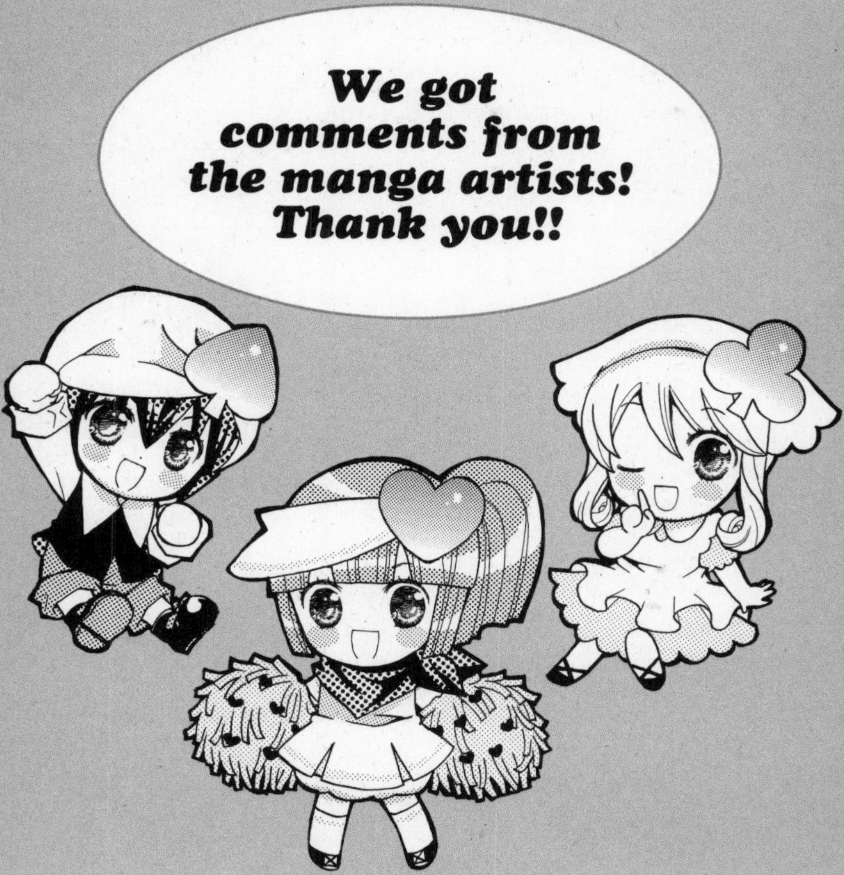
We got comments from the manga artists! Thank you!!

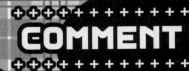

COMMENT

I'm so sorry about
the bad manga!! Hee hee, is
it too late to be flustered about what
I did? (° □° ;)
But I was very happy to be able to
draw my favorite Guardian Characters ♡
Please invite me again if there is
another opportunity!!
Je t'aime ♡ ♡

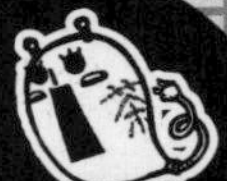

Sakyou

Hello. It was very fun to
be able to participate in the
"Shugo Chara Chan!" manga!
I get nervous when I draw other
people's characters...
But I was happy I was able to draw
Mahimahi with them!
Thank you very much!

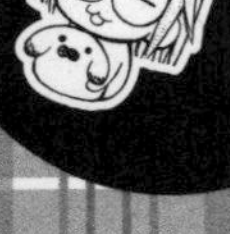

Ema Toyama

Since Naph-naph is a good friend of mine, I worked hard to draw this manga ☆ But I had difficulty with simple problems such as shaping Ran right, or which screentone to use. But at least PEACH-PIT liked "Barber Hair Raiser," so I guess it was worth it.

+ + + + + + + + + + + + + + + +

Miyuki Eto

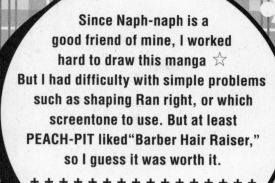

The Guardian Characters are so cute and I love them, so I'm happy I got to work on this collaboration.
I got to imagine that they were going to be with my characters, and it was fun.
Thank you for the opportunity!

+ + + + + + + + + + + + + + + +

Yuriko Abe

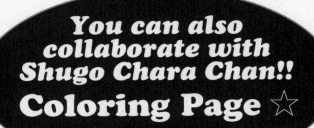

You can also collaborate with Shugo Chara Chan!!
Coloring Page ☆

You can photocopy these pages and color them! Will you be able to make it come out nice?

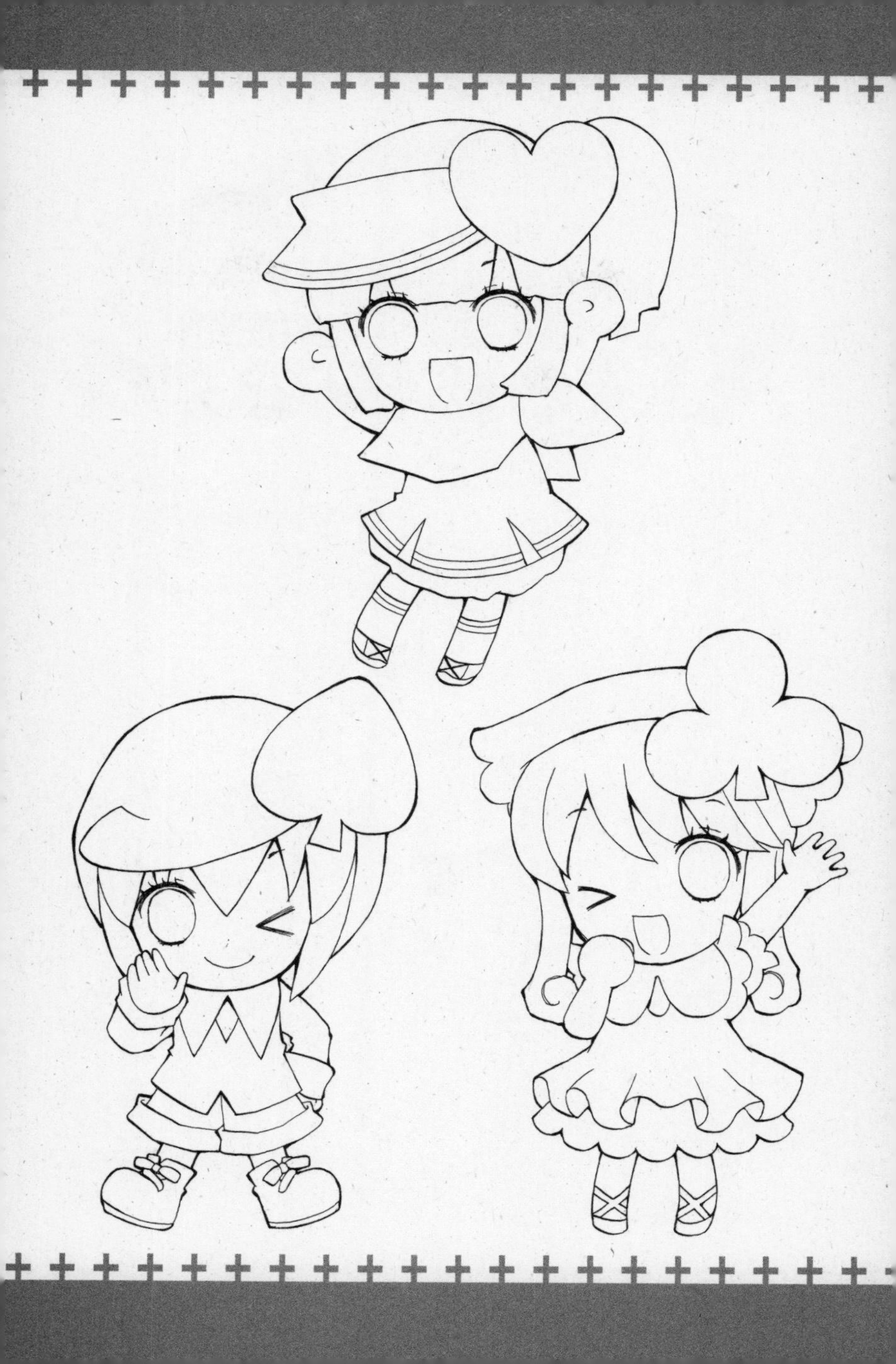

Afterword

"Shugo Chara Chan!"
came about as a spin-off series for
"Shugo Chara!" We enjoyed reading the
different stories by the various artists as one
of the many readers like you. And we're very
happy that the stories were published
into a series.
Thank you so much!

PEACH-PIT

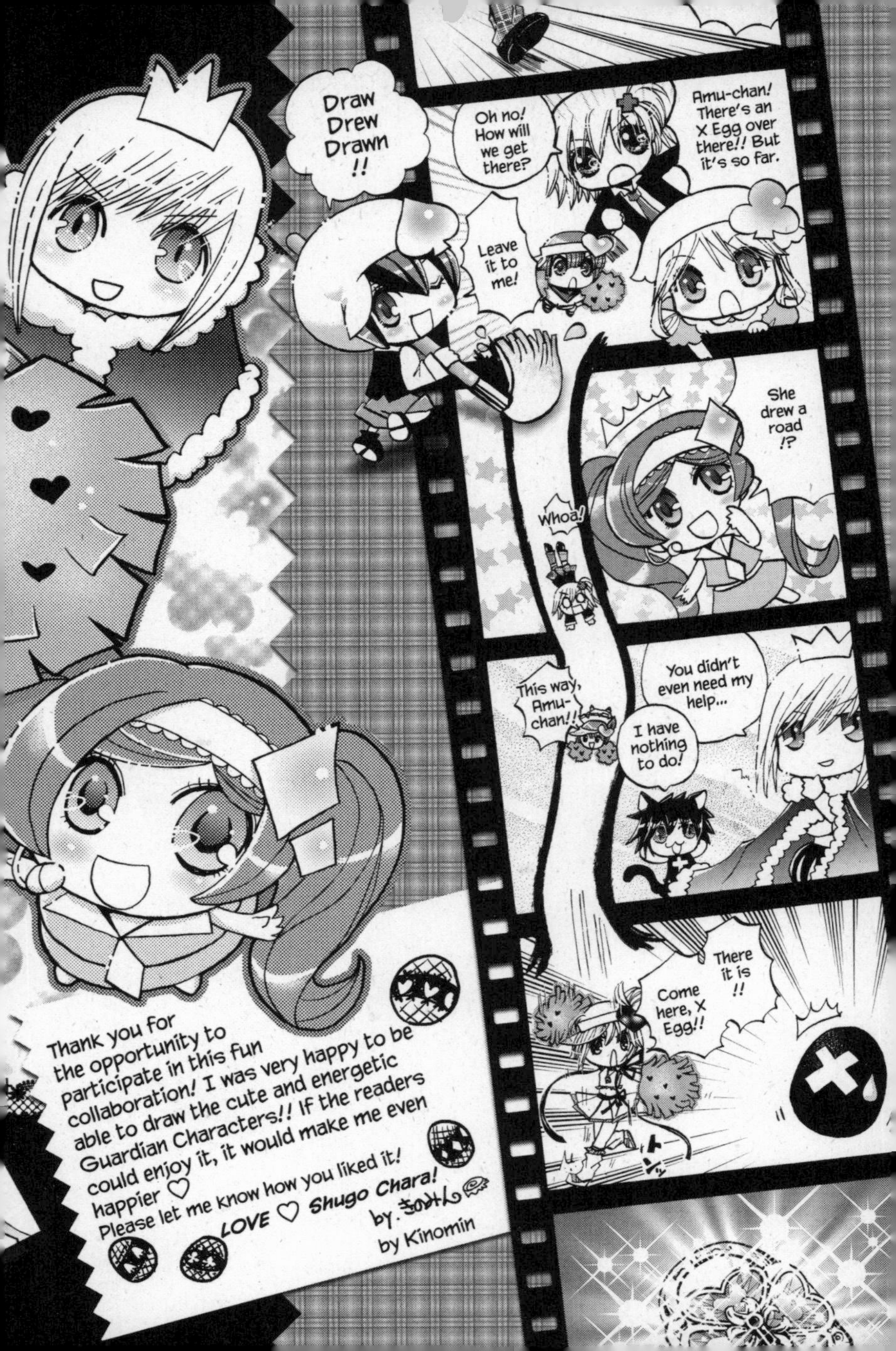

Amu-chan! There's an X Egg over there!! But it's so far.
Oh no! How will we get there?
Leave it to me!
Draw Drew Drawn !!
She drew a road !?
Whoa!
You didn't even need my help...
I have nothing to do!
This way, Amu-chan!!
There it is !!
Come here, X Egg!!
Thank you for the opportunity to participate in this fun collaboration! I was very happy to be able to draw the cute and energetic Guardian Characters!! If the readers could enjoy it, it would make me even happier ♡
Please let me know how you liked it!
LOVE ♡ Shugo Chara!
by Kinomin

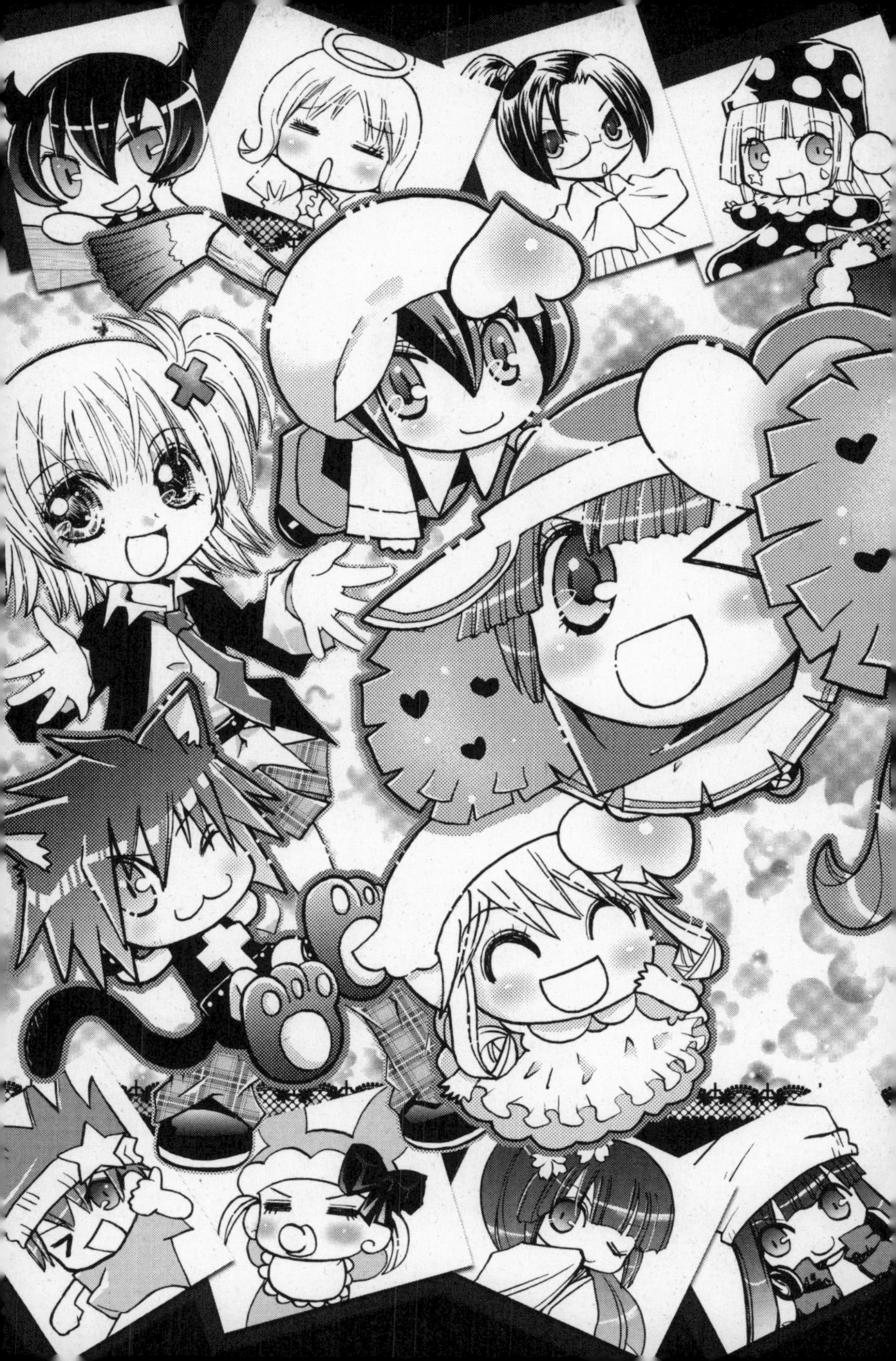

AFTERWORD

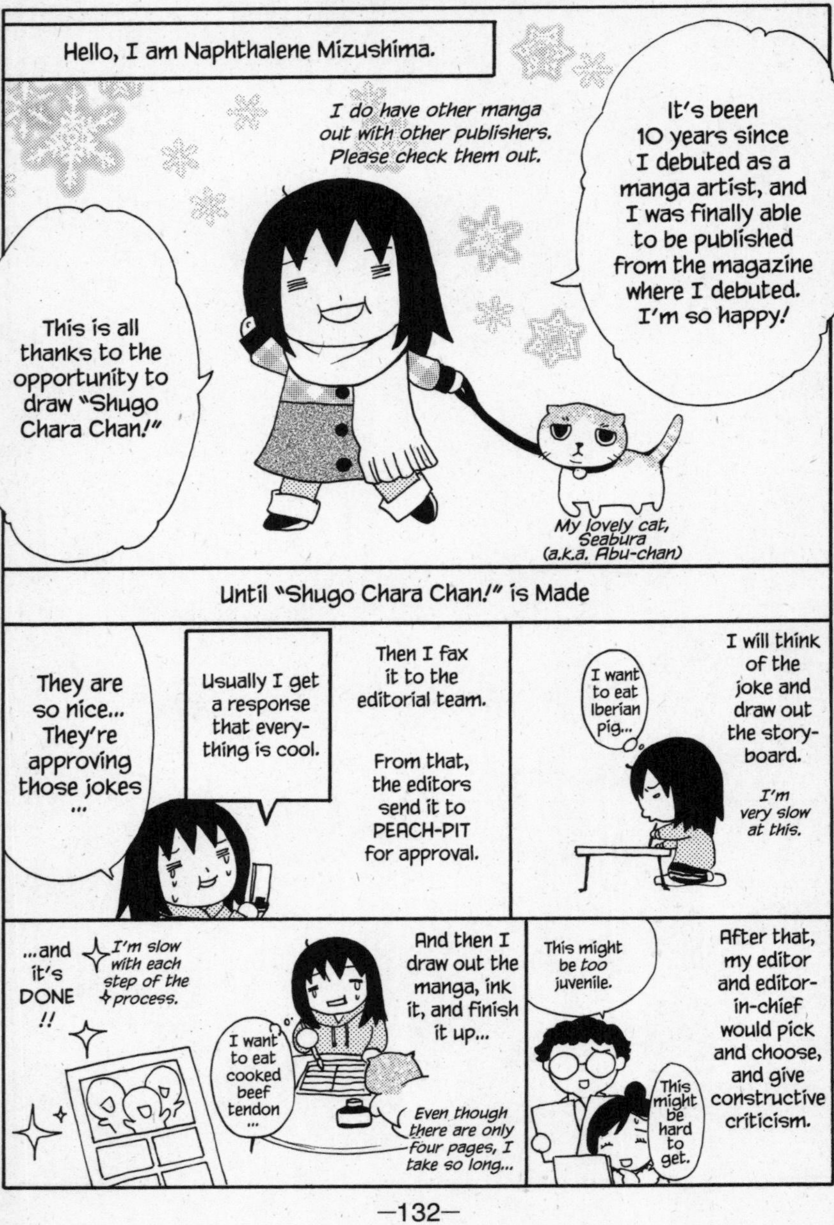
Hello, I am Naphthalene Mizushima.
It's been 10 years since I debuted as a manga artist, and I was finally able to be published from the magazine where I debuted. I'm so happy!
I do have other manga out with other publishers. Please check them out.
This is all thanks to the opportunity to draw "Shugo Chara Chan!"
My lovely cat, Seabura (a.k.a. Abu-chan)
Until "Shugo Chara Chan!" is Made
I will think of the joke and draw out the story-board.
I want to eat Iberian pig...
I'm very slow at this.
Then I fax it to the editorial team.
From that, the editors send it to PEACH-PIT for approval.
Usually I get a response that every-thing is cool.
They are so nice... They're approving those jokes ...
After that, my editor and editor-in-chief would pick and choose, and give constructive criticism.
This might be too juvenile.
This might be hard to get.
And then I draw out the manga, ink it, and finish it up...
I want to eat cooked beef tendon ...
Even though there are only four pages, I take so long...
...and it's DONE !!
I'm slow with each step of the process.

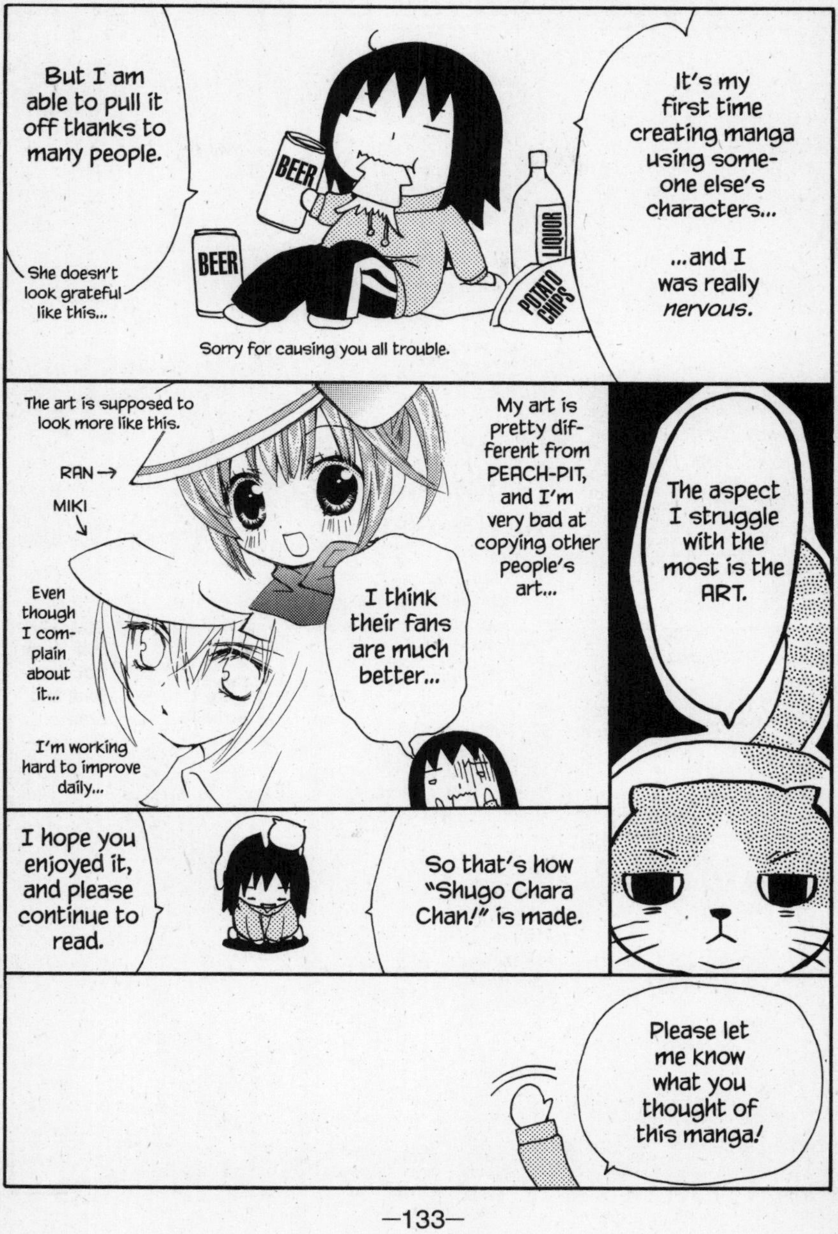
It's my first time creating manga using some-one else's characters...
...and I was really *nervous.*
But I am able to pull it off thanks to many people.
She doesn't look grateful like this...
BEER
BEER
LIQUOR
POTATO CHIPS
Sorry for causing you all trouble.
The aspect I struggle with the most is the ART.
My art is pretty dif-ferent from PEACH-PIT, and I'm very bad at copying other people's art...
I think their fans are much better...
The art is supposed to look more like this.
RAN →
MIKI
Even though I com-plain about it...
I'm working hard to improve daily...
So that's how "Shugo Chara Chan!" is made.
I hope you enjoyed it, and please continue to read.
Please let me know what you thought of this manga!

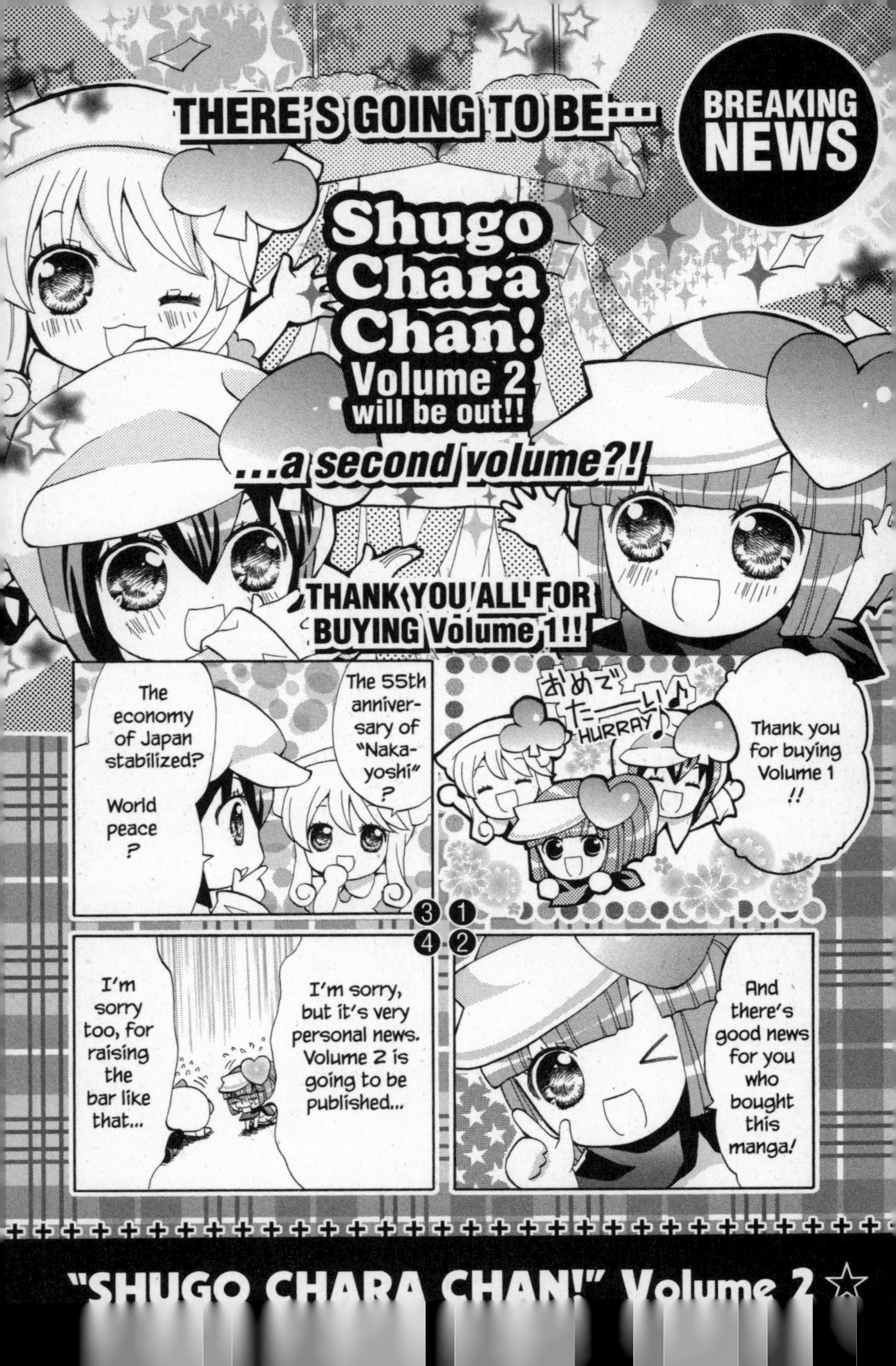
BREAKING NEWS
THERE'S GOING TO BE…
…a second volume?!
Shugo Chara Chan! Volume 2 will be out!!
THANK YOU ALL FOR BUYING Volume 1!!
Thank you for buying Volume 1 !!
おめでたーーい♪
HURRAY
And there's good news for you who bought this manga!
The 55th anniversary of "Nakayoshi"?
The economy of Japan stabilized?
World peace?
I'm sorry, but it's very personal news. Volume 2 is going to be published...
I'm sorry too, for raising the bar like that...
"SHUGO CHARA CHAN!" Volume 2 ☆

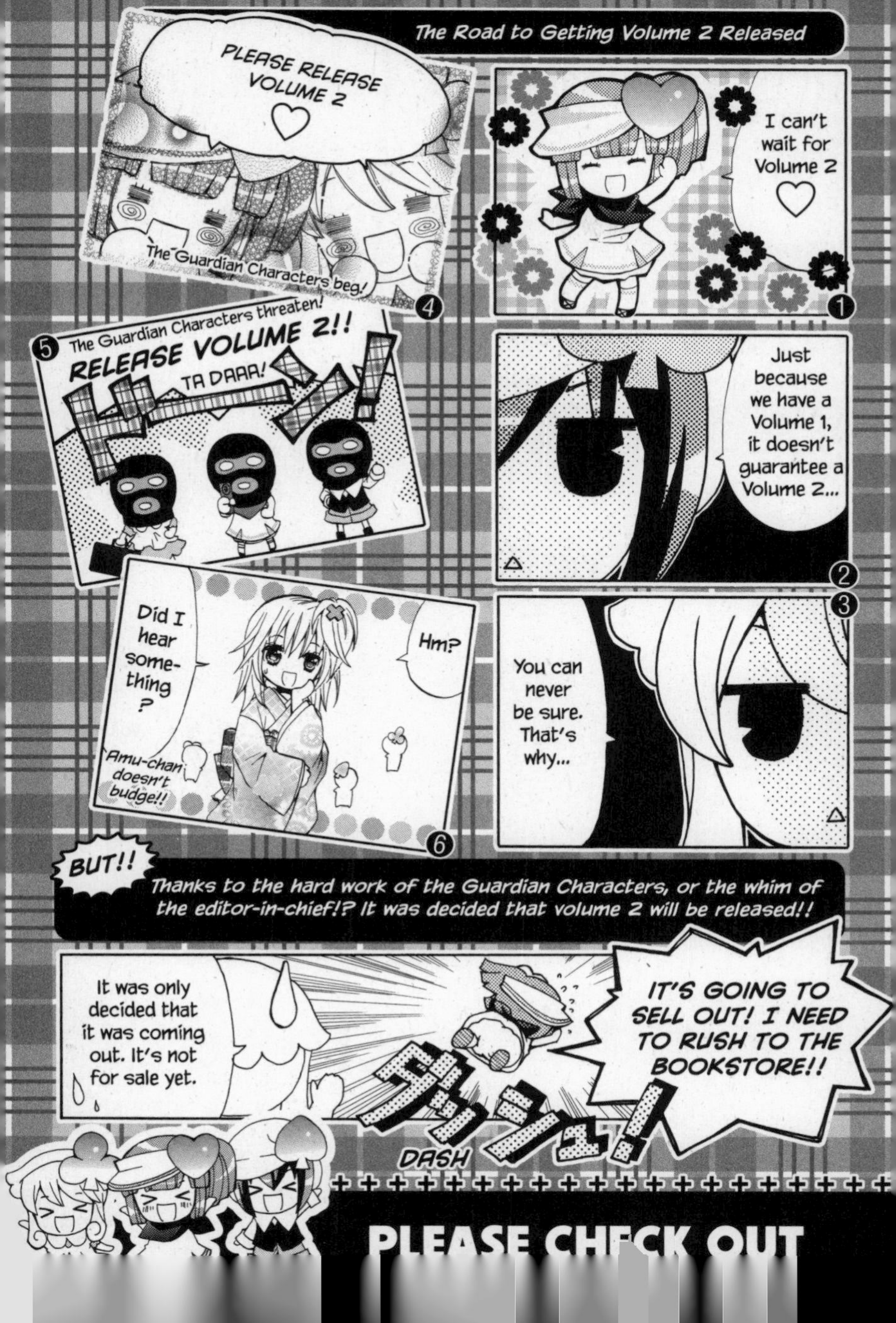
The Road to Getting Volume 2 Released
I can't wait for Volume 2 ♡
Just because we have a Volume 1, it doesn't guarantee a Volume 2...
You can never be sure. That's why...
PLEASE RELEASE VOLUME 2 ♡
The Guardian Characters beg!
The Guardian Characters threaten!
RELEASE VOLUME 2!!
TA DAAA!
Hm?
Did I hear some-thing?
Amu-chan doesn't budge!!
BUT!!
Thanks to the hard work of the Guardian Characters, or the whim of the editor-in-chief!? It was decided that volume 2 will be released!!
IT'S GOING TO SELL OUT! I NEED TO RUSH TO THE BOOKSTORE!!
DASH
It was only decided that it was coming out. It's not for sale yet.
PLEASE CHECK OUT

About the Creators

PEACH-PIT:
Banri Sendo is born June 7, ***Shibuko Ebara*** is born June 21. They are a pair of emini Manga artists working together. Currently running "Shugo Chara!" on "Nakayoshi."

Naphthalene Mizushima
Born February 2. Aquarius. Currently running "Shugo Chara Chan!" on "Nakayoshi."

Kinomin
Born October 26. Scorpio. Currently running "Shugo Chara Chan! Kids ★ " on "Yahoo! Kids."

Translation Notes

Japanese is a tricky language for most Westerners, and translation is often more art than science. For your edification and reading pleasure, here are notes on some of the places where we could have gone in a different direction with our translation of the work, or where a Japanese cultural reference is used.

Oden, page 6
Oden is a Japanese dish served during the winter. arious ingredients, including eggs, daikon radish, and fish cake, are boiled in a flavored broth.

Tsundere, page 8
Tsundere is a term for a personality or characteristic trait of a person who is standoffish or aloof who becomes loveable and adorable in different situations. This characteristic first started in Japanese video games featuring girls (dating- simulation games), then moved on to anime and manga, but it's now used widely in mass media.

Bento, page 14
Bento is the term for "boxed lunch" in Japanese. It usually consists of rice, a side dish of meat or fish, vegetables, and either a pickled dish or dessert.

Tamagoyaki, page 15
A tamagoyaki is a fried egg grilled thinly on a frying pan and rolled into a cylindrical shape. It is a common side dish in bento. epending on preference, a tamagoyaki can be flavored with rice vinegar, sugar, soy sauce, salt, black pepper, et al.

Umeboshi, page 15
Umeboshi are pickled ume, which are a type of plum. Umeboshi is quite common in Japan, and can often be found in boxed lunches, placed in the center of a bed of rice to make it look like the Japanese flag. Umeboshi isare very salty and sour. It is made by putting ripe ume in a barrel with salt.

Niboshi, page 20
Niboshi are dried small fish that can be eaten or used to make soup stock.

Flower, page 36
In Japanese, the word for flower is "hana." "Hana" is also a homonym for nose.

Host, page 41
In Japan, a host refers to a male who pours drinks and offers conversation to female customers at a bar, known as a host club. A typical host would be wearing a dark suit, collared shirt with the collar sticking out from under the suit, ewelry, and be very tanned with bleached hair.

Takoyaki, page 43
Takoyaki is a grilled ball with a piece of octopus in the middle. It is made on a grill and shaped into half- circles. You whisk some flour, water, and egg and pour it into the hot grill. You then put a piece of octopus, some cut up green onion, and grill for a bit. The

hardest part is flipping over the mix to make a ball. You use a takoyaki pick, which is similar to an ice pick, but thinner.

Yukata, page 43
A Yukata is a kimono worn mainly in the summer. It is made of lighter fabric than kimonos, and has fewer garments underneath. The word yukata comes from the words "bath" and "clothing." uring old Japan, people wore clothing to take a bath, and something simpler and lighter than a yukata was worn. Eventually, people came to wear it loosely after a bath, and in modern Japan, people wear it at hot-spring Japanese hotels, festivals, or ust simply around their house during summer.

Goldfish Scooping, page 45
oldfish Scooping is a common game at festivals in which there is a shallow pool filled with goldfish, and the customer tries to catch them with round wires that are wrapped with thin paper. The customer needs to catch the goldfish before the paper rips.

Mouse Tail Firework, page 47
The mouse tail firework acts the same way as the round Spinners in the United States. It is named so because the Japanese versions are shaped like a mouse's tail, unlike the round Spinners, which are cylindrical in shape.

Snake Firework, page 48
A snake firework's embers stretch out when it is lit up, looking like an emerging snake that is appearing.

Omikoshi, page 48
The omikoshi is a portable shrine in which the people of the community used to carry around the local god so that the god could see their community.

Tsukkomi, page 66
In Japanese comedy, especially with comedian duos, the comedians are separated into a tsukkomi and a boke. A boke is a person who would say something stupid or nonsensical, and the tsukkomi would react to the boke's comment. A tsukkomi's typical move is to ab the boke playfully.

Yakisoba, page 67
Yakisoba is fried noodles, usually flavored with sauce similar to Worcestershire sauce.

DAIGO STARDUST, page 70
The person in the last panel is AI O STA UST, also known simply as AI O. He is the vocalist for the rock band "B EAKE ." He started a trend of posing with his arms crossed, saying, "Wish!" He is always wearing fingerless gloves, which started a trend around the time that this manga was published.

Nabe, page 71
Nabe is a term that refers to various pot dishes in Japan. Common ingredients of a nabe include vegetables such as nappa cabbage, mushrooms, green onions, tofu, and meat. The actual word "nabe" means "pot."

Shugo Chara Chan! Kids★ , page 73

Shugo Chara Chan! Kids ★ was a collaborative pro ect between the Shugo Chara! property and Yahoo! Kids. Yahoo! Kids was a kids' version of Yahoo! JAPAN, featuring links of sites targeted toward children. The search was also filtered, so that one couldn't search for adult-related material.

Nakayoshi, page 79

Nakayoshi is the monthly sho o manga mazazine published by Kodansha. Shugo Chara! and Shugo Chara Chan! were both published in Nakayoshi.

Peak, horn, antlers, page 82

In Japanese, the word for peak in whipped cream is "tsuno." "Tsuno" is also a homonym for horns and antlers.

Kotatsu, page 84

A kotatsu is a table covered with a blanket, with a heat generator attached to the table to keep one s feet warm. In the winter it is really hard to get out of.

Tanabata, page 101

Tanabata is a festival held annually on July 7. It is to celebrate the meeting of the stars ega and Altair, who are separated by the Milky Way "river." They are allowed to meet once a year on July 7. It is custom to put slips of paper with wishes on bamboo leaves.

Datemaki, page 102

A datemaki is a Japanese food made by mixing minced white fish or shrimp with egg, mirin, and sugar, grilling it, then rolling it up. It is served during New Year's.

Mirin is a sweet kind of rice wine that is used as a condiment. Sometimes, mirin is used for cooking in place of sugar or soy sauce. It is also popular because, when used on fish, it erases the fish's smell."

Kimono, page 117

A kimono is a traditional Japanese garment that resembles a robe. It is wrapped around the body and layered in the front; a long piece of cloth (known as a sash) is tied around to keep it in place.

Zashiki-warashi, page 117

ashiki-warashi is a Japanese yokai (supernatural creature in Japanese folklore) that originates in Iwate Prefecture. This yokai looks like a child with bobbed hair.

ANIMAL LAND

MAKOTO RAIKU

WELCOME TO THE JUNGLE

In a world of animals where the strong eat the weak, Monoko the tanuki stumbles across a strange creature the like of which has never been seen before - **a human baby!**

While the newborn has no claws or teeth to protect itself, it does have the rare ability to speak to and understand all the different animal.

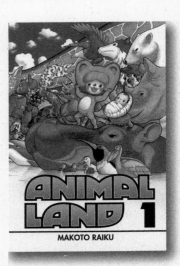

Special extras in each volume! Read them all!

RATING OT AGES 10+

VISIT WWW.KODANSHACOMICS.COM TO:
• View release date calendars for upcoming volumes
• Find out the latest about new Kodansha Comics series

Animal Land © Makoto Raiku/KODANSHA LTD. All rights reserved.

SHUGO CHARA!

PEACH-PIT

CREATORS OF *DEARS* AND *ROZEN MAIDEN*

PEACH-PIT
CREATORS OF DEARS AND ROZEN MAIDEN
SHUGO CHARA!
1

Everybody at Seiyo Elementary thinks that stylish and supercool Amu has it all. But nobody knows the real Amu, a shy girl who wishes she had the courage to truly be herself. Changing Amu's life is going to take more than wishes and dreams—it's going to take a little magic! One morning, Amu finds a surprise in her bed: three strange little eggs. Each egg contains a Guardian Character, an angel-like being who can give her the power to be someone new. With the help of her Guardian Characters, Amu is about to discover that her true self is even more amazing than she ever dreamed.

Special extras in each volume! Read them all!

VISIT WWW.KODANSHACOMICS.COM TO:

- **View release date calendars for upcoming volumes**
- **Find out the latest about new Kodansha Comics series**

A Kodansha Comics Trade Paperback Original

Shugo Chara Chan! volume 1 copyright © 2008 PEACH-PIT, Naphthalene Mizushima, Kinomin, Sakyou, Ema Toyama, Miyuki Eto and Yuriko Abe
English translation copyright © 2011 PEACH-PIT, Naphthalene Mizushima, Kinomin, Sakyou, Ema Toyama, Miyuki Eto and Yuriko Abe

Published in the United States by Kodansha Comics, an imprint of Kodansha USA Publishing, LLC, New York.

Publication rights for this English edition arranged through Kodansha Ltd., Tokyo.

First published in Japan in 2008 by Kodansha Ltd., Tokyo.

ISBN 978-1-935-42995-1

Original cover design by Akiko Omo

Printed in the United States of America.

www.kodanshacomics.com

9 8 7 6 5 4 3 2 1

Translator: Satsuki Yamashita
Lettering: Vince Sneed

TOMARE!

止まれ
[STOP!]

You're going the wrong way!

Manga is a completely different type of reading experience.

To start at the *beginning*, go to the *end*!

That's right! Authentic manga is read the traditional Japanese way—from right to left. Exactly the *opposite* of how American books are read. It's easy to follow: Just go to the other end of the book, and read each page—and each panel—from right side to left side, starting at the top right. Now you're experiencing manga as it was meant to be!